The urban experience

A sourcebook

English, Scottish and Welsh towns, 1450-1700

The urban experience

A sourcebook

English, Scottish and Welsh towns, 1450-1700

edited by

R. C. Richardson
Head of the History and Archaeology Department,
King Alfred's College, Winchester

and

T. B. James
Senior Lecturer in History and Archaeology,
King Alfred's College, Winchester

**Manchester
University Press**

Copyright © R. C. Richardson and T. B. James 1983

Published by Manchester University Press
Oxford Road, Manchester M13 9PL, UK
and
51 Washington Street, Dover, N.H. 03820, USA

British Library cataloguing in publication data
The urban experience.
   1. Cities and towns – Great Britain – History
  I. Richardson, R. C.   II. James, T. B.
   941'.009'732   HT133
ISBN 0–7190–0900–6

Library of Congress catalogue card number
82–62244

Library of Congress cataloguing in publication data
applied for

Printed in Great Britain by
Butler & Tanner Ltd, Frome and London

CONTENTS

2 THE ECONOMY 33

PREFACE

There is no mistaking the great upsurge of interest in urban history which has taken place in this country over the last generation and the lively debate which has surrounded it. At the level of both general surveys and monographs manifest gaps which once existed in the historian's knowledge have now been filled and urban history has emerged as a recognisable and coherent discipline in its own right. Regular conferences on the subject have taken place since 1966, and *The Urban History Yearbook*, founded by the late Professor H. J. Dyos of Leicester University, began publication in 1974. Books and articles in the field continue to grow in quantity and in sophistication. A further indicator of growth in the subject is that in 1975 no fewer than fifty-eight British universities and polytechnics were offering courses in urban history and they were joined in 1977 by the Open University.[1] As far as the pre-industrial period is concerned, the excellent bibliography in Peter Clark, *The Early Modern Town: a reader* (1976) provides a convenient guide to recent achievements of research and re-interpretation. Students of the early modern town are well served both by textbooks and by case studies.[2]

It is true to say, however, that the growing literature on urban development in the late Middle Ages and early modern period has not included a satisfactory sourcebook. The main thrust of the classic three-volume collection of *Tudor Economic Documents* by Tawney and Power (1924) lay elsewhere, and similarly the very title of the more recent volume by Joan Thirsk and J. P. Cooper (*Seventeenth-Century Economic Documents* (1972)) makes clear that the student could expect to find urban history represented there only as one theme among many. On the other hand, the specifically urban documentary collection published in conjunction with the Open University course on early modern towns (*Towns and Townspeople, 1500–1780* (1977)) was too short and too restricted in its geographical and thematic coverage to provide anything more than the briefest of introductions. A more substantial sourcebook has clearly been needed for some time and the present volume arises from that conviction. It is also the direct product of its editors' teaching experience in that both of them have planned and taught early modern urban history courses at first degree level.

The documentary collection which follows has three principal aims.

The first is to highlight major features of the economic, social and political development of urban communities between 1450 and 1700. In addition the period covered by the sourcebook embraces major demographic changes. The book begins in 1450 with the population of England perhaps at its lowest point since the Conquest, while the succeeding decades saw towns filling up once again with people, until in the seventeenth century they could scarcely take any more. The editors have been conscious of the need to convey something of the rich variety of their subject and of the danger of choosing examples to support only a narrow preconceived view. So although, for instance, urban crisis and decline in the fifteenth and sixteenth centuries – a topic at present being much debated by historians – is undoubtedly one of the themes firmly represented in this selection, it takes its place alongside others.[3]

The second aim is to offer documentary examples from the widest possible spectrum of urban experience from the growing range of towns (London, the regional capitals, ports, market towns, spas, dockyard towns, and so on) in different parts not just of England, but of Scotland and Wales as well. Early modern Scotland was not so highly urbanised as England, and politically Scotland was perhaps less stable than England with more resultant damage to the towns. Town politics, too, developed at a different pace north of the border. The merchants took longer to establish their hegemony in Scottish than in English and Welsh towns. Gild authority was not so heavily eroded in Scotland as in England, and in the seventeenth century the gilds were able to ensure offices for their deacons on the town government of the larger burghs. However, the history of the Scottish gilds remains to be written, although some fine series of records are coming to light at Perth and elsewhere. The smaller size of the Scottish burghs result-ed in their suffering more keenly from the demographic, economic and political fluctuations of the pre-industrial world. The Reformation came later to Scotland than to England and Wales, but after 1559 the religious scene in Scotland was utterly transformed along Calvinist lines. However, in spite of all the differences of chronology and degree which can be dis-cerned in the development of Scottish burghs, their inhabitants suffered from many of the same difficulties as their English and Welsh counterparts. The documents selected below from Scotland illustrate both the similar-ities and differences. Thus the Scottish experience in the period up to 1700 provides a valuable yardstick to remind the reader of the importance of pre-industrial regional differences, of which the language of the Scottish documents included in this selection is just one striking example.

The third aim of this collection is to indicate the scope of the different categories of evidence available to the historian of this subject. The records of the Scottish towns, where they have been gathered together, contain similar town books, charters, taxation records to those found in the south. However, the Scottish burghs have their uniquely valuable kirk session and presbytery records which are an unrivalled source for the social historian.

No sourcebook, however bulky or comprehensive, is designed to be used in isolation, and this one — in at least two senses — is no exception. First, the book will be of greatest value when used in conjunction with modern historians' surveys of and monographs on the urban experience of this period. Among the important topics included in this selection one could mention, for instance, the political allegiance of towns in the later fifteenth century, the urban impact of the Reformation, the diversification and regulation of economic activity, town/countryside relations, the growing importance of London, the effects of plague, political accommodation and resistance to changing régimes in the seventeenth century, and the growth of social institutions and leisure. These are examples only, and to find his way through the selection the reader is referred not only to the table of contents but to the detailed index. The second way in which the book is designed not to be self-contained is that by identifying all the documents we have chosen the reader is enabled to follow up the extracts printed here and to find for himself other examples of the same kind of evidence.

Much of the documentation offered here — reflecting the range of what is available — is necessarily administrative in one sense or another and so conveys an official view (either central or local) of the issues under discussion. Corporation archives are the richest repository for this subject. The preponderance of documents concerned with government, justice, economic regulation and religion is no doubt unavoidable. None the less, we hope that the available range of essentially private records is well represented. The reader will find, for example, wills and inventories, correspondence, petitions, rentals and accounts, as well as (in Chapter One) a good selection from the writings of contemporary topographers and historians, and examples of art work and cartography. Changes in the physical appearance of towns, as well as changes in economy, society and politics, receive attention in this collection.

The structure of the book — thematic chapters each with their own internal chronology — is self-evident and requires no further explanation. In compiling this sourcebook the present editors rapidly came to appreciate the problems of selection. There was so much material available, so much ground to cover, and somehow it had to be distilled to a manageable size and yet still clearly satisfy the three guiding principles we enunciated at the outset. Documents which were originally in Latin are offered here in

English translation. There are many extracts rather than complete texts. In other respects, however, editorial intervention has been kept to a minimum. (Editorial glosses in the text are enclosed in square brackets). Definitions of obsolete words are provided. Capitalization generally and punctuation and spelling occasionally have been modernized when this appeared necessary in the interests of clarity. The collection draws both on previously unpublished material and on documents printed in Record Society volumes.

The main editorial division of labour has been a chronological one, Dr James being responsible for the pre-1600 material and Dr Richardson for the seventeenth-century extracts. Ultimately, however, the book is a joint venture in the full sense and the editors stand equally responsible for the book as a whole; the decision not to divide the volume at 1600 into two completely separate halves was one that was deliberately and willingly taken. Cross-reference between extracts in different parts of the book will enable the reader to explore long-term trends and to make comparisons and contrasts.

Both editors gratefully acknowledge the assistance they have received at every stage from archivists, librarians and others, and the encouragement of the publishers. They owe a particular debt to the Institute of Historical Research in London where much of the research for this volume was carried out. For permission to reprint material in extract form we are grateful to the following publishers, record societies, and record offices: Bristol Record Society, British Society for the History of Pharmacy, Buckinghamshire Record Society, Cambridge Antiquarian Society, Chetham Society, City and Royal Burgh of Edinburgh, Cumberland and Westmorland Antiquarian and Archaeological Society, Dugdale Society, Essex Record Office, Eyre-Methuen Ltd., Gulliver Publishing Company, Historical Manuscripts Commission, Isle of Wight Record Office, Kent Archaeological Society, Kent Archives Office, Lancashire Record Office, Leicester City Council, Liverpool Public Libraries, Manchester University Press, Norfolk Record Society, Northamptonshire Record Society, Oxford Historical Society, Oxford University Press, Oxfordshire Record Society, Record Society of Lancashire and Cheshire, Royal Historical Society (Camden Series), Scottish Burgh Records Society, Scottish Historical Society, Somerset Record Society, Southampton Record Office, Southampton Record Series, Staffordshire Record Society, Stratford-upon-Avon Record Office, Suffolk Record Office, Suffolk Records Society, Surrey Record Society, Surtees Society, University of Wales Press, Wiltshire Record Office, Wiltshire Record Society, Worcestershire Historical Society, Yale University Press, Yorkshire Archaeological Society.

April 1982   RCR   TBJ

References

1   P. Clark, *The Early Modern Town: a Reader* (1976), p. 1. See also H.
     J. Dyos (ed.), *The Study of Urban History* (1968) and A. Sutcliffe
     'The condition of urban history in England', *The Local Historian*, XI
     (1974), 278–84.

2   For surveys see, for example, C. Platt, *The English Medieval Town*
     (1976), A. R. Bridbury, 'English provincial towns in the later Middle
     Ages', *Economic History Review*, 2nd ser. XXXIV (1981), P. Clark
     and P. Slack, *English Towns in Transition 1500–1700* (Oxford, 1976),
     J. Patten, *English Towns 1500–1700* (Folkestone, 1978), and A.
     MacInnes, *The English Town 1660–1760* (1980). Good examples of
     modern monographs are C. Platt, *Medieval Southampton* (1973), A. D.
     Dyer, *The City of Worcester in the Sixteenth Century* (Leicester,
     1973), W. T. MacCaffrey, *Exeter, 1540–1640* (2nd ed., Cambridge,
     Mass., 1976) and P. Clark (ed.), *Country Towns in Pre-Industrial
     England* (Leicester, 1981).

3   See P. Clark and P. Slack (eds.), *Crisis and Order in English Towns,
     1500–1700* (1972); R. B. Dobson, 'Urban decline in late medieval
     England', *TRHS.*, 5th Ser., XXVII (1977), 1-22; A. D. Dyer, 'Growth
     and decay in English towns, 1500–1700', *Urban History Yearbook
     1979*, 60–72; C. Phythian-Adams, 'Urban decay in late medieval
     England', in P. Abrams and E. A. Wrigley (eds.), *Towns in Societies*
     (Cambridge, 1978), 159–85; C. Phythian-Adams *et al.*, *The Tra-
     ditional Community under Stress* (Milton Keynes, 1977).

GLOSSARY

almain rivets   light armour
alnage (ulnage)   measurement of cloth by the ell; official measurement
  and inspection of quality of woollen cloth
appurtenance   appendage to property
backsyde   rear yard or garden
bailie   chief magistrate of a burgh (Scots); alderman
beadle   junior parish or town official with responsibility for keeping
  order
blackfriars   Dominican friars
borough   a fortified place; a chartered community with structured government; a habitation larger than a village
brake   bracken
bruche   see burgh
burgage   tenure in towns whereby land was held for a rent
burgess   strictly an inhabitant of a borough possessing full municipal
  rights
burgh   (Scots) see borough
burh   see borough
cade   a cask or barrel (especially for herrings)
calenderer   one who smoothed or pressed cloth
cell   monastery dependant on a larger house
chantry priest   endowed for chanting mass, often for the soul of the
  founder
cognizance   hearing or trying a case
commonalty, 'comyntye'   a body corporate
cordwainer   shoemaker
common council   town council composed of burgess officials
corselet   type of body armour
court leet   periodical court of record held originally by the lord of its
  manor or his steward to hear residents' problems
danegeld   land tax originally (supposedly) levied to protect England
  against depredations
deacon   (Scots) head of an incorporated craft; Presbyterian official
  appointed to deal with secular affairs of the congregation
domus civica   town house, gild hall

doom judgement

dirge first word of antiphon at Matins in the office of the dead, the name adopted for that service

drugget wool

ell measure of cloth, England 45 inches, Scotland 37.2 inches

escheat confiscated goods or lands which revert to the lord

eyre circuit court held by justices

fee feudal holding

firkin small cask

foreigner an outsider, distinct from a stranger or alien

frankpledge system by which each member of a tithing was answerable for the good conduct of any one of its members

freeman member of a borough community with defined rights, sometimes equivalent to, sometimes inferior to those of a burgess

frieze(s) kind of coarse woollen cloth

gestronmaker (? gesseronmaker) light armour maker

gild, guild a confraternity or association formed for mutual aid and protection. Usually craft-based, but in the later Middle Ages socio-religious gilds existed.

gild merchant a confraternity, not necessarily entirely composed of merchants, which in the later Middle Ages in certain towns merged with the town government to become one body.

greyfriars Fransiscans

habeas corpus a writ requiring the presence of a person before a judge or in court for a purpose specified in a writ.

higgler itinerant dealer

hogshead large cask

Hostmen monopoly merchants (of Newcastle)

huckster hawker, petty retailer

infangthief right of manorial lord to try and amerce a thief

landgavel land-tax, ground rent

lastage port duty or market toll

law day day for a meeting of a court

league measure of distance, perhaps three miles

li pound

livery distinctive form of dress worn by retainers; provision or allowance made to followers

madder dye from *rubia tinctorum*

marchpanes marzipan

mark money of account, 13*s* 4*d*

mercer seller of small wares, or seller of silk and costly textiles

murage tax levied for building or repairing walls
murrey mulberry coloured cloth
ob halfpenny
ordinary set meal at an inn
piepowder (orig. from *pede pulverosus* or *pied poudreux*) court which heard merchants' disputes at markets and fairs
poldavis coarse canvas or sacking
pontage a toll levied (ostensibly) for the upkeep of bridges
provost (Scots) head of town government
pullen poultry, poultry flesh
reeve local official
replevin recovery of goods taken subject to a court hearing
scot and lot town tax at proportional rate to defray expenses
sir title of honour of knight, baronet or ordinary priest
soke and sac(k) customary rights of jurisdiction which belonged to the lord of the manor
stallage fine levied for right to erect a stall
staple town or place appointed by royal authority where a body of merchants could enjoy exclusive right of purchase of specific classes of goods for export
stranger a non-townsman, one from outside; alien
subsidy financial aid granted by parliament to meet special needs
tenement land or real property held by tenure
tod measurement by weight of wool
tonnage and poundage tax payment per ton, or tun, and per pound sterling
trental set of thirty requiem masses; payment for such masses; sometimes 'month's mind', commemoration on thirtieth day after burial
tronage weighing of goods, or tax for weighing goods
usher under master at school
watch and ward performance of originally feudal duty of a watchman
whittawer one who prepares white leather
will and testament instructions, usually written, for distribution of real and personal property after death

Inverness

Aberdeen

Perth • St Andrews
Stirling
Edinburgh
Glasgow
Lanark
Berwick
Ayr

Newcastle-
upon-Tyne

Carlisle

Kendal

Lancaster York

Preston Leeds
Ormskirk Blackburn Hull
Liverpool Manchester
Beaumaris
Chester Chesterfield

Nottingham

Lichfield Leicester King's Norwich
Lynn Great
Birmingham Coventry Peterborough Yarmouth
Bury
St Edmunds Aldeburgh
Worcester Northampton Cambridge
Stratford- Bedford Ipswich
upon-Avon Colchester
Gloucester Chelmsford Harwich
Haverfordwest Oxford High Maldon
Pembroke Tenby Great Wycombe
Marlowe London
Reading Gravesend Queenborough
Bristol Calne Kingston Rochester Canterbury
Bath Marlborough upon Thames Maidstone Faversham
Devizes Guildford Tunbridge
Wells Wells
Bridgwater Wilton Winchester Lewes Rye
Salisbury Southampton
Exeter Newport Portsmouth

0   km   100

1

Contemporary topographers and historians

1 CONTEMPORARY TOPOGRAPHERS AND HISTORIANS

1. William Worcestre's histories of some English towns, 1479

Of Norwich

Edward the Elder, son of king Alfred, a most victorious prince, among other noble works restored the *burh* which in Saxon was formerly called *Burghchester* and now Norwich, but which in the British tongue is named Kaergwelyn after king Gwytelinus who first founded that city with its castle, and gave it the name of 'the blanch flour castel' from its beauty.

Julius Caesar was not the first builder of that castle, but he caused various fortifications to be made there, as he did in every city whose name includes 'Chester', as one may suppose for example Chichester, Winchester, Rochester, and others. King Edward the Elder, when his time had come, was buried in the New Minster of Winchester which is now called Hyde Abbey.

Southampton

Hampton was named by Arviragus king of the Britons, who slew the Roman Hamon by the sea-shore in the place where the town of Hampton stands. On this account it was called Hampton in the time of Gwyder King of the Britons who refused to pay tribute to the Romans and who was afterwards slain by Claudius Caesar the Roman at Portchester town.

John H. Harvey (ed.), *William Worcestre: Itineraries*
(Oxford, 1969), 211

2. An Italian description of London, 1497

Now I must write somewhat more fully about the town of London, since it is the capital of the whole kingdom. First of all its position is so pleasant and delightful that it would be hard to find one more convenient and attractive. It stands on the banks of the river Thames, the biggest river in the whole island, which divides the town into two parts and forms the border of the county of Kent, the country and district which extends from

Dover to London. The town itself stretches from east to west, and is three miles in circumference. However its suburbs are so large that they greatly increase its circuit.

It is defended by handsome walls, especially on the northern side, where they have recently been rebuilt. Within these stands a very strongly defended castle on the banks of the river, where the king of England and his queen sometimes have their residence. There are also other great buildings, and especially a beautiful and convenient bridge over the Thames, of many marble arches, which has on it many shops built of stone and mansions and even a church of considerable size. Nowhere have I seen a finer or more richly built bridge.

Throughout the town are to be seen many workshops of craftsmen in all sorts of mechanical arts, to such an extent that there is hardly a street which is not graced by some shop or the like which can also be observed by everyone at Milan. This makes the town exceedingly prosperous and well-stocked, as well as having the immediate effect of adding to its splendour. The working in wrought silver, tin or white lead is very expert here, and perhaps the finest I have ever seen. There are also very many mansions, which do not, however, seem very large from the outside, but inside they contain a great number of rooms and garrets and are quite considerable. Six-inch oak beams are inserted in the walls the same distance apart as their own breadth and walls built in this way turn out to be made of the same material as the houses I described in Maastrich.

All the streets are so badly paved that they get wet at the slightest quantity of water, and this happens very frequently owing to the large numbers of cattle carrying water, as well as on account of the rain, of which there is a great deal in this island. Then a vast amount of evil-smelling mud is formed, which does not disappear quickly but lasts a long time, in fact nearly the whole year round. The citizens, therefore, in order to remove this mud and filth from their boots, are accustomed to spread fresh rushes on the floors of all houses, on which they clean the soles of their shoes when they come in. This system is widely practised not only by Londoners but also by all the rest of the island's inhabitants, who, it seems, suffer from similar trouble from mud.

There are a great many churches, but the most important of them all is St Paul's Cathedral, which is very magnificent and was built at great expense. Its roof is all made of lead, a practice that can be seen in many other buildings also. Merchants from not only Venice but also Florence and Lucca, and many from Genoa and Pisa, from Spain, Germany, the Rhine valley and other countries meet here to handle business with the utmost keenness having come from the different parts of the world. But the chief exports of this island are wool and fabrics, considered the best in the world, and white lead, for the island is more freely endowed with these commodities than any other country. By sea and the Thames goods of all kinds can be brought to London and taken from the city to other destinations.

> Andreas Franciscius, *Itinerarium Britanniae*, printed in *Two Italian*
> *Accounts of Tudor England*, trans. and publ. by C. V. Malfatti
> (Barcelona, 1953), 31–5, 36–7

3. An ideal of town distribution and planning, from *Utopia*, 1516

There be in the ilande liiii large and faire cities, or shiere townes, agreyng all together in one tonge, in lyke maners, institucions and lawes. They be all set and situate alyke, and in al poyntes fashioned alyke, as farforthe as the place or plotte sufferethe. Of these cities they that be nigheste together be xxiiii myles asonder. Againe there is none of them distaunte from the nexte above one dayes jorneyeye a fote. ... The precinctes and boundes of the shieres be so commodiously appoynted oute, and set fourthe for the cities, that none of them all hathe of anye syde lesse than xx myles of grounde, and of some syde also muche more, as of that part where the cities be of farther distaunce asonder. None of the cities desire to enlarge the boundes and limites of theire shieres.

Of the cities

Of them all Amaurote[1] is the worthiest and of most dignitie. For the resideu knowledge it for the head citie, because there is the counsell house ... The citie of Amaurote standeth upon the side of a lowe hill in fashyon almost foure square. For the breadth of it beginneth a litle beneth the toppe of the hill, and still continueth by the space of two miles untill it come to the ryver of Anyder. The length of it, which lieth by the rivers syde, is sumwhat more. The river of Anyder ... before the citie is half a myle broade ... and fortie myles beyond the citie it falleth into the Ocean sea. Ther goeth a bridge over the river made not of piles or of timber, but of stonewarke with gorgious and substancial arches at that part of the citie that is farthest from the sea: to the intent that shippes maye passe along biefor all the side of the citie without let. They also have an other river which ... runneth downe a slope through the middes of the citie into Anyder. And because it riseth a litle withoute the citie the Amaurotians have inclosed the head springe of it, with stronge fences and bulwarkes, and so have joined it to the citie. This is done to the intente that the water should not be stopped nor turned away, or poysoned, if their enemies should chaunce to come upon them. From thence the water is derived and conveied downe in cannels in bricke divers wayes into the lower partes of the citie ... The citie is compassed aboute with a heighe and thicke stone walle full of turrettes and bulwarkes. A drie diche, but deape, and brode, and overgrowen with bushes, briers and thornes, goeth aboute thre sides or quarters of the citie. To the fourth side the river it selfe serveth for a ditche. The stretes be appointed and set furth very commodious and handsome, both for carriage and againste the windes. The houses be of faire and gorgious building, and on the strete side they stande joined together in a long rowe through the whole strete without any partition or separation. The stretes be twentie fote brode. On the backe side of the houses through the whole length of the streete, lye large gardens inclosed rounde withe the backe parte of the streetes. Everye house hathe two doores, one into the streete, and a posterne doore on the backsyde into the garden. Whoso will, maye go in, for there is nothing within the houses that is private, or anie mans owne ... The houses be curiouslye builded after a gorgious and gallante sorte, with three storyes one over another. The outsides of the walles be made either of harde flinte, or of plaster, or els of bricke, and the inner sydes be well strengthened with tymber work. The roofes be plaine and flat, covered with a certen kinde of plaster that is of no coste, and yet so tempered that no fyre can hurte or perishe it, and withstandeth the violence of the wether better than any leade. They kepe the winde oute of their windowes with glasse, for it is there much used, and somehere also with fine linnen cloth dipped in oyle or ambre, and that for two commodities. For by thys meanes more lighte cometh in and the winde is better kepte oute.

[1] This is a somewhat idealised view of More's London.

J. R. Lumby (ed.), *More's Utopia* (1716 edition, rp. Cambridge, 1902), 69, 72–6

4. University towns and other Scottish burghs, *c.* 1520

The chief city in Scotland is Edinburgh. It has no river flowing through it, but the Water of Leith, half a league distant, might at great expense be diverted for the purpose of cleansing the city; but, after all, the city itself is distant from the ocean scarce a mile. Froissart compares Edinburgh to Tournay or Valenciennes; for a hundred years, however, the kings of Scots have had their residence almost constantly in that city. Near to Edinburgh – at the distance of a mile – is Leith, the most populous seaport of Scotland. On the descent thither is a small village, very prosperous, inhabited by weavers of wool – which gives its name to the best cloths in Scotland. Then there is Saint Andrews –where there is a university, to which no one has as yet made any magnificent gift, except James Kennedy, who founded one college, small indeed, but fair to look at and of good endowment. Another university is in the north, that of Aberdeen, in which there is a noble college founded by a bishop, Elphinston by name, who was also the founder of the university. There is, besides, the city of Glasgow, the seat of an archbishop, and of a university poorly endowed, and not rich in scholars. This notwithstanding, the church possesses prebends many and fat; but in Scotland such revenues are enjoyed *in absentia* just as they would be *in praesentia,* – a custom which I hold to be destitute at once of justice and common sense. I look with no favour on this multitude of universities; for just as iron sharpeneth iron, so a large number of students will sharpen one another's wits: Yet in consideration of the physical features of the country, this number of universities is not to be condemned. Saint Andrews, the seat of the primate of Scotland, possesses the first university; Aberdeen is serviceable to the northern inhabitants, and Glasgow to those of the west and south.

There is, in addition, the town of Perth, commonly called Saint John or Saint John's town, the only walled town in Scotland. Now if towns in general had even low walls, I should approve of it, as a means of restraining the robbers and thieves of the realm. The Scots do not hold themselves to need walled cities; and the reason of this may be, that they thus get themselves face to face with the enemy with no delay, and build their cities as it were, of men. If a force twenty thousand strong were to invade Scotland at dawn, a working day of twelve hours would scarcely pass before her people were in conflict with the enemy for the nearest chief gathers the neighbouring folk together.

John Major, A History of Greater Britain as well England as
Scotland (Scottish Historical Society Publications, X, 1892), 28–9

5. Leland visits Exeter and two small Welsh towns, 1535—43

There be diverse fair streates in Excester, but the high streate, that goith from the west to the est gate, is the fairest. In this streate be *castella, aquaeductus, et domus civica.* There be xv paroche chirchis in the towne. The cathedrale chirch of S. Peter and Paule: the cimiterie wherof having 4 gates is environid with many fair housis. The college house, wher the cantuarie prestes lyith, made of late tyme by John Rese dean of St. Burianes. The Vicares College. The Carnarie chapelle in the cemitery, made by one John Tresurer of the cathedrale chirch of Excester. A chapelle in the cimiterie. There was a priorie of S. Nicolas, a celle to Bataille-Abbay, in the north side of the toune. Joannes de Grandisono bisshop of Excester made an hospitale of S. John, and endowid it with landes. This hospitale is hard by the est gate. There is an other poore hospitale in the toun wherin yet sik men be kepte. There was an house of Gray Freres bytwixt the north and west gate neere the towne waulle, now a plain vacant ground caullid Frerenhay. Bytten Bisshop of Excester remevid thens the Gray Freres, and buildid them an house a litle without the south gate. There was an house of Blake Freres in the north side of the cemiterie of the cathedrale chirch, but withoute the close. The Lorde Russelle hath made hym a fair place of this house. There appere 2. fragmentes of inscriptions of the Romaines sette by chaunce of later tymes in the town waulle renewid on the bak side of this house sumtyme longging to the Blak Freres. One of them standith in the tower of the waul, the other is in the waull hard by the tower. The suburbe that lyith without the est gate of Excester is the biggest of al the suburbs of the towne, and berith the name of S. Sithewelle, where she was buried, and a chirch dedicate ther to her name.

Pembroke standith upon an arme of Milford, the wich about a mile beyond the towne creketh in that so that it almost peninsulatith the toune that standith on a veri maine rokki ground. The toune is welle waullid and hath iii. gates by est, west and north, of the wich the est gate is fairest and strongest, having afore hit a compasid tour not rofid, in the entering wherof is a portcolys *ex solido ferro.* The castel stondith hard by the waul on the hard rokke, and is veri larg and strong, being doble wardid. In the utter ward I saw the chaumbre wher king Henri the VII. was borne, in knowlege wherof a chymmeney is new made with the armes and badges of king Henri the VII. In the botom of the great stronge rownd tower in the inner ward is a mervelus vault caullid the Hogan. The toppe of this round towr is gatherid with a rofe of stone almost *in conum*, the top wherof is keverid with a flat mille stone. In the toune be a ii. paroche chirchis, and one in the suburbe. Montaine a celle of Blak Monkes in the suburbe is suppressid. The toune hath bene welle buildyd, and the est suburbe hath bene almost as great as the toun, but now it is totally yn ruine.

Tenby town stondith on a main rokke, but not veri hy, and the Severn Se so gulfeth in about hit, that at the ful se almost the thirde part of the toune is inclosid with water. The toune is strongeli waullid, and welle gatid, everi gate having his portcolis *ex solido ferro*. But that gate that ledith to Cairmardin ward is most semeliest, as circulid without with an embatelid but open rofid towr, after the fascion of the east gate of Pembroke. Without this gate is a preti suburbe. In the middes of the town is a faire paroche chirch. The toun it selfe lakkith fresch water, wherfore *utuntur importata*.

L. T. Smith (ed.), *The Itinerary of John Leland in or about the Years 1535– 43* (1907), I, 228; III, 115–17

6. William Lambarde attempts to classify towns by their names, 1576

How to discerne of townes by the ending of their names.
Such therefore, as were then numbred in the inferiour sort and degree, are commonly founde to have their names to ende, either in -bye, -tun, -ham or -sted. Bye, signified a dwelling, as byan, did to dwell: Tun which we now sounde (ton) and (towne) was derived of their woorde (tynan) to tyne, or inclose with a hedge: Wic and wice (for they bothe be one) was used for a place upon the edge of the sea or river, and was borowed of the Latine woord (*vicus*) though it be spoken wic: for the Saxons (having no single v consonant in all their alphabet) used to sound it as double w: making of vinum, ventus, and via, wine, wynd, and way.

Ham, properly signified a covering, and (by metaphore) a house that covereth us: This woord, we here call (home): but the northren men (not swarving so farre from the original) sounde it still (heam).

Finally, by (sted) they meant a seate, or standing by a river, deriving it (happily) from the Latine woord (*status*): and by -thorpe or -dorpe, a village, yet used in the lower Germaine.

Againe, such towns and dwellings as then were of greater price and estimation (either for the worthinesse of the owner, or for the multitude of the inhabitants, or for the strength or beautie of the building it selfe) had their names shut up commonly with one of these five particles, -ceaster, -biry, -burgh, -healle, or -weorth: Chester denoted a walled or fortified place, being the same both in woorde and weight that the Latine (*castrum*) is: Bury, or -biry was used for a court, or place of assembly: Burh (now also -burgh, and sometimes -burrough) is none other in sounde or substance, than *pyrgos* in Greeke, which we now call a towre, of the Latine name (*turris*): Healle, or (as we now speake it) hall, is all one with the Latine *aula*, or Greek aulē: Weorth (which also is now spoken woorth) signified *atrium*, a base court, or yarde, such as is commonly before the better sorte of houses. (Some derive weorth of the German word (*werd*) a poole). And thus much generally, and for this purpose, may suffice: for, to deale thorowly herein, belongeth rather to a peculiar dictionarie, than to this kinde of treatie and discourse.

William Lambarde, *A Perambulation of Kent* (1576), 376–7

7. Notable events recorded in the town chronicle of Perth, 1580–90

The entrie of the worthie and nobill king James the Saxt within Perth the 28 day of Maij 1580.

Mr John Row departed, minister at Perth in the 1580 yeir of God October 16.

Mr Patrick Galloway minister, admitted thairto 25 of Apryle 1581 yeiris; he tuik his woyage to be minister to his maiestie the 11 of Februar 1589 yeiris.

The erle of Morton regent, beheadit at Edinburgh.

The dounfalling of fyve bows of the brig of Tay, on the 14 day of Januar 1582 yeiris.

The Justice air halden at Perth, be king James the Saxt the 6 of Julij 1582 yeiris.

Pest in Perth the 24 day of September 1584 yeiris, continewit to August 1585 yeiris quharin at the plesore of God, departed this lyff, fourteen hundred and twenty seven persons young and auld therby.

The entrie of the erllis of Mar and Angus in Striviling, against his maiestie, at palm sondie 1585.

His sacred maiesties marriage in Denmark be my lord marischall, ambassador, the 20 day of August 1589.

Thair arryval at Leithe the first of May 1590 and crownit quene the 17th of the same monethe. Her entrie to Perth the 23 of Junii 1591.
A plague among the bestiall 1590.

James Maidment (ed.), *The Chronicle of Perth 1210–1668*
(Maitland Club, X, Edinburgh, 1831), 4

8. William Camden praises the city of Worcester, 1586

The Severn with a slow course as it were admiring passeth by Worcester the chief town of this shire, seated on its bank: and it really deserveth admiration both for its antiquity and beauty.

This city was, in all probability, built by the Romans, when to curb the Britains who dwelt beyond Severn, they planted cities at convenient distances all along upon its east-bank, just as they did in Germany on the south-side of the Rhine. It is seated upon an easie ascent from the river, over which lieth a bridge with a tower upon it. It was anciently fenced with lofty Roman walls, as an old parchment-roll informs us; and hath to this day a good firm wall. But its glory consists in its inhabitants; who are numerous, courteous, and wealthy, by means of the cloathing trade; in the neatness of its buildings, the number of churches, and most of all, in the episcopal see, which Sexuulfus bishop of the Mercians placed here A.D. 680. building of a cathedral church in the south part of the city, which hath often been repair'd, and by the bishops and monks hath been lengthened westward, a little at a time, almost to Severnside.

In the year 1113 a casual fire, which consumed the castle, burnt the roof of the church also. During the civil wars in k. Stephen's reign, it was fired once and again, but suffered most when the king took the city, which he had unadvisedly put into the hands of Walleran Earl of Mellent; but at that time he could not carry the castle. However, it still rose out of the ashes with greater beauty, and hath flourished under an excellent government, managed by two bailiffs chosen out of 24 citizens, two aldermen and two chamberlains, with a common council consisting of 48 citizens more. As to the geographical account of it, its longitude from the west meridian is 21 degrees, 52 minutes, and hath the north pole elevated 52 degrees and 12 minutes.

William Camden, *Britannia* (1695), 518–19

9. A town plan of Chelmford, 1591

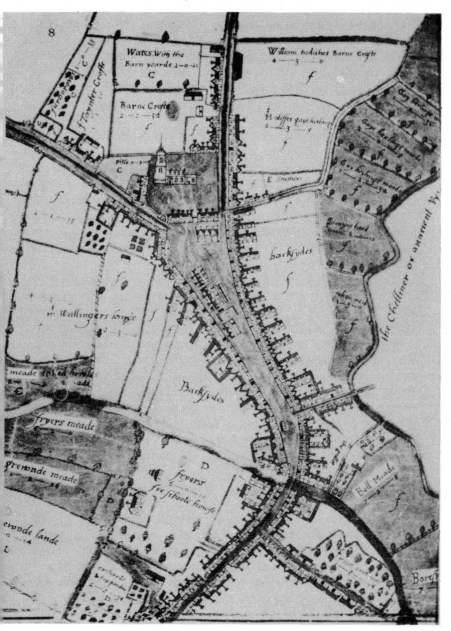

By courtesy of Essex County Records Office

10. John Stow defends London's pre-eminence, 1598

I have shortly to answer the accusation of those men, which charge London with the loss and decay of many (or most) of the ancient cities, corporate towns, and markets within this realm, by drawing from them to herself alone, say they, both all trade of traffic by sea, 'and the retailing of wares and exercise of manual arts also. Touching navigation, which I must confess is apparently decayed in many port towns, and flourisheth only or chiefly at London, I impute that partly to the fall of the Staple, the which being long since a great trade, and bestowed sometimes at one town and sometimes at another within the realm, did much enrich the place where it was, and being now not only diminished in force, but also translated over the seas, cannot but bring some decay with it, partly to the impairing of havens, which in many places have impoverished those towns, whose estate doth ebb and flow with them, and partly to the dissolution of religious houses, by whose wealth and haunt many of those places were chiefly fed and nourished. I mean not to rehearse particular examples of every sort, for the thing itself speaketh, and I haste to an end.

As for retailers, therefore, and handicraftsmen, it is no marvel if they abandon country towns, and resort to London; for not only the court, which is now-a-days much greater and more gallant than in former times, and which was wont to be contented to remain with a small company, sometimes at an abbey or priory, sometimes at a bishop's house, and sometimes at some mean manor of the king's own, is now for the most part either abiding at London, or else so near unto it, that the provision of things most fit for it may easily be fetched from thence; but also by occasion thereof, the gentlemen of all shires do fly and flock to this city; the younger sort of them to see and show vanity, and the elder to save the cost and charge of hospitality and house-keeping.

For hereby it cometh to pass, that the gentlemen being either for a good portion of the year out of the country, or playing the farmers, graziers, brewers, or such like, more than gentlemen were wont to do within the country, retailers and artificers, at the least of such things as pertain to the back or belly, do leave the country towns, where there is no vent, and do fly to London, where they be sure to find ready and quick market. And yet I wish, that even as many towns in the low countries of King Philip do stand, some by one handy art, and some by another; so also that it might be provided here that the making of some things might (by discreet dispensation) be allotted to some special towns, to the end, and although the daintiness of men cannot be restrained. which will needs seek those things at London, yet other places also might be relieved, at the least by the workmanship of them.

Thus much then of the estate of London, in the government thereof, in the condition of the citizens, and in their power and riches. Now follow the enumeration of such benefits as redound to the prince and this realm by this city: in which doing I profess not to rehearse all, but only to recite and run over the chief and principal of them.

Besides the commodities of the furtherance of religion and justice, the propagation of learning, the maintenance of arts, the increase of riches, and the defence of countries (all which are before showed to grow generally by cities, and be common to London with them), London bringeth singularly these good things following.

By advantage of the situation it disperseth foreign wares (as the stomach doth meat) to all the members most commodiously.

By the benefit of the river of Thames, and great trade of merchandise, it is the chief maker of mariners, and nurse of our navy; and ships (as men know) be the wooden walls for defence of our realm.

It maintaineth in flourishing estate the countries of Norfolk, Suffolk, Essex, Kent, and Sussex, which as they lie in the face of our most puissant neighbour, so ought they above others to be conserved in the greatest strength and riches; and these, as it is well known, stand not so much by the benefit of their own soil, as by the neighbourhood and nearness which they have to London.

It relieveth plentifully, and with good policy, not only her own poor people, a thing which scarcely any other town or shire doth, but also the poor that from each quarter of the realm do flock unto it, and it imparteth liberally to the necessity of the universities besides. It is an ornament to the realm by the beauty thereof, and a terror to other countries, by reason of the great wealth and frequency. It spreadeth the honour of our country far abroad by her long navigations, and maketh our power feared, even of barbarous princes. It only is stored with rich merchants, which sort only is tolerable; for beggarly merchants do bite too near, and will do more harm than good to the realm.

It only of any place in this realm is able to furnish the sudden necessity with a strong army. It availeth the prince in tronage, poundage, and other her customs, much more than all the rest of the realm.

It yieldeth a greater subsidy than any one part of the realm; I mean not for the proportion of the value of the goods only, but also for the faithful service there used, in making the assess, for no where else be men taxed so near to their just value as in London; yea, many are found there, that for their countenance and credit sake, refuse not to be rated above their ability, which thing never happeneth abroad in the country. I omit that in ancient time the inhabitants of London and other cities were accustomably taxed after the tenth of their goods, when the country was assessed at the fifteenth, and rated at the eighth; when the country was set at the twelfth, for that were to awake a sleeping dog; and I should be thought *'dicenda, tacenda, locutus,'* as the poet said.

It only doth and is able to make the prince a ready present or loan of money.

It only is found fit and able to entertain strangers honourably, and to receive the prince of the realm worthily.

Almighty God (*qui nisi custodiat civitatem, frustrà vigilat custos*) grant that her majesty evermore rightly esteem and rule this city; and he give grace, that the citizens may answer duty, as well towards God and her majesty, as towards this whole realm and country. Amen.

H. B. Wheatley (ed.), *The Survey of London
by John Stow* (1912), 495–7

11. The history of cities in England: the view of an Elizabethan antiquarian, 1598[1]

The first city of name in England is Totnes in Devon, for that by opinion of writers Brute landed there, and within that town is a great stone, as London stone, whereon the report is, that Brute reposed himself, when he first landed there. It is at this day governed by a mayor and bailiffs.

Hollingshed is of opinion that there were greater store of cities, towns, and villages in old time than there are at this day: and he doth vouch Ranulf, monk of Chester, who telleth of a general survey made 4 W. C. and that there were to the number of 52000 towns, and 45002 parishes; but by the assertions of such as write in our time concerning that matter you shall not find above 17000 towns and villages in the whole; which is but little more than a fourth part of the aforesaid number.

It appeareth by the records belonging to the cathedral church of St. Peter in Exon, that the bishops see for Devon was first at Kirton, and from thence after removed into Excester; which Kirton is but a little village at this day, and hath but one church.

I have divers antiquities in coin stamped at several towns in England, the ancientest whereof is a British piece of gold, whereon is *Camuladunum*, which Hollingshed taketh to be Colchester, but Mr. Camden taketh it to be Malden in Essex, the town where the King's mint was kept. In the days of king Æthelstane there is mention that there should be a mint for coins in

Canterbury, Rochester, London, Winton, in the street of Lewes, in the street of Hastings, Chichester, Hampton, and diverse others.

[1] On the Elizabethan Society of Antiquaries (of which the author of this extract was a member) see May McKisack, *Medieval History in the Tudor Age* (Oxford, 1971) and K. Sharpe, *Sir Robert Cotton, 1586–1631: History and Politics in Early Modern England* (Oxford, 1979).

Joseph Holland, 'For the antiquity of cities in England'
(1598), J. Ayloffe (ed.), *A Collection of Curious
Discourses* (1775), I, 38–9

12. Cornish towns and townspeople, 1602

From gentility, we will descend to civility, which is or should be in the townesmen. Those in Cornwall do no more by nature, then others else-where by choyce, conceive themselves an estranged society from the upland dwellers, and cary, I will not say a malice, but an emulation against them, as if one member in a body could continue his wel-being without a beholdingnes to the rest. Their chiefest trade consisteth in uttering their petty marchandises, & artificers labours at the weekly markets. Very few among them make use of that oportunity, which the scite upon the sea proffereth unto many, for building of shipping, and traffiking in grosse: yet some of the easterne townes piddle that way, & some others give themselves to fishing voyages, both which (when need requireth) furnish her maiesties navy with good store of very serviceable mariners.

There are (if they be not slaundered) that hunt after a more easie then commendable profit, with little hazard, and (I would I could not say) with lesse conscience. *Anno 32. H 8.* an act of parliament was made for repayr-ing, amongst others, the borough townes of Launceston, Liskerd, Lostwithiel, Bodmyn, Truro, and Helston in Cornwall, but with what fruit to their good, I cannot relate.

Within late yeeres memorie, the sea-coast townes begin to proclaime their bettering in wealth, by costly encrease of buildings, but those of the inland, for the most part, vouch their ruined houses, and abandoned streets, as too true an evidence, that they are admitted no partners in this amendment. If I mistake not the cause, I may with charitie inough wish them still the same fortune: for as is elsewhere touched, I conceyve their former large peopling, to have bin an effect of the countries impoverishing,

[*to p. 17*]

13. Bristol and York mapped by Speed, *c.* 1610

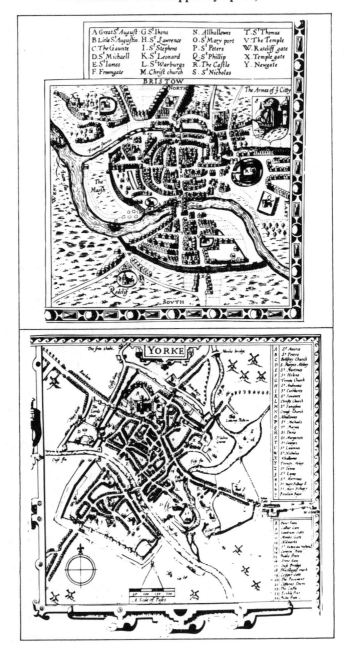

while the invasion of forraine enemies drave the sea-coast inhabitants to seeke a more safe, then commodious abode in those inland parts.

Richard Carew, *The Survey of Cornwall* (1759), 65–6

14. Berwick in 1634

Junii 25. – We arrived about five clock at Barwicke, where we passed a very fair, stately bridge over Tweede, consisting of fifteen arches, which was built by king James, and, as it is said, cost £17,000 ... This town [is] seated upon the main sea, the Northern Ocean, and seems to be almost environed with the sea.

The haven is a most narrow, shallow, barred haven, the worst that I have seen; it might be made good, a brave and secure haven, whereas now only one little pink of about forty ton belongs unto it, and some few fishing-boats. There being, therefore, no trade in this town, it is a very poor town, many indigent persons and beggars therein. Here were the strongest fortifications I have met with in England, double-walled, and out-works of earth, and the outer walls like unto Chester walls, and without the inner walls a deep and broad moat well watered; the inner walls of invincible strength, stone walled within, and without lined with earth about twenty yards thick, with bulwarks conveniently placed to guard one another, like unto the Buss, Bergen, Antwerpe, or Gravelin: these were begun by Queen Mary, finished by Queen Elizabeth, but something in decay: these walls environ the town.

A stately, sumptuous, and well-seated house or castle was here begun by the last Earl of Dunbar, where the old castle stood; but his death put an end to that work. Here was a most stately platform propounded and begun; a fair long gallery joiced not boarded, wherein is the largest mantle-tree I have seen, near five yards long of one piece; this leaded over, which gives the daintiest prospect to the sea, to the town, to the land, and the river. This, with much lands hereabout, was bestowed upon him by king James, who left all his lands to his daughter and heir, who married the now Earl of Suffolk. This town is seated on the north side of Twede, and is placed upon the sloping of a steep hill. They speak of three hundred and sixty salmons taken at one draught, and ordinarily about eighty, and one hundred, or one hundred and twenty, at one draught. We lodged at the Crown, were well used; 8*d* ordinary, and 6*d* our servants, and great entertainment and good lodging, a respective host and honest reckoning.

[*to p. 19*]

15. London from Bankside engraved by the Czech Wenceslaus Hollar, 1647

A. M. Hind, *Wenceslaus Hollar and his Views of London and Windsor in the Seventeenth Century* (1922)

26 Junii. – Upon Friday we departed from Barwicke, which, though it be seated in Scottland, yet it is England, and is annexed to the crown of England by act of Parliament, and sends two burgesses to the Parliament-house, and here the country is not reputed Scottish, until you come to a town, four miles distant from Barwick, called Ayten.

E. Hawkins (ed.), *Travels in Holland, the United*
Provinces, England, Scotland and Ireland, 1634–5
by Sir William Brereton Bart (Chetham Society:
I, 1844), 94–6

16. The topography, economy and government of Newcastle-upon-Tyne in 1649

The Sand-hill

Now let us describe unto you the other streets and markets in this town. First of the Sand-hill, a market for fish, and other commodities; very convenient for merchant-adventurers, merchants of coals, and all those that have their living by shipping. There is a navigable river, and a long quay or wharf, where ships may lie safe from danger of storms, and may unload their commodities and wares upon the quay. In it, are two cranes for heavy commodities, very convenient for carrying of corn, wine, deals, &c. from the quay into the water-gates, which are along the quay-side, or into any quarter of the town.

In this market-place are many shops and stately houses for merchants, with great conveniences of water, bridge, garners, lofts, cellars, and houses of both sides of them. Westward they have a street called the Close. East, the benefit of the houses of the quay-side.

In this Sand-hill standeth the town-court, or guildhall, where are held the guilds every year by the mayor and burgesses, to offer up their griev-ances, where the mayor keepeth his court every Monday, and the sheriff hath his county-court upon Wednesday and Friday.

In it is kept a court of admiralty, or river-court, every Monday in the afternoon. This is a court of record for inrolling of deeds and evidences. There is a court of Pie-powder, during the said two fairs, Lammas and St. Luke; all the privileges and power, that a court-leet can have, are grant-ed to this court.

Under the town-court is a common weigh-house for all sorts of com-modities. King Henry the Sixth sent to this town, as to other cities and towns, brass weights according to the standard.

Near this is the town-house, where the clerk of the chamber and chamberlains are to receive the revenues of the town for coal, ballast, salt, grind-stones, &c.

Next adjoining is an alms-house, called the Maison de Dieu, built by that noble benefactor Roger de Thornton.

Above which is the stately court of the merchant-adventurers, of the old staple, resident at that flourishing city of Antwerp in Brabant, since removed to the more northern provinces under the states. Their charters are ancient, their privileges and immunities great: they have no dependence upon London; having a governor, twelve assistants, two wardens, and a secretary ...

The middle parts of the town

Next up street is the street called the Side. In the lower part of it standeth a fair cross, with columns of stones hewn, covered with lead, where are sold milk, eggs, butter, &c.

In the Side are shops for merchants, drapers, and other trades. In the middle of the Side is an ancient stone-house, an appendix to the castle, which in former times belonged to the Lord Lumleys, before the castle was built, or at least coetany[1] with the castle.

Next up the town north, is Middle-street, where all sorts of artificers have shops and houses.

The west-side of this street is the oatmeal-market.

On the east side of it is the flesh-market, I think the greatest market[2] in England for all sorts of flesh and poultry that are sold there every Saturday; the reason is not the populousness of the town that makes it, it is the people in the country, within ten miles of the town, who make their provision there; as likewise all that live by the coal-trade, for working and conveying coals to the water: as also the shipping which comes into this river for coals, there being sometimes three-hundred sail of ships. In this market are kept two fairs in the year, for nine days together; one of them at that remarkable time of the year, the first of August; the other is held, the eighteenth of October, upon St. Luke's day.

Next above north, is the big[3] and oat market every Tuesday and Saturday in the week.

In which street is an ancient house, with a large gate, called the Scots Inn, where the kings, nobility, and lairds of Scots lodged, in time of truce or league with England.

[1] Of the same age.   [2] Except Leadenham market in London.   [3] i.e. barley.

Chorographia: or a Survey of Newcastle-upon-Tyne (1649),
Harleian Miscellany, (1809), III, 276–7

17. William Smith describes the city of Chester. 1656

The famous and ancient city of Chester standeth upon the river of Dee, on the west side of the countrey of Cheshire; as also, on the west part of England, (for which cause it is of some called Westchester) distant 16. miles south-east from the main Sea, 20. miles east from Denbigh, 30. north from Shrewsbury, 36. north-west from Stafford, 44. west from Darby, and 55. south from Lancaster.

The walls

The walls of the city contain at this present day, in circuit, two English miles; within the which, in some places, there is certain void ground, and corn-fields, whereby (as also by certain ruines of churches, or such like great places of stone) it appeareth, that the same was in old time all inhabited. But look what it wanteth at this day within the walls, it hath without, in very fair and large suburbs.

The gates

It hath four principal gates, the East-gate towards the east; the Bridge-gate towards the south; the Water-gate towards the west; and the North-gate towards the north.

These gates in times past, and yet still, according to an ancient order used here in this city, are in the protection or defence of divers noble-men, which hold or have their lands lying within the county palatine. As first, the Earl of Oxford hath the East-gate, the Earl of Shrewsbury hath the Bridge-gate, the Earl of Darby the Water-gate, who in the right of the castle of Hawarden (not far of) is steward of the county palatine; and the North-gate belongeth to the city, where they keep their prisoners.

Besides these four principal gates, there are certain other lesser, like postern-gates, and namely St. John's Gate, between East-gate, and Bridge-gate; so called, because it goeth to the said church which standeth without the walls.

The East-gate is the fairest of all the rest; from which gate, to the banes, which are also of stone, I find to be 160. paces of geometry. And from the banes, to Boughton, almost as much.

The bridge

The Bridge-gate is at the south part of the city, at the entring of the bridge, commonly called Dee-bridge; which bridge is builded all of stone, of eight arches in length: At the furthest end whereof, is also a gate; and without that, on the other side of the water, the suburbs of the city, called Hond-bridge.

Sheriffs

The sheriffs (as also the Maior) on the work-dayes, go in fair long gownes welted with velvet, and white staves in their hands. But they have violet and scarlet for festival dayes.

The common hall

Not far from the Pendice, towards the Abbey Gate, is The Common Hall of the City. Which is a very great House of Stone: and serveth instead of their guild-hall, or town-house.

The rowes

The buildings of the city are very ancient; and the houses builded in such sort, that a man may go dry, from one place of the city to another, and never come in the street; but go as it were in gallaries, which they call, the Roes, which have shops on both sides, and underneath, with divers fair staires to go up or down into the street. Which manner of building, I have not heard of in any place of christendome. Some will say, that the like is at Padua in Italy, but that is not so. For the houses at Padua, are builded as the suburbs of this city be, that is, on the ground, upon posts, that a man may go dry underneath them; like as they are at Billingsgate in London, but nothing like to the Roes.

The Mercers Row

It is a goodly sight to see the number of fair shops, that are in these Rowes, of mercers, grocers, drapers and haberdashers, especially in the street called, The Mercers Row. Which street, with the Bridge street, (being all one street) reacheth from the high crosse to the bridge, in length 380 paces of geometry, which is about a quarter of a mile.

Conduits of fresh water

There are certain conduits of fresh water. And now of late (following the example of London) they have builded one at the high crosse in the middest of the city, and bring the water to it, from Boughton.

Daniel King, *The Vale Royall of England, or the County*
Palatine of Chester illustrated (1656), 37, 40

18. Beaumaris, *c.* 1669

This town was built by Edward I. in the 23rd year of his reign, A. D. 1295, in a place called Bonover Marsh, and it was walled about and strengthened with a castle on the east end thereof to awe the Welsh. Some will have it called from Bimaris, as Horace calls Corinth Bimaris Corinthus, Hor: Lib. 1. Od. 7, from the meeting of two seas or tides near the place. Others from the French Beau and Marais, a beautiful marsh.

In this town take a view of 5 things (viz.), the church, the school, castle, sea and port adjoining, borrough and corporation, together with its liberties, franchizes, and government thereof. ...

The town of Beaumaris was incorporate by Edward 1st., and that by charter dated at Berwick-on-Tweed on the 10th. Sept. 24th. of his reign, whereby he granted, 1st., that the town of Beaumaris should be a free borough, and that the men of the same town should be free burghers. 2d., that the constable of the castle should be mayor of the town. 3d., That 2 bailiffs should be chosen at Michaelmas yearly. 4, That they shall have a free prison in the castle, and shall have cognizance of all trespasses except the case of life and member. 5, That all lands assigned to the borough shall be diswarrened and disafforested; and that no Jews shall dwell there. 6, That they shall have a guild of merchandize with haunce and other customs and liberties to such a guild appertaining. 7, That no sheriff shall enter there for any plea or plaint. 8, That the villeine of any person shall dwell and hold land in the borough, paying scott and lott for a year and a day without claim or challenge, and from thence-forth shall be coerced and call'd again by his lord, but remain free in said town; and that he shall have sock and sack and theane and infangthiefe. 9, That the burgesses of the said town shall be quit of toll, lastage, passage, murage, pontage, stallage, danegeld, and gaywitt, and all other customs and exactions through the king's dominions. 10, That the said burgesses and their goods shall not be arrested within the king's lands and power, for which they be not sureties or principal debtors. 11, That if any of the said burgesses die testate or intestate, their goods shall not be confiscated to the king, but their heirs shall have the same. 12, That the burgesses shall not be convicted by any foreigners for any matter but by English burgesses, except it be for matters touching the commonalty of the said borough, and then they are to be led by the customs of ye city of Hereford.

The town and suburbs are divided into 4 wards (viz.) Castle Street Ward, Church Street Ward, Watergate Ward and Wrexham Street Ward, a constable to each ward. In Wrexham Street Ward there is a street call'd

Rating Row (or as corruptly call'd Rotten Row), so call'd because in old times when the castle was garrison'd the provisions coming from the country were rated there for the use of ye garrison. ...

The borough was first govern'd by a constable, alderman, and two bailiffs, but since the renewal of the charter in Elizabeth's reign there is only a mayor and two bailiffs. The first mayor on the new charter was Richard Bulkly, Esq., after Sir Richard. It had a recorder, a town clerk, a coroner, two serjeants at mace, two church wardens, one to be chosen by the 24 burgesses, the other by the minister of the town, accountable only to the town court, and not to the consistory court of Bangor for their yearly accounts, a privilege they claim by prescription. Two sidesmen, two common appraisers, two searchers and sealers of leather, two scavengers, two burleigh men or overseers of the hedges, ditches, and inclosures about the town. One water bailiff, a bailiff for each of the 4 wards, and one bailiff for the liberties. One beadle.

J. Fisher (ed.), *Tours in Wales by Richard Fenton* (Cambrian Archaeological Association, 1917), 275–6, 304–5

19. Kendal, as depicted by Daniel Fleming, 1671

This town is a place of excellent manufacture, and for civility, ingenuity, and industry so surpassing, that in regard thereof it deservedly carrieth a great name. The trade of the town makes it populous, and the people seem to be shaped out for trade, improving themselves not only in their old manufactures of cottons, but of late of making of drugget, serges, hatts, worsted, stockins, &c., whereby many of the poor are daily set on work, and the town much enriched. The inhabitants are generally addicted to sobriety and temperance, and express a thriftiness in their apparrel, the women using a plain tho' decent and handsome dress, above most of their neighbours. They count it much for their credit, that their town hath dignified barons, earls, and dukes, and several of them of the blood royal with the title thereof. ...

It is fortified on the east side with a fair old castle, the antient seat of some of the lords of this town ... and on the west side of this town is defended (opposite to the said castle), with an old fort or artificial hill, a great height called Castle How-hill or Battle-place. ... This corporation was antiently an alderman town, but being changed in King James 1st reign, it hath ever since been a mayor town, and is now (1671) prudently governed by James Sympson Esq., mayor thereof, Willm. Guy, Edwd. Turner, To. Towers, Tho. Fisher, Wm. Potter, Tho. Jackson, John Park, Tho. Turner, Stephen Birkett, James Troughton, Willm. Collinson, and John Jefferson, aldermen of the said town, with 20 common council men, assisted by Tho. Braithwaite Esq. recorder, and Mr. Allan, town-clerk, and two attornies, who still attend at their sessions and courts of record; herein are also a sword-bearer, two serjeants-at-mace, two chamberlains, three constables, and six overseers for the poor. In this town are seven companies, viz. mercers, shearmen, cordwainers, tanners, glovers, taylors, and pewterers, each of which companies hath a warden, chosen every year, and sworn to see to their several trades, and the observation of their orders, having also each of them a several hall, or place belonging to the said companies. Here is quarterly a general sessions of the peace holden for this town by the mayor, recorder, and two senior aldermen, who are all justices of the peace for this corporation by their charter. ... Its a great market for all sorts of provision, &c., on every Saturday, and fairs for cattle on 25th April and 28th October. The country about this town is very pleasant and fruitfull, abounding with corn and grass well enclosed, and well stor'd with good houses, woods, and rivers, divers of them empty themselves into Kent, and with it after a few miles travel incorporate with the ocean.

G. F. Duckett (ed.), *Fleming's Description of the County of Westmorland, 1671* (Cumberland & Westmorland Antiquarian & Archaeological Society, Tract Series, I, 1882), 8–11

20. Thomas Baskerville in Norwich, 1681

As to Norwich it is a great city and full of people. I cannot say which is the bigger, Bristol or Norwich, but of the two I think Norwich. It hath 34, some say 35 churches, and those for the most part not small, but large and well built of free-stone and flint. I told, as I stood upon the castle yard myself 28 towers, of these Christ Church, the cathedral is chief, situate in the lower parts of the town not far from the river; it hath a tall spire or steeple in the middle and 2 small spires at the West end front, with thick bulky pillars in the body of the church, like those of Wells in Somerset, and so is the cloister adjoining containing like that, a church-yard within it. The bishop hath now a large ancient house hard by the church, but by the ruins which Mr. Burton the school-master shewed us, it hath been much bigger. Dr. Reynolds the late bishop of this diocese hath built to the now standing part of the house a very fine chapel, and as I remember lies buried in it. Bishop Sparrow, late of Exeter, is now the present bishop of the diocese ...

This city is encompassed with an ancient flint wall, with towers at convenient distance for defence, and gates for entrance, and this wall is of such extent that within the compass of the city are many gardens, orchards, and inclosures, so that a man may boldly say it hath the greatest inclosures of any town in England. There are also on the other side the river some forts or towers of stone, where they may cross the river with chains of iron to hinder the passage of boats.

Here also remains the ruins of a very stately castle, built on the top of an eminent hill in the midst of the town, over-topping all the rest of the city, and to this castle, surrounded with deep dikes, there is an entrance by one bridge having only one great and entire arch under it, of such a vast breadth and height that it surpasses any of the bridges in Yorkshire, over the river Wharfe or elsewhere. A little way from this castle on the opposite side of a hill, is the chief market place of this city, and this being the only place where all things are brought to be sold, for the food of this great city, they not as in London allowing markets in several places, make it vastly full of provisions, especially on Saturdays, where I saw the greatest shambles for butchers' meat I had ever yet seen, and the like also for poultry and dairy meats, which dairy people also bring many quarters of veal with their butter and cheese, and I believe also in their seasons pork and hog-meats. These people fill a square of ground on the side of a hill twice as big Abingdon market place. They setting their goods in ranges as near as may be one above another, only allowing room for single persons to pass between; and above these the butchers have their shambles and such kind of people as sell fish, of which there was plenty of such kinds as the seas hereabouts afford, viz. crabs, flounders, mackerel, very cheap, but lobster for sea fish and pike or jack for river fish, were dear enough. They asked me for one pike under 2 foot, 2s 6d, and for a pot of pickled oysters they would have a shilling. Here I saw excellent oat-meal which being curiously hulled looked like French barley. With great store of ginger-bread and other edible things. And for grain in the corn market, which is on the other side the market-house, as large for space of ground as that on which the dairy people stand, I saw wheat, rye, oats, malt ground and not ground, French wheat, and but little barley, because the season for malting was over.

Their chief market-house stands in the midst of this great market-place, now very full of people and provisions, being circular or round in form, having chained to the several pillars thereof bushels, pecks, scales, and other things for the measuring and weighing of such goods as are brought to the market. And over against this declivity where the market people stand is a fair walk before the prime inns and houses of the market place, called the gentlemen's walk or walking place, which is kept free for that purpose from the encumbrance of stalls, tradesmen, and their goods. About the middle of this walk is the sign of the 'King's Head,' where we lay, Mrs. Berne, a widow, then landlady, who keeps a good ordinary on Saturdays for 12 pence meat, where we dined in the company of many gentlemen ... Here is also in the compass of this market place a fair town-hall, where the mayor and his brethren with the livery-men of this city keep a great feast, presenting the ladies that come thither with marchpanes to carry away. They have also fine shows in the streets, in some measure like that of the Lord Mayor's Day of London and, as Mr. Burton told me, one of the eminent scholars of his school does usually make an elegant speech to the mayor and his brethren as they pass by, richly clad in their scarlet robes.

The chief trade of this famous town mostly consists in making stuffs, and worsted stockings, they in these sorts of manufactures excelling all other places. As to the river, it is not so broad as the Thames below Oxon, yet the boats that trade between this and Yarmouth usually carry between 20 and 30 tons ...

Here is in this city an order the like is no where else to be found in any town in England, and that is, the butchers are obliged to sell the meat they kill the fore part of the week by Thursday night, for on a Friday night speaking to our landlady for a joint of mutton to be roasted for our suppers, she told us it was not to be had. And this they do to oblige the fishermen to bring plenty of fish from the sea, as also to make good the sale of that kind of food, so that, as some gentlemen of Yarmouth told me, they many times there for that reason have but bare or scanty markets of fish.

'Thomas Baskerville's Journeys in England temp. Car. II',
Historical MSS. Commission, 13th Report, Appendix Pt. II,
Portland Mss. (1893), II, 268–70

21. Preston, towards the end of the seventeenth century

This burrough is much adorned with its large square or market-place, as likewise with the streets thereof, which are so spacious from one end thereof unto the other, that few of the corporations of England exceed the same, either for streets or market-place. In the midle of the burrough is placed an ample antient and yet well beautifyed gylde or town hall or toll bothe, to which is annexed, at the end thereof, a counsell chamber for the capitall burgesses or jurors at their court days, to retire for consultation, or secretly to retire themselves from the comon burgesses or the publiq root of people, as occasion shall require.

The publiq hall hath a decent cheq, and above it an elevated bench, whereat the three portmotes or the two leet days and the grand leet or court of election for new magistrates, sitts the mayor, aldermen, and such gentry as attends those meetings, and likewise at their court of common pleas, held each 3 weeks, for deciding suites and controversies ... Under this hall are ranged two rows of butchers' shopps on either side, and row at either end, where victualls are exposed dayly for the use of man, excepting Sundays, as also weekly on the public market dayes (&c.) Wednesday, and Saturday, and Friday being ever a market for fish, butter, and cheese, as likewise in the evening for yarn; Wednesday likewise being a market for fish, butter, and cheese: And upon Saturday, as soon as light appeare, is the market bell for linnen cloth; when ended, yarn appears, bread and fish of all sorts, butter and cheese; as formerly, the fish all in a row upon the fish stones, and places adjacent; their butter, cheese, and pullen, and potters about the butter crosse, in the end of Cheapside market; and bread nere unto the fish market.

The cattell market ordinarily in the Church-street, and upon the Saturday only; their horse market in the Fishergate, and begins about the ending of their market for cattell.

The swyne market over against the church; their sheep early upon the west side of the market-square, above the shoomakers' stalls; and the leather cutters, earthern vessell, in Cheepside, and wooden vessell in the west end of the market-place, below the barley market. The upper corn market, beginning at one of clock, upon the corn bell ringing; here standeth for sale rowes of wheat, rye, oats, in their distinct fyles and orders; below them towards the west is the barley and bean market, placed in distinct and well ordered rowes, in which place, before the corn comes into town, was hydes and skinns exposed to sale untill 9 or 10 aclock. Below the fish stones standeth the stalls of hardwaremen, with all sort of iron instruments; in the midst of the market-place, aside the barley market, are the stalls for brass and pewter; and higher above them, ranges of stalls for pedlars and cloth cutters, hosiers and the like: yet notwithstanding all these varyetys of wares and merchandizes, thus exposed, most of the burgesses or inhabitants of the burrough have shops about the market-place and in other streets, in their houses or nere their lodgings, were the several companyes of tradesmen dayly expose wares to sale ...

> Richard Kuerden, *Brief Description of the Borough and Town of Preston*, ed. J. Taylor (Preston, 1818), 4–8

22 The journeys of Celia Fiennes: Tunbridge Wells, 1697, and Portsmouth

Tunbridge Wells

They have made the wells very comodious by the many good buildings all about it and 2 or 3 mile round, which are lodgings for the company that drinke the waters, and they have encreased their buildings so much that makes them very cheape; all people buy their own provision at the market which is just by the wells and furnish'd with great plenty of all sorts flesh fowle and fish, and in great plenty is brought from Rye and Deale etc., this being the road to London, so all the season the water is drank they stop here which makes it very cheape, as also the country people come with all their back yard and barne door affords, to supply them with, and their gardens and orchards which makes the markets well stored and provision cheape, which the gentry takes as a diversion while drinking the waters to go and buy their dinners it being every day's market and runns the whole length of the walke, which is between high trees on the market side for shade and secured with a row of buildings on the right side which are shopps full of all sorts of toys, silver, china, milliners, and all sorts of curious wooden ware, which this place is noted for the delicate neate and thin ware of wood both white and Lignum vitæ wood;[1] besides which there are two large coffee houses for tea chocolate etc., and two roomes for the lottery and hazard board; these are all built with an arch or pent house beyond the shops some of which are supported by pillars like a peasa [piazza], which is paved with brick and stone for the drye walking of the company in raine ...

There is at the lower end of the walke, which is a broad space before you come to the walls of the wells, where is a large sun dial set up on severall steps of stone; thence you go straight along to a chapple[2] ... There are severall buildings just about the well where are severall apothecary's shops there is also a roome for the post house; the post comes every day and returns every day all the while the season of drinking the waters is, from London and to it, except Mondayes none comes down from London, so on Satturdayes non goes up to London. You pay a penny Extraordinary for being brought from Tunbridge town which is 4 mile distance, that being a post town, you likewise have the conveniency of coaches every day from London for 8 shillings apiece dureing the whole season and carriers twice a week.

There are severall bowling-greens about the wells one just at it on Mount Sion, and another up the hill called Mount Ephraim, where is also a large chapple ... There is severall other bowling greens at a distance off a mile or two fitted for the companys lodging, there, as Rust Hall and Southborough. They have all houses to the greens so the gentlemen bowle, the ladies dance or walke in the green in the afternoones, and if wet dance in the houses, there being musick maintained by the company to play in the morning so long while they drink the waters and in the afternoon for danceing. There are severall good taverns at the walks and all about to supply good wine, and brew houses for beer and bakers for bread, but some of them come from London and spoyle the market by raiseing the price, so the higlers and hucksters in a great measure. This whole Country is full of stone and iron; the earth is clay and sand.

[1] Tunbridge ware was made from beech or sycamore inlaid with other woods.
[2] The church of King Charles the martyr.

Portsmouth (visited sometime before 1691)

From a hill just above Cowes that runns along by the Sea-side you may easily see Spitt-head and St. Hellens Point and all the shipps that lay along the road and that lay in Portsmouth Haven; from Ride[Ryde] is 3 leagues to Portsmouth: I pass'd it in an hour. Portsmouth is a very good town well built with stone and brick. It's not a large town, there are walls and gates about it and at least eight bridges and gates without one another with ditches which secures it very strongly to the land-ward; to the sea the fortifications are not so strong. There is a platform with guns and pallisadoes; there is a good dock for building shipps, but about 6 mile off at Burston [Bursledon] and Red bridge are the best shipps built; there are most of the great shipps lye at anchor here.

I was a board the Royall Charles [Charles II's flagship] and the Royal James which are fine shipps, the roomes spacious for length and breadth but not high. There was a large chappel and cabbin with damaske furniture.

The Castle at Portsmouth is not great; it's rather called the King's House where is a great deal of armes. I was in the dineing roome where King Charles the Second met Queen Katherine and was marryed to her and set the crown on her head; there from that roome out of double doores goes a long wooden bridge to the plattforme. Just by is Southsea Castle which is wash'd round by the sea and pretty deep water att spring tides. It looks very fine but think its but of little Strength or Service.

C Morris (ed.), *The Journeys of Celia Fiennes* (1949),
132–5, 53

23. A general survey of the origins of cities and boroughs, 1704

When for my own private satisfaction I first began to inquire into the original constitution of burghs, in this and foreign nations, what they were, and whence their great liberties, and privileges. In our ordinary writers, whosoever they were, that discoursed of them as they came in their way, I found little else but prescription, and pretended usage and possession time out of mind, vouched for the great independent rights they have claimed, and do challenge.

And truly by the notion these writers have, and their readers cannot but have, of them, according to their informations, they seem to have been æternal, or at least coæval with the Creation, and so many ready wrought, and framed, small commonwealths, lifted out of the chaos, and fixed upon the surface of the earth, with their walls, gates, town or gild-halls, courts, liberties, customs, privileges, freedoms, jurisdictions, magistrates and officers, in their formalities, and all extravagant, uncontroulable, and absolute powers, and absurd rights, they have of late years pretended to.

But, whoever will seriously peruse this treatise, shall find the dates of their originals, and gradual augmentations, and must confess they have nothing of the greatness and authority they boast of, but from the bounty of our ancient kings, and their successors, notwithstanding any other confirmations, or acquired right, they may allege, and acknowledge that prescription, and pretended immemorial customs or usages avail not, when there are charters or other records which shew, that in this case (of what weight soever they may be in other,) they are mere conjectures, words of course, and the popular assertions of such men, as either knew not how, or would, or for their more gainful imployments could, not look into those great monuments of antiquity, and discoverers of truth.

And therefore I have opposed matter of fact, through the whole discourse, to these fond imaginations, and easie notions, and for the clearer demonstration of what I intended to evince, have produced all the instances of cities, burghs, and towns in both the books called Domesday-Books, from whence I could receive any satisfaction of the condition and import of burghs and burgesses in the Saxon times, without any particular deductions from these instances, or remarks upon them.

'Tis easie for any man that will but note them to observe, that according to the modern way of speaking, they then made but a small figure in the nation, to be sure the burghs were not distinct common-wealths, or governments, nor the burgesses statesmen, or people of much interest, whatsoever some popular and factious writers, who scrible by rote, and according to their own fancies, have delivered to the contrary.[1]

[1] On Robert Brady, the author of this extract, see D. Douglas, *English Scholars, 1660–1730* (2nd ed., 1951) and J. G. A. Pocock, *The Ancient Constitution and the Feudal Law* (Cambridge, 1957).

Robert Brady, *An Historical Treatise of Cities and Burghs or Boroughs* (2nd edition, 1704), preface

2

The economy

24. Some Gloucester properties with their owners and occupiers past and present, 1455

The abbot of Saint Peter holds a tenement near there wherein N. Skinner and Leus, tailor dwell ...

L.[1] The same abbot holds a tenement with appurtenances at the eastern corner of Castle Lane, wherein William Carter, skinner, dwells: wherein Ralph of Todenham and William Lorimer dwelt in the times of Henry III and Edward I. And he renders for landgavel 14*d* ...

The abbot of Saint Peter holds in fee there on the western side of Castle Lane three tenements lying together, wherein Richard Skinner, N. Brinklow and Thomas Ferrour dwell ...

L. The infirm poor of the Hospital of Saint Bartholomew hold a tenement with appurtenances, wherein the wife of Thomas Hyat dwells: which William Dyues and William of Northampton, tanner, held in the time of Henry III; Margaret Ide in the time of Edward I; the heirs of the said Margaret in the time of Edward II. And they render by year for landgavel 14¼*d* ...

L. The Prior of Saint Bartholomew holds a tenement with appurtenances there towards the bridge; which Alice Spick held in the time of King Henry III; Simon Skinner in the time of king Edward I; the same prior in the time of king Edward II and afterwards; wherein John Hoskins, tailor, dwells. And he renders therefor for landgavel 14¼*d* ...

[1] 'L' indicates a payer of landgavel.

W. H. Stevenson (ed.), *Rental of the Houses in Gloucester AD 1455* (Gloucester, 1890), 19–51

25. Coastal distribution of imports and local goods at Southampton, 1469

	Custom	Cranage and Wharfage
11 Oct. Ship, John Stollocke, master Vyncent Tehy & Wat Jamys, owners, in. Anchorage and Keelage free.		
John Jamys, burgess, 2 barrels soap, 1 barrel green ginger, 2 C. linen cloth	free	free
Vyncent Tehy, burgess, 1 sack hemp, 1 cwt. frying-pans, 3 C. stockfish, 3 full cauldrons, 2 barrels soap	free	free
John Aport, citizen of Nova Sarum, 3 sacks hemp, 9 cwt., £6	6d	1½d
6 barrels cork	6d	1d
2 barrels green ginger; 80 lb., £2	3d	1d
Goslyn of Wynchester, 1½ sacks hemp; 4½ cwt., £3	9d	½d
1 barrel oil; 30 gall.	3½d	½d
1 bale madder	2d	½d
Henre Tayler, 1 barrel oil; 22 gall.	2½d	½d
2 barrels salmon	1s 0d	1d
1 C. stockfish	2d	
6 firkins salt eels, £1 6s 8d	4d	½d
1 barrel soap, 16s 8d	2½d	¼d
Edmond Gradclyfe, 1 bale hemp; 300 lb., £2 5s 0d	6d	½d
1 bale madder	2d	½d
2 barrels soap, £1 13s 4d	5d	½d
2 full cauldrons, 6s 8d	2d	
Clement Glose, 8 balets woad	8d	2d
John Tardyffe, ½ barrel lathnails, £1 6s 8d	4d	½d
1 maund; 12 doz. hats, £2	6d	½d
12 Oct. Water Jamys, burgess, 2 bales madder, 4 barrels cork, 4 barrels soap, 2 bales hemp, 2 C. linen cloth	free	free
Boat of John Dagebell, out		
John Smyth, 2 C. iron	1d	
Boat of Thomas Shelow, out		
Thomas Avanne, burgess, 1 butt wine	free	2d
1 bale madder; by crane	free	1d

D. B. Quinn and A. A. Ruddock (eds.), *Port Books of Southampton 1469–70* (Southampton Record Society, XXXVII, 1937), 2–3

26. 'Moonlighting' by shoemaker journeymen at Norwich, 1490

Assembly on the Feast of St Matthew 6 H. VII. [21 Sept. 1490].
It is agreed that the bill of the shomakers craft shall be enacted according to the effect of that bill. And whosoever of the said craft shall act to the contrary, he shall forfeit six shillings and eight pence, and they shall be divided in this form, viz. one part to the community and the other part to the craft. Which same bill, word for word follows.

To our right honourable mastres, the Meire and his brethern aldermen, and to our good mastres and weelwillers of the common cownsell of the cite, sheweth to your grete discrecions the poor artificers and craftymen of shomakers of the seid cite, that wher dyvers jornymen and servaunts of the seid crafte gretly disposed to riot and idelnes, whereby may succede grete poverte, so that dyvers dayes wekely whan them luste to leve ther bodyly labour till a grete parte of the weke be almost so expended and wasted, ayenst the avauntage and profight werely of them self and of ther mastres also. And also contrary to the lawe [of] god and good guydyng temporall, they labour qwikly toward the Sondaye and festyvall dayes on the Saterdayes and vigils ffro iiij of the clock at after none to the depnes and derknes of the nyght foloweng. And not onely that synfull disposicion but moche warse so offendyng in the morownynggs of such festes, and omyttyng the heryng of ther dyvyne servyce; Wherfor prayeth the seid artificers hertyly, that the rather for goddys cause and also that vertuous and true labour myght help to the sustentacion of the seid crafte, that by your generall assent may be ordeyned and enacted for a laudable custume, that none such servaunt or jornyman from hensforth presume to occupye nor werke after the seid howre in vigeles and Saterdayes aforeseid, upon peyne by your discrecions to be sette for punyshment alsweel of the seid artificers for ther favoryng and supportyng, as for the seid jornymen so werkyng and offendyng.

W. Hudson and J. C. Tingey (eds.), *Records of the City of Norwich* (Norwich, 1906), II, 104

27. A deceitful wool merchant at Nottingham, 1516

February 13, 1515–16

William Green, tailor, complains of Richard Halam of a plea of deceit, etc. And whereupon the same William, by William Edmundson his attorney, says that whereas the aforesaid Richard, on the 20th day of September, in the seventh year of the reign of our Lord the present King here at Nottingham, etc., sold to the aforesaid William Green 16 tods of wool, warranting the said 16 tods to be good, pure and clean wool, whereas as an actual fact there were two pounds of sand in each tod of the said sixteen tods of wool; and so the same Richard Halam has falsely deceived the said William Green therein: whereby he says that he is injured and has damage to the value of 40s; and therefore he brings suit, etc. And the aforesaid Richard comes in his proper person; and says that [blank]

W. H. Stevenson (ed.), *Records of the Borough of Nottingham*
(Nottingham, 1882–1914), III, 137

28. Local apprentices gain a monopoly of artisan craft work at Guildford, 1522

Memorandum by the discretion of George Parkehurste nowe beyng mayer of the town and borough of Guldefford John Perkyns, John Shyngylton, John Stoughtton, Thomas Blanke, William Hamond, Thomas Atkynson, Thomas Barne, Thomas Olyver, Robert Katerykke, Oswald Roger, John Daburne, Robert Snellyng, Henry Langley, John Smallpece & Richard Romppe brethern with the hole comyntye of the same hathe made this composicion frome this daye forward to endure for ever that William Hamond thelder nor none other freman no forener inhabitanttes or dwelleres within the brough of Guldefford afore sayd schall nott frome thys daye forward occupye the occupacion of a fuller nor shereman within hys house or dwellyng place nor within this towne nor other place no non other hond occupacion what so ever hit be or here after maye be onlesse he hathe ben bownded apprentice unto the sayd hond crafte or occupacion or by reason of maryage.

Enid M. Dance (ed.), *Guildford Borough Records, 1514–1546*
(Surrey Record Society, XXIV, 1958), 12–13

29. The overland distribution of goods from Southampton in early January 1529[1]

Thuresday the ij off January. Item Wylliam Arnolde & Thomas Elderfelde in with iij loods off clothe to West Hall pontage iiij*d*. Item John Knollman to Romsey with iij cades off heryng for Mr. Bull custom i*d* ob. & ij heds off raysones & iij topenots[2] off fygs custom ij*d* pontage i*d* [Total] iiij ob. Item Wylliam Rokell to Sarum with i cade off heryng & i hed off raysones & ij C off oryngs upon ij hores. In custom i*d* pontage i*d* [Total] ij*d*.

Fryday the iij off January. Item Thomas Elderfelde to Kyngston with i tun off wyne for Harry Huttoft B[urgess] custom fre brocage viij*d* pontage i*d* [Total] ix*d*. Item John Shebell to Sarum with i h[ogs] h[ead] of trane[3] for Wylliam Jamys B custom fre iij heds off fygs & vi topots for Mr. Chafyn & viij heds off raysones custom by see brocages iiij*d* pontage i*d* [Total] v*d*.

Satresday the iiij off January. Item John Wren to Burford with ij cades off heryng & i C. & dm. [i.e. half] off garlycke custom fre brocages iiij*d* pontage i*d* & in with iiij loods off woll pontage iiij*d* [Total] ix*d*.

[1] Some editorial intervention has been necessary here to render the accounts more easily understood. Pontage was paid per cart or animal; custom varied according to the goods and the status of the merchant; brokage varied with the distance the goods were being taken. A wide variety of measures and containers were used.

[2] Toppet, topkin: a basket for fruit.

[3] Trane oil, from whale blubber, or fish oil.

(Southampton Record Office, SC 5/5/33)

30. Provision of beer, bread and candles at Edinburgh, 1529–31

Broustarris [Brewers] — It is statute and ordanit be the provest [chief magistrate of the burgh], ballies [aldermen], and counsall that na brouster na dry tapster [brewer or retailer] in this burgh tak apone hand to sell ony derrar aill fra Monunday furth at nixt cummys na[than] xvi*d* the galloune and [th]at it be gud and sufficient aill of the price forsaid commonlie tilbe sauld till [to] the kingis liges under the pane of viij*s* for the first falt the secund falt deling of thair aill and the thrid falt to bring thar caldrone or kettellis to the [town] crose and ding [pierce] thame throw with ane puncion [punch] and spane [ban] thame fra the operatione for yer and day.

Baxtarris [Bakers] — Item it is statute and ordanit be the provest, ballies and counsall that all baxtaris within this burgh baik thar braid gud and sufficient stuff weill bakin and dryit and [th]at the ij*d* laif [loaf] wey xviij uncis and the broune breid offerand [in proportion] tharto wnder the pane of ane wnlaw the first falt and fra thine [thence] furth deling of thar breid. And that na huckstar [hawker] within this toune tap nor sell ony quhite [white] breid in for buthis [booths] fra Monunday furth under the pane of eschaeting of the breid and banassing of thaim the toune and [th]at ilk baxtar haif bot ane buth to sell his breid in allanerlie and his awin merk apone his breid.

Candilmakaris. — Item it is statute and ordanit be the provest, ballies and counsall that all maner of parsonis candilmakaris within this burgh that thai mak thair candill that thai sell till [to] our soverane lordis legis of gud and sufficient stuff baith weyk [wick] and tallone [tallow] and sufficient werkmanship and [th]at thai sell the pund thairof commonlie for vj*d* the rag weyk and v*d* the *lib* [pound] hardis weik and at thai haif thair ballance and wechtis baith les and mar and be redy till sell the samyne in pundis and half pundis in houssis and utouth [outwith] gif thai pas apone the hie gait [road] under the pane of viij*s* for the first falt and the secund falt eschaet of thair stuff and the thrid falt spanyng [banning] of thar operatione and quhen thai pas throu the toune that thai be honestlie tursit [packed] under the panis forsaid and [th]at na candilmaker melt thair tallone on the forgait under the said panis.

P. Hume Brown (ed.), *Scotland Before 1700 from Contemporary Documents* (Edinburgh, 1893), 197–8

31. Accounts of a Bristol merchant's import/export trade, begun in 1546

1546 John Spark of Newenham in the Forrest of Deane
yeman owith the 24 day of Marche £11 for the rest &
closyng up of his cowmpt fo. 230   £11
Itm. more the same day for 3 tand hides 12*s*   12*s*
Itm. the 4th day of June £6 16*s* 8*d* & is for a ton of the
Rendry iren[1] to be pd. at Seynt Jamistide next   £6 16*s* 8*d*
Itm. the 20 day of July £4 10*s* & is for 3 hogshedes Gascon
wyne at £6 the ton   £4 10*s*
Itm. the same day £20 which my wif delyver to hym in
redy monney for to by tand hides for me   £20

Itm. the 3 day of September £7 13s 4d for 2 buttes seck	£7 13s 4d
Itm. for a h'd iren after £7 the ton, montith	£1 15s
Itm. the 17 of September 1547 d'd & paide to hym in ready monney £20	£20
Itm. the last day of November 1547 pd. to John Spark in Bristowe £20 14s in redy monney	£20 14s
1547 Itm. the 24 of Marche anno 1547 £3 18s 4d for a butt of seck	£3 18s 4d
1548 Itm. the 13 day of Aprell £4 for a butt seck & £7 10s for a pipe of wull oyle	£11 10s
Itm. £10 which my wif d'd to hym the 25 of July	£10
Itm. the 23 of Augost my wif delyverd unto hym £40 for to by sekyns & lether	£40
Itm. the 10th day of September my wif paide to hym	£20
Memorandum Itm. the 26 of July £4 for a butt of seck, £3 16s 8d	~~£4~~ £3 16s 8d
Itm. the 22 day of Augost 45s & is for 1 h'd iren after £9 the ton	£2 5s
~~Itm. the 7 day of September for 2 buttes 1 pipe & 2 h'd lery cask-price~~	
Itm. the 17 day of October anno 1548 pd. to hym £20 13s 4d	£20 13s 4d
Itm. the 15 day of Marche 1548 paide to hym in redy money £5	£5
Itm. the 15 day of Aprell 1549 £9 6s 8d which is 16 nobles for a butt of seck & £4 for 2 h'd Gascon wyne	£9 6s 8d
Itm. £6 which I paide for his hows in Newneham	£6
Itm. the 13 daye of July paide to hym 49s 4d	£2 9s 4d
Itm. the last day of Augost 1549 £20 for so myche he r. of my wif in ready monney	£20

S.   £248

[1] From Spain.

J. Angus and J. Vanes (eds.), *The Ledger Book of John Smythe 1538–1550* (Bristol Record Society, XXVIII, 1975), 289

32. Vagaries of weather and resultant price fluctuations observed from Liverpool, 1567

This yere was a pleasaunt sedyng off all corne, and after suche a fervent heate and drught succedyd that it was great plentie of all kynd fuell, specially turffe and coole. And the market of all corne, but wheat and rie, did riese to a dowbtfull opynyon of all people, soe as all England over the people dreadyd an excessive charge of hey and other fodder for the cattle off all the land. At Weyryngton [Warrington] this yere was a loode of hey sold for xvs, that is, a mean market loode. And as God Almyghtie, gyver of all goodnesse, off his frie mercie, of us undeservyd and not lokyd fore, abowt [blank] daye of Julie send us suche pleyntie of pleasaunt weyther, wyth rayne, and moderate rayen continewyng from day to daye and tyme to tyme, all August, and after in September, that corne haye fuell and all kynd of victuals fell and came downe to reasonable price, to the great laud and praise of God, the comforte of all faythfull Christians, as, to wete, all excepte covetuouse fermers and avariceous storers of all townes and countreis, hopyng to engross all provision in theyre possession: it soe pleased God it provyd a great plentie of [blank] but onlie monye and gold.

J. A. Twemlow (ed.), *Liverpool Town Books, 1550–1862*
(Liverpool, 1918), I, 341–2

33. Only burgesses to be free to enter the gilds at Canongate, Scotland, 1567

None to be frie of the Craft till he be burges
The quhilk daye It is statute be the bailleis and Counsall that in all tymes to cum that nane of the diaconis ressaif onye freman with thame anent thair craft afoir he be admittit burges be the baillies And quhatsumevir deacone dois in the contrare heirof fra this daye furthe salbe poyndit for that man burgeschip that sall happin to be admittit viz. four pundis sasone as knawlege beis haid be the saidis bailleis and Counsall and na ferder delaye to be haid thairof.

Miscellany of the Maitland Club (Maitland Club, LI.2,
Edinburgh, 1840), 303

34. Apprenticeships, with tools, at Northampton, 1567–8

M[emorandum] Henry Stokes the sone of John Stokes, of Kettilby in the Countie of Lecetor husbondman put himself Covenaunt servant to George Harrison of Northampton shuesmith with him to dwell from the feast of Seynt John baptyste 1567 unto the end of vij yeres, and at the ende of vij yeres to give Henry Stokes a sledy, a buttres, a paire of bellos, a paire of pynsons, iij hammers, a vice, a byckhorn,[1] and at every of two of the last yeres shall give him xijd a quarter in monye. Mr. Edward Masky then beinge Maior of Northton.

M[emorandum] at the feast of all saintes 1568 Giles Amasko the son of John Amasko of Cartmell in the countie of Lancashire hathe put himself covenaunt servant with Roger Haskyn of Northampton taylor for ix yeres with doble apparrell a paire of sheres and a pressinge yron and pleege, Giles Slatier Cristofer Benloos of Kendall.

[1] A two-ended anvil.

C. A. Markham and J. C. Cox (eds.), *Records of the Borough of Northampton* (Northampton, 1898), II, 322

35. Attempts to exploit aliens' skills at Norwich, 1568

Court on Saturday, 6 March [1568]
Vyncent Tesmonde, Symond Sallett and Thomas Tesmonde, white tawers, beyng sworne and deposyd do complayne and saye that on Tewesdaye beyng St Mathies even [23 Feb.] last paste they went to the howse of one Peter Byllett a straunger dwelling in the parisshe of St. Mary of Coslany to know and understande the manner and waye of pullyng the shepskynnes according to souche order as was taken before Mr. Mayour. And the sayde Peter Byllett very stowtely aunsweryd and sayde that he couldenot be in reste but moche disquyeted and trobled. And in talke betwyn them the sayde Byllett called the sayde Vyncent Tesmonde and Thomas Tesmonde bothe knaves, and that he wolde not teach neyther them nor none of ther servauntes to pelte woll onles they wilbe prentyses for iiijer. or fyve yeares. And hereupon there ys commaundement geven that neyther the sayde Peter Byllett nor yet eny other straunger shall engrosse or by eny wolskyns in the market nor of eny bocher at eny tyme after. And hereupon he ys comyttyd to prison.

W. Hudson and J. C. Tingey (eds.), *Records of the City of Norwich* (Norwich, 1906), II, 184

36. A mixed cargo at Rye, 1574

In the *Jhesus* of Rye, burden 25 tons, of which John Gillians is master, entered 21st day of May.

From Loie Etchard of London, native, for one horsepack containing 225 lbs. nutmegges, value £37 10*s*.   Custom and Subsidy 37*s* 6*d*
[Attestation illegible.]

From Olliver Fisher of London, native, for 2 horsepacks containing 500 lbs. pepper, value £41 13*s* 4*d*.

One fardell containing 400 ells of canvas, [value] £10.

600 realmes making 300 bundles browne paper, [value] £10.

Total value £61 13*s* 4*d*. Subsidy £3 1*s* 8*d*
Attested: Wm. [?] Didsbury for Oliver Fisher.

From Thomas Rucke, native, for 10 bagges grene woad containing 1,500 lbs., value £7 10*s*.   Subsidy 7*s* 6*d*
Attested: [   ]

From Nicholas Purvage of Rye, native, for one fardell containing 300 ells course browne canvas £7 10*s*.

Two small bagges containing 100 lb. hoppes, value 10*s*.

Total value £8. Subsidy 8*s*
Attested: Nicholas Pourvage.

From William Votamare, alien, for one ballet containing 50 ells canvas, value £25.   Custom 3¾*d*; Subsidy 1*s* 3*d*
Attested: Vinson [   ] for William Watemare.

From Edmund Tindall of Rye, native, for one fardell containing 100 ells canvas, value 50*s*.   Subsidy 2*s* 6*d*
Attested: his mark.

From Christopher Falloies of Rye, alien, for one casse containing 4 demi pesses searges of Winchelsey, value £3.   Custom 9*d*; Subsidy 3*s*

200 realmes browne paper making 100 bundelles, [value] £3 6*s* 8*d*.

Custom 10*d*; Subsidy 3*s* 4*d*
Attested: Christophle de Falloize.

From John Binglei of London, native, for one fardell containing 200 ells browne canvas, value £5.   Subsidy 5*s*
Attested: Wm. Bragden for John Bingleye.

From John Challener of London, native, for three horsepacks containing 650 lbs. capiton' thread course, value £21 13*s* 4*d*.

One fatt making one horsepack and one fardell containing 9½ gross Vandome gloves, [value] £11 8*s*.

11 doz. lb. peacinge thread, value £14 13*s* 4*d*.

4 doz. Latten gold ballaunces, value 13*s* 4*d*.

1 gross Spectackelles casses, value 10s.
50 lbs. copper thread, value £6 5s.   Total value £33 10s. Subsidy 33s 6d

R. F. Dell (ed.), *Rye Shipping Records, 1566–90* (Sussex Record
Society, LXIV, 1965–6), 18

37. Distribution of market towns in Kent, 1576

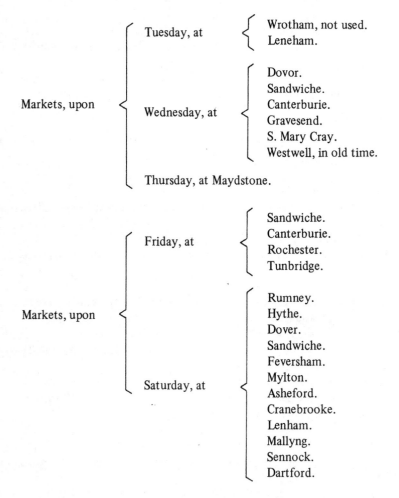

Markets, upon

Tuesday, at — Wrotham, not used.
Leneham.

Wednesday, at — Dovor.
Sandwiche.
Canterburie.
Gravesend.
S. Mary Cray.
Westwell, in old time.

Thursday, at Maydstone.

Markets, upon

Friday, at — Sandwiche.
Canterburie.
Rochester.
Tunbridge.

Saturday, at — Rumney.
Hythe.
Dover.
Sandwiche.
Feversham.
Mylton.
Asheford.
Cranebrooke.
Lenham.
Mallyng.
Sennock.
Dartford.

William Lambarde, *A Perambulation of Kent* (1576), 53

38. The occupational structure of Kendal, 1578–9

Twelve severall companyes

1 Chapmen marchannts and salters may choise ij$^{o\cdot}$ wardons wheroff th'one to be yearly a chapman thother a marchannt or salter.

2 Marcers and drapers lynnen and woollen may choise ij$^{o\cdot}$ wardons wherof th'one to be a mercer thother a wollen or lynnen drap or a m'cer occupyinge wollen drapye.

3 Shearmen fullers dyers websters may choise iiij$^{or\cdot}$ wardons and all to be shearmen yearlye.

4 Taylers imbrodyrers and whilters[1] may choise iiij$^{or\cdot}$ or ij$^{o\cdot}$ wardons all to be tayllers yearlye.

5 Cordyners coblers and curryers may choise iiij$^{or\cdot}$ or ij$^{o\cdot}$ wardons all beinge cordyners yearly.

6 Tanners sadlers and girdlers may choise ij$^{o\cdot}$ wardons whearoff one to be a tanner and thother a sadler or girdler yearlye.

7 Inholders and alehowsekepers and typlers[2] may choise iiij$^{o\cdot}$ wardons wheroff ij$^{o\cdot}$ to be inholders and other ij$^{o\cdot}$ alehowsekepers.

8 Butchers and fishers may choise ij$^{o\cdot}$ wardons bothe to be butchers yearlye.

9 Cardmakers[3] and wyerdrawers may choise ij$^{o\cdot}$ wardons and bothe to be cardmakers yearly.

10 Surgons scryvyners barbors glovers skynners parchem^{t} and poyntemakers may choyse ij$^{o\cdot}$ wardons thone to be a glover yearlye.

11 Smythes iron and hardwaremen armerers cutlers bowyers fletchers spuryers potters pannrs plumbrs tynkers pewterers and metallers may choise ij$^{o\cdot}$ wardons wheroff one to be a blaksmythe ye'lye.

12 Carpenters joyners masons wallers sclaters thatchers glasiers paynters pleysterers dawbers[4] pavers myllers and cowpers may choise ij$^{o\cdot}$ wardons wherof th'one to be a carpent^{r} or joyner.

[1] To welt is to border or hem.
[2] Beerhouse keepers.
[3] These craftsmen made cards, or combs of leather and wire for carding wool.
[4] Builders of clay or mud walls, mixed with straw.

R. S. Ferguson (ed.), *The Boke off Recorde or Register of Kirkbie Kendall* (Cumberland and Westmorland Antiquarian and Archaeological Society, Extra Series, VII, 1892), 110–11

39. Dyeing and sealing cloth at Norwich 1584

Assembly on Friday, 26 June 26 Eliz. [1584]
An act for new commodities.

Forasmucheas the commodities made and wrought within this cittie beeyng dyed within the same cittie have not been well and woorkmanly dyed and dressed by reason whereof the merchauntes tradyng the same ar greatly hindered and the sayd commodities thereby ar lyke to grow owt of request yf speedy reamidie bee not therefore provyded. This day therefore it is ordeyned and enacted by the whole consent of the maiour, shreeves, citizens and commonaltie as hereafter followeth.

Clothes to be engrayned − In primis, that no dyer shall die uppon any clothes used to bee calendred any of these colors followeng, vidz. crymson, purple, murrey or read but in grayne, nor any tawnyes but in mather and waod, and shall sette uppon everie grayned cloth a letter for his name with a sealle and a **G** for grayned uppon payne for everie cloth dyed to the contrarie vs.

The calenders to have a sealle − Item, that before the first day of July next commeng everie calendrer shall have a sealle with their severall mark where with they shall sealle all clothes wch they shall calender beeyng perfectly dyed and well dressed upon payn that every calendrer shall lose for everie cloth other wyse sealled xij*d*.

No clothes to bee sealled but engrayned clothes − Item, that the calenders shall not sealle to their knowledge any purples, crymsens, murryes or reades but suche as bee dyed in grayne nor any tawnes but such as shalbe perfectly mathered and waodded uppon payne to forfeyt for everie cloth sealled to the contrarie xij*d*.

Defective clothes punysheable − Item, that every cloth beeyng found defective eyther in dyeng, blackeng or dressing, after it bee tacked or sealled by the calendrer or his servauntes may bee tryed by three merchauntes and three dyers to the end the fault may be punysshed according to the quantitee of the offence.

W. Hudson and J. C. Tingey (eds.), *Records of the City of Norwich* (Norwich, 1906), II, 148−9

40. Complaints against the Company of Hostmen, Newcastle-upon-Tyne, 1603

The Complaintes of the Towne against the said Fraternitie

1. First that their incorporacion was graunted for the benefitt of the towne, and procured at the costes of their common treasure, whereof the burgesses are more then five hundred, and the oastmen that reape the benefitt thereof fewer then fortye.

2. Secondly, that noe burgesse since their said corporacion can be admitted into the fraternitye wthout excessive fynes.

3. Thirdly, that before the same incorporacion the burgesses might buy seacoles at 6s a chaldron, or under, in the country, and ship them at their pleasure. Since the said incorporacion all cole mynes are ingrossed, and noe keeles or vessells can be had to laye aborde such coles, whereby the plenty of coles is abated and the price inhaunced for the proffitt of the oastmen & the preiudice of the towne & commonwelth.

4. Fourthly, that before the same incorporacion all maisters of ships might buy and barter wth any burgesse for the best and cheapest cole. Since the same incorporacion they are restrayned to buy of any but ostemen, and enforced to take such cole, and of such price and persons, as the oastmen appoint.

5. Fiftly, that the same oastemen, for the same purpose, have devided their trade into foure quarters, and agreed what quantity of cole every oasteman of every quarter shall make and utter, and at what price, and that the gayne of any one should be distributed amongst them all.

6. Sixtly, they have agreed at what rate poore collyers, cariage men, and keele men shall worke and carry cole; and have abridged their wages to their extreame impoverishment and excessive charge of the towne.

7. Seaventhly, that by colour of a tolleracion in their charter for ships of soe greate burthen as could not conveniently approche the towne to lade and unlade farr beneath it, they permitt all sortes of vessells to be there laded and unladed, contrary to the statue and to the impoverishment of the burgesses and the prejudice of the Kinges customes.

8. Eightly, that they ingrosse the most parte of corne and other merchandizes brought into the said port, by bartering of cole, and imediatly sell the same corne and merchandizes to burgesses and country men at excessive prices, to the encrease of dearth and impoverishment of the commons, both of the towne and the countrye.

Extracts from the Records of the Company of Hostmen of Newcastle-upon-Tyne (Surtees Society, CV, 1901), 19–20

41. Enforcing standard weights and measures. Devizes, 1617

Whereas divers and sundrie abuses and misdemeanors have ben and are daylie comitted within this boroughe by the wayinge of fleshe victuall, butter, cheese, grease and other comodityes – put to sale in the ffayres and marketts in the boroughe and att other tymes att the private wayte of certayne persons – burgeses and inhabitants of the boroughe, whereby not onely the King's Maties [Majesty's] standard beames provided wthin the boroughe for indifferencye betweene [party and party] are much prejudiced, but also His highness's subjects are ofte tymes defrauded by meanes of such private wayinge of the comodityes above menconed. For reformacon whereof and to the intent that from henceforthe falcityes & deceipts by unjust and unlawful waights and measures may be prevented; the maior & burgeses, being his Majesty's farmer of the standard waights & measures within the boroughe and whot are by the lawes of this realme charged with the care thereof, have provided a comon beame with wayght agreable with his Highnes's standard for the publike waighinge of fflesh, victuall &c brought to this boroughe to be solde. Thereupon it was ordered decreed and established (by the maior &c) that noe person or persons, burgeses or inhabitants of this boroughe, shall bringe to be solde in this borough in grosse or by waight any of the comodityes before menconed other than such as they doe ordinarilye sell by retail in their shopps, to waye any of the comodytyes at any private beame in the boroughe, but shall bring all such comodytyes soe exceedinge the wayght of six pounds to be waighed at the comon beames. For the waighinge thereof respectively, the waigher shall not take above twoe pence for the waight of one hundred, and for the waight of halfe hundred once pence, for the waight of a quarterne of one hundred a halfe penye, and for the waight of halfe quarterne of the hundred and under, not above one farthinge, upon payne that every one offending to forfaict for each offence the some of six shillings and eight-pence the one moytye [half] thereof to be to the use of the maior and burgeses the other moytye for reparacons of the caweswayes of the borough.

B. H. Cunnington (ed.), *Some Annals of the Borough of Devizes* (Devizes, 1925), I, 55

42. The expense of repairing the harbour and sea defences at Ayr, Scotland, 1622

Anent the supplicatioun gevin in be James Blair, commissioner for the burgh of Air, in name of his said burgh, shawing that thair herbarie and haill bulwarkis ar becum ruinous and licklie to fall doun and perish whitche will tend to the overthrow of the toun, thair tred consisting for maist pairt be the sey, and thairfore desyring licence to purches ane new gift of the impost grantit to theme of before be oure Soverayne Lord for repairing and uphalding of thair said harberie and bulwarkis, as at mair lenth is contenit in thair supplicatioun givin in theranent. The said commissioneris of borrowis findis thair desyre ressonable and thairfore grantis licence to the said burgh to impetrat of oure Soverayne Lord ane gyft of the impost in maner specifiet in the impost grauntit to the said burgh in anno 1587 and that for the spaice of nyntein yeires efter the expyring of the said gift; provyding alwayis the said burgh at the finishe and expyring of the said impost mak compt to the borrowis of thair intromissioun, as lykwayis that they bestow the soumes collectit to the reparatioun of thair said herberie and bulwarkis foresaid.

J. D. Marwick (ed.), *Extracts from the Records of the Royal Burghs of Scotland, 1615–76* (Edinburgh, 1878), 134

43. The regulation of fishing in Oxford, 1623

At this Counsell it is ordered with the consent of all fishermen and boatemen of the cittye, uppon solemne warninge this day appearing, that noe freeman of this cittye shall betwixt the last daye of February and the first daye of June groape or take with their hands any crawefish, trouts, chubbs, or any other fishe in any the waters of this citty uppon paine of 40s, the one halfe to be imployed for the benefitt of the cittye and the other to the person that shall informe the same.

Alsoe it is ordered that noe freeman of the citty shall lay or use any flewe or dryve or drawe in any of the waters of the citty in any yeare after the last daye of February untill the mayor and bailiffs shall have had their fishing dayes accordinge unto the auntient usage of the citty, uppon paine of 40s to the uses in the former order expressed.

Alsoe it is ordered that noe freeman that shalbe owner of shall carry or convey any claye, earth, gravell or other

Port Meade or any other the wasts and grounds of the cittye without the licence of the mayor and bayliffs under the seale of the citty, upon paine of 40s.

Alsoe it is ordered that every freeman having any boate uppon any the water of the citty shalbee answerable for all the acts and deeds of such as shalbe wafted, ferryed or conveyed in his boats, as well concerninge publique offences donne in the waters, fishinge and game of swanns, as particuler trespasses done upon the lands neare adjoyninge unto the sayd waters; and shall within 14 dayes next after warninge unto them geeven make payment and satisfaction of all multes, penalties and forfeitures for all the offences that shalbe donne in or uppon the sayd game of swannes, waters and fishings by any the parties that shalbe soe wafted, ferryed or conveyed in any of their boats, as yf themselves had donne the same offences; and for private trespasses such recompense unto the parties wronged as the mayor, bailiffs and comminalty shall appointe, under paine of 40s for the use of the mayor.

It is likewise ordered that noe person shall at any tyme of the yere drawe with any pitchnett in any of the waters belonging to the cittye, nor shall sett any pitchnett in any parte of the cittie's water betweene the King's mills called the castle mills and Binsey, upon paine of 40s.

H. E. Salter (ed.), *Oxford Council Acts, 1583–1626* (Oxford Historical Society, LXXXVII, 1928), 314–15

44. Ordinances of the merchant gild of Carlisle, 1624

1. First that undermaisters give warneing to the company to appear in our chamber or guild hall on yr quarter dayes and at other tymes upon occasion. That our dinner daye be kept as hath been accustomed upon Sunday before Michaelmas. No under maister is to have his dinner ffree ffor his attendance. Every one to paye for his brotherhood yearlie to-wardes the charges of the dinner for strangers invyted 4d quarterlye. Those that be absent at our quarter dayes to yeald their consent to anie good order made as though they were present.

2. None to open shopp windoes upon Sundayes or other festivall dayes. Our quarters to be duelye kept ffriday after Saint Peter, fridaye before Michelmas, ffriday before Candlemas, and ffriday before Low Sunday. Maisters to give warneing to the company upon occasion. None to take an apprentice but to a merchant.

3. Noe distresse to be taken but to be delivered again upon payment.

The occupation to goe to the church at the buriall of the departed.

3. The youngest to reverence their elders: no foriner or outman to be taken partner or admitted to use the trade.

4. Boundering of the kinges moor none to have the dinner but by due course and for obteyning a fee. Apprentices to be enrolled quarter day next date of his indenture. None to use his ancestors unreverentlie. None to sell sickles or sythes or anie other merchantize suffred to be sould by strangers, but onelie at the two faires.

5. None fforyner or stranger suffred to sell anie merchandyse but in tyme of our faires. None to [sell] cottons or frise under couller ffor Scottes men. Every apprentice to pay for his enrolement VI*d*, to the clarke. None to speake before his elder have spoken. Every fforryner absent at our quarter dayes without lawfull excuse amerced XII*d*.

6. All those that doe trayde to pay every quarter daye twelve pence. No Scotes man suffered to retaile eyther in market or houses. Every apprentice being admitted a brother VI*s* 8*d*.

7. No apprentice to be taken under 14 years of age the master giving over trayding must offer his apprentice to the occupation.

8. None suffred to take an apprentice onles he use and exercise the trade ...

R. S. Ferguson and W. Nanson (eds.), *Some Municipal Records of the City of Carlisle* (Cumberland & Westmorland Antiquarian and Archaeological Society, 1887), 94–5

45. A petitioner requests that he be allowed to change his trade. Maldon, 1629

The petition of Henry Childerley and Anne his poore wife

To the right worshipfull the King's Majestie's bayliffes of his auncient borrowgh towne of Maldon, together with the Justices and Aldermen of the same incorporation, Henry Childerley of Maldon aforesaid, taylerr, together with Ann his said wiffe in all humble manner sheweth unto your good worshipps:

That whereas your poore petitioner Henry Childerley was borne in this towne and brought upp all his younge tyme with his aged ffather for the helpe and comfort of his said ffather. And your worshipps doe all knowe did spend that his younge tyme with him whearein he shoulde as well have advantaged himselfe in travill to have seene and learned workmanship as also to have gayned something towards his maytenance. And sithence the death of his said ffather hath beene much hindered and over charged by the longe and teadiouse sicknesses of his wiffe and children and is nowe much charged with one childe which hath longe beene and yet is visitted with much sicknesse.

And further may it please your worshipps to understand that in regard there are soe many tayllers in this towne that your poor pititioner hath nor cannot gett sufficient worke to sett himselfe on worke of his said trade for the mayntenance of him, his wiffe and children. Whearefore the premisses considered in your judiciall and charitable understanding and judgment, the said Henry and Ann his said wiffe doe heereby ernestlie request and most humblie intreate that your worshipps wolde be pleased to grant to yor poore pititioners your lycence wheareby they may be authorised after the manner of a cookeshopp in the howse wherein they nowe dwell to dresse and make readie fleshmeate and ffish respectivelie, holsome and good fitt and decent for his Majestie's subjects and the same to them together with breade and midde beere within the said howse to vend and sell at reasonable rates hopeing thereby that by their paynes and honest endeavours to gaine themselves some parte of their maytenance. Whereby they hope by God's grace not to be at any tyme heereafter either themselves or theirs chargable to the towne or parish whearein they live, but the reather heereby to shewe their willingnesse accordinge to their abillitie to give to such as want. And heerein yor poore pittitioners and their children ever will and shalbe bound to praie God for your worshipps longe liffe and prosperitie. And thus in all submission doe humblie take their leaves.

Essex County Record Office. Maldon records. D/B 3/3/199

46. Cornering the market in Blackburn, 1629

*Blackburn. To the right worshipful Sir Richard Houghton and others
his Majesty's Justices of Peace within this hundred of Blackburne,
The humble petition of the poore inhabitants of Blackburne*
Sheweth unto your good worships that not manie yeares agoe there was usually sould and bought in open markette 30, 40, or 50 measures of meale everie markett day to the helpe, nourishment and relieffe of your petitioners and other poore distressed people within or neare the afforesaid towne. But now soe it is, may it please your worshipps and in

consideration of your petitioners impoverishment, that there is many lycensed badgers [i.e. dealers] within this hundred and especially one Lawrence Hargreaves who doth commonly badge, carrie and transport much kind of grayne either into forraine parts or for his better proffit maketh sale thereof in Burnley not frequentinge anie open markett but doth unjustlie enrich himselfe against all equitie and good conscience and contrarie to the statute in that case provided to the overthrowe and impoverishment of your petitioners and many more who cannot buy one halfe pecke of meale or lesse (if the greatest need required). And furthermore, if it please your worshipps, your petitioners standing in greate need of [horses] and cannot procure the same for money in regard of the multiplicitie of badgers who having not horses of theire owne to ffitt theire carridges but hyring att greater rates doth cause with the former this miserable complaint of your petitioners. For redresse whereof may it please your worshipps to take or order such course as may bee thought fittinge or agreeinge to your worshipps, the good of the commonwelth and the betteringe of your petitioners. And your petitioners, as in duetie bounden, will continually pray for your worshipps' health and happines long to continue.

Lancashire Record Office. Quarter Sessions records.
QSB/1/61/36

47. Family businesses in Nottingham, 1654

1654, Tuesday, December 19
Order for Buttchers' stalls. — Ytt is ordered by this Companie, thatt when anie Buttcher shall dye thatt holds a stall or shopp from the towne, thatt then his wyefe or sonne shall hould the same stall or shopp, they usinge the same trade, otherwaies the towne to dispose thereof to him or them thatt will give moste for the stall or shopp: this order to bee lykewise to them thatt houlds a stall in the Spice-chambers.

W. H. Stevenson (ed.), *Records of the Borough of Nottingham*
(Nottingham, 1882–1914), V, 284

48. Regulation of the town lands, Calne, 1657

ember 1657. Whereas the commons belonging to the borough of have been of late sold at a low rate by those who could not stock commons themselves so that many countrymen adjacent to the said borough, by buying the said commons at a low rate, have stocked more cattle in the commons than the townsmen, and at the breach of thother feildes of Calne aforesaid have depastured their said cattle with the rest of the hurd, whereby the said feildes are suddenly eaten upp, and the commoners aforesaid having little benefit thereby, and whereas also of late there have been very few milch kine kept in the said commons, it is ordered and agreed by the burgesses and other inhabitants and commoners whose names are subscribed that from henceforth the said commons shall be stocked with horse beasts and rother beasts as well, that is to say one horse upon three beast leaze, and such horse to have the towne marke of Calne, or in default thereof putting in any horse into each of the fresh commons before the rother beasts are putt in, such partie owning the said horse shall forfeit and loose two shillings to be paid to the guild stewards to be distributed amongst the resydue of the said commoners for every such default or putting in before the said beasts as aforesaid contrary to this order, and being further refractory to this order shall for that year loose his or her common. And if any person or persons violate this order any actions to be brought shall be prosecuted at the cost of the said burgesses and commoners.

It is likewise ordered and agreed that for the ensuing year one of the said burgesses shall be hayward or overseer of the commons so that this order may be the better observed and kept. For his pains he shall have one horse common and 4*d* for every beast. Afterwards yearly the hayward shall be one of the commoners taking his turn.

It is also agreed that for every horseleaze in the winter season there shalbe six sheepe stocked upon every such horseleaze unstocked, and also that no countryman shall have any benefit of stocking the commons with horse or beast unless the commoners and townsmen first refuse to stock.

It is further agreed that no person shall stock more than 2 horses or 3 beasts unles be those which have commons of theire owne for the stocking of more and unles there are commons to be spared to the intent that every commoner which will stocke may, and that for every horse which comes in 2*s* shall be paid to the guild stewards, and for every beast 8*d* according to the old custom, and likewise 6*d* for every horse at St. Martin's tide from those wishing to winter horses in the Portmarsh, and for every sheep 2*d*; all which sums are to go towards defraying the common charges in and about the said town and commons.

It is also agreed that the winter lease of the Alders be sold in manner and form as formerly at the time and place accustomed, and the money thereof be employed as formerly; and also that the said commons be hained at St. Mathias' day.

It is also agreed that the guild stewards shall have for their pains 6*s* 8*d* each in lieu and satisfaction of 20 sheep lease which they had formerly enjoyed.

A. W. Mabbs (ed.), *Guild Stewards Book of the Borough of Calne, 1561–1688* (Wiltshire Record Society, VII, 1953), 103

49. Petition of the stocking makers of Leicester, *c*. 1674

Sheweth that the petitioners have for divers yeares last past, employed themselves in the buying and combing of wooll and in getting the same to be spun and knit up into stockings, to be sold to hosiers, and other retailers by which meanes they have wrought up yearly about 200 todds of wooll, used great quantityes of oyle and soap, and kept constantly at work about 2000 poore people men, women, and children of the towne of Leicester and adjacent villages, to the great advantage of the towne and country, to the support of the petitioners and their familyes, and to the inabling of them to beare a great part of the publick taxes. And although the employment before mencioned is no trade within any statute, nor any man by law prohibitted the exercise thereof in any citie or towne corporate of England, yet divers freemen of Leicester perceiving that the petitioners have brought the said employment to a considerable manufacture, do nowe endeavour to engrosse the same wholly to themselves, and to turne it into a monopoly and by unjustifiable ordinances to exclude the petitioners from the free exercise of their calling. And albeit that at the generall sessions of the peace lately holden for the said burrough, it was after serious advise and consultacion with the Grand Jury adjudged that it was lawfull for the petitioners to keep on their said employment, and ordered that they should not be molested therein, yet severall of the said freemen do attempt the procureing of some order of this Common Hall to hinder the petitioners from the further exercise of their calling. And for the accomplishing of their designes do use these false suggestions: that the petitioners do not give the spinners and knitters sufficient wages, and so the work is slightly done, and the commodity brought into discreditt, but if the petitioners may be prohibitted and some of the freemen onely use the calling, they will give greater wages. They will employ none but the best spinners and knitters, and they will have all the yarne wound on clock reels that so it may be perceived whether good or not, and no stockens made but such as shall be very good. To which the petitioners do answere and humbly offer theis following consideracions. 1. That it is improbable that when a very great number of those that set the poor on worke shall be restrayned those few which are left shall give greater wages to the poore then are given now when the worke folks will be as many still and fewer masters to imploy them. 2. If the goodnes of the work be the thing the freemen aim at. They may now take the best worke folks, give greater wages if they please, make better worke and out sell the petitioners and none can hinder them. 3. If none but the best work folks be set on work, then the children can never be taught, and the manufacture in short time will perish. 4. It is not the curious makeing of a few stockens, but the generall makeing of many that is most for the publick good, for that sets more people on work, as well children as others, and when the stockens are made up and sorted there are amongst them some for all sorts of people and the buyer is able to judge of them and to give prices accordingly. If none but fine stockens be made the poore must go without. 5. And as to the clock reeles there will be great inconveniency in them; for every workwoman is to buy such a reele, which many are not able to doe. And then when the yarn is spun, it is halfe as much labor as the spining to winde it on such a reele and when it is in skaines from off the reele it is five times as much labor to double it out of the skaine as it would be to do it off the spooles, and it often happens that the skaines are so tangled that they can never be doubled at all. 6. The viewing of the yarne in the skaine is altogether needles, for any man in doubling the yarne from off the spooles can judge of the work sufficiently. 7. That driving the petitioners out of the towne (if it could be effected) would be much to the dammage of the towne and hinder above 1,000 poore people of the work they now have, for the petitioners and all the rest that follow the imployment are not able to set all the poore on work now, and if your petitioners should be restrained the rest cannot set halfe of them on work. 8. Divers persons who by reason of some disasters and losses have been forced to leave off their trades, and widdowes after the death of their husbands, have learned and taken up this imployment and thereby have maintained themselves and their familyes, which otherwise they could not have done, which advantage or privilledge will be taken away, if the imployment be confined to a small number as some endeavour. 9. If there be no law extant by which the petitioners can be restrained, how safe can it be to contrive ordinances or by lawes to hinder the publicke good? 10. If the increaseing of a manufacture to the height be everywhere adjudged a publick proffit, that ought to be advanced rather than the gratifying of a few because freemen.

The premisses considered the petitioners humbly pray that this assembly will not act anything which may tend to the prohibitting of the petitioners from the exercising of the said calling.

H. Stocks and W. H. Stevenson (eds.), *Records of the Borough of Leicester* (Cambridge, 1923), IV, 536—8

50. The economic condition of Lanark, Scotland, in 1692

Lanerick, the nynth day of May 1692. Compeired befor James Fletcher, provost of Dundie, and Alexander Walker, baillie of Aberdeen, commissionars appointed by the conventione of the royall borrowes for visiting the wholl royall burghs by west and south the river of Forth, the present magistrats and towne clerk of the said burgh of Lanerick, who gave in an accompt of their patrimonie and comon good, together with an answer to the said visitors instructiones, as followes:—

1. As to the first article, it is answered that ther comon good *communibus annis*, will amount to 1550 lib. Scotts, and that ther debts extends to the sowme of 5920 lib. monie forsaid.

2. As to the second article, it is answered that they have no mortificationes.

3. As to the third article, it is answered that they are not concerned therein.

4. As to the fourth article, it is answered that they have no seaport nor occasion for it.

5. As to the fyfth article, it is answered that they have produced their theasaurers bookes for fyve preceding yeares, which hes been considered be the saides visitors as in answer to the first, and have found by the ballance of the saides fyve yeares at the adjusting of ther accompts for 1691 ther theasurer debitor to them in the sowme of three hundred pounds Scots, and that ther eiquies with clerks and other dewes extends to fourty eight pounds Scots mony which is annuallie payed.

6. As to the sixt article, it is answered that they have no forraigne [trade], and that ther inland trad consists of fourty pack of wooll they vent yeirly or thereby, and some inconsiderable trade they have by

retailling goodes which they bring from Glasgow, Lithgow, and other royall burghs, and that they vent about a tunn of French wine or therby yearly, and ane inconsiderable quantity of seck and brandie, and that they vent and consume about eighteen bolls of malt weekly.

7. As to the seaventh article, it is answered that have they no ships, barks, boats, or ferrie boats belonging to them.

8. As to the eight article, it is answered that they are neither owners nor pairtners of any ships, barks, or boats belonging either to burghs royall, of regality or barronie, nor are they concerned in trade with unfree burghs.

9. As to ninth article, that ther cess is paid by a tax on ther inhabitants.

10. As to the tenth article, it is answered that their minister's stipends is payed out of the teinds of the paroch, and that ther schoolmaster and all others ther publiet servants are payed and mantained out of the comon good.

11. As to the elleaventh article, it is answered that ther publict works are supported and mantained out of the comon good.

12. As to the twelth article, it is answered that the houses are in reasonable good conditione, and that the rents of the best and warst of ther houses will be twixt eighteen pounds and sex poundes, and that they have few or no houses inhabited by strangers.

13. As to the threteenth article, it is answered that they have four yearly fairs, each of two dayes containwance, and a weekly marcat, the customs of all which are a pairt of ther comon good as in answer to the first article.

14. As to the fourteenth article, it is answered that the following burghs of barronie and regality are within ther precinct, viz., Hamiltoun, Steven, Stounehouse, Lesmahego, Carlock, Carnwath, Carstairs, Douglass, Roberttowne, Bigger, Lamingtoun, Craufurd and Craufurd John, who have all weekly marcats and severall fairs of great value, and the house rents and trade of most of them are better then ther owne.

15. As to the fyfteenth article, it is answered that ther fynes, burgers admissions, and other casualties are but inconsiderable and applyed for the use of the burgh.

This is the trew accompt of the state and conditione of the said burgh of Lanerk in answer to the above writtin instructiones, as it is given up, upon oath, by the saids magistrats and toune clerk, undersubscryveing, to the best off ther knowledge, to the saids visitors, place, day and dait forsaid. [Signed] : Ja. Weir, bailly, Rob. Huntar, baillie, R. Dick, clk.

Extracts from the Records of the Royal Burgh of Lanark
(Glasgow, 1893), 240–1

51. The Scottish towns recognise the value of an open-door policy for skilled immigrants, 1696

The conventione haveing considered how far it is the intrest of the royall borrowes to accept of all michanicks of all sorts, whether forraigne or native, to come to the severall burghs of this kingdome and to set up ther, for payment of such a sowme as shall be aggreed upon, and to grant them the priviledges and freedomes of ther severall incorporationes, and in respect the good toun of Edinburgh hes been allwayes in use to take in any tradsmen of singular airt (who maks applicatione to the toun councill) to any of ther respective incorporationes, gratis, and allowes them ther privieledges and freedomes, doe therefore recommend to all the royall borrowes to doe the same and to deal discreitlie with any persone or persones so qualified that offers himself to come in.

J. D. Marwick (ed.), *Extracts from the Records of the Convention of the Royal Burghs of Scotland, 1677–1711* (Glasgow, 1880), 210

52. Extracts from the town rental of Newport (Isle of Wight), 1700–1

A rentall of the town rents of the burrough of Newport beginning from Lady Day 1700 and ending at Lady Day 1701

High Street

Walter Swetman's executor for a garden	1s	0d
William Stephens Esq. for Hazards	10s	0d
Jane Trattle for Martendale	3s	4d
Edward Trattle, butcher	5s	0d
Mr Roman for Minghams	15s	4d
John Sweet	7s	0d
Mr John Cheek	2s	0d
Mr Roman for a tenement under the tower	2s	4d
Mrs Moore for the corner house at lower end of High Street		2d
Mr Roman for his dwelling house and shopps	£2 0s	0d
and for Mr Coleman's	£1 5s	0d
John Adams for his shopp	6s	8d
Mrs Coleman for Lamberts	13s	4d
Martha Newland	6s	0d

Widdow Eeles	6s	0d
Mr Ridge's butcher's shopp	6s	8d
Mr Talmidge's butcher's shopp	6s	8d
Mr Thomas Read's butcher's shopp	6s	8d
John Alexander's shopp	6s	8d
Catherine Whitehead for tricketts	19s	0d
and for an incroachment with her wall there	[	?]
Mr Gother for his building against the town hall	5s	0d
and for the porch and pales there	[	?]
[Sub-total]	£9 14s	[?]

Mr Reynold's house, shopp and window	4s	0d
Mr Brassatt's bulk		2d
The roome under the Townhall staires	10s	0d
Widdow Stocknell for an incroachment with		
the wall of her house	1s	0d
Mrs Elizabeth Downe for her porch		8d
Nicholas Norton's bulk		6d
Mrs Reynolds for ground taken out of the river		2d
and for standing of the elme		2d
Widdow Jolliff's porch		4d
Henry Harris's bulk		6d
William Talmidge for an incroachment with a wall		6d
The like with his house in the beast markett	2s	6d
and for setting out the signe		6d
Mr Dove for his saltchest		6d
The bugle porch		4d
George Love for standing of his shopp	2s	0d
Mrs Reynolds for the ground where the elme stands	2s	0d
Widdow Sellars for her hall window		4d

Sea Street

Mr Moore for one storehouse		4d
and for another storehouse	6s	8d
Brown's tanhouse	2s	0d
Mrs Mouncher's tenement	6s	2d
Mr James Grant	1s	4d
and a storehouse and ground late Mary Hall's		8d
Mr William Stephens his storehouse	3s	0d
[Sub-total]	£2 6s	2d

Mr Grant's marsh		4*d*
The fountaine	£2	1*s* 0*d*
Mr Mathew's storehouse		1*s* 8*d*
Mr Francis Searle for the ooze		1*s* 0*d*
Mr Grant for Little London		10*s* 0*d*
Mr Hall for ground taken out of the river		2*s* 0*d*
Mrs Reynold's storehouse		4*s* 4*d*
Widdow Mersham's tenement		5*s* 2*d*
Mrs Mary Hall	£2	0*s* 0*d*
and for ground taken out of the river		2*s* 0*d*
Ann Hayles for her porch		2*d*
Mr Grant for the royalty of the haven	£5	0*s* 0*d*
Mrs Down's storehouse		1*s* 0*d*

Isle of Wight Record Office. Newport records. NBC 45/124

53. Rates charged by Thames watermen, 1702

Rates signed and agreed upon by the Privy Council and the Lord Mayor and Court of Aldermen to be taken by watermen

	Oars	Skuller
From London to Limehouse, Newcrane, Shadwell Dock, Bell wharf, Ratcliff cross	1*s*	6*d*
From London to Wapping Dock, Wapping New stairs, Wapping Old stairs, The Hermitage, Rotherhith Church stairs, Rotherhith stairs	6*d*	3*d*
From St Olaves to Rotherhith Church stairs and Rotherhith stairs	6*d*	3*d*
From Billingsgate to St Saviour's Mill	6*d*	3*d*
From St Olaves to St Saviour's Mill	6*d*	3*d*
All the stairs between London Bridge and Westminster	6*d*	3*d*
From either side above London Bridge to Lambeth, Fox hall	1*s*	6*d*
From Whitehall to Lambeth, Fox hall	6*d*	3*d*
From Temple, Dorset stairs, Blackfriars stairs, Paul's Wharf to Lambeth	8*d*	4*d*
Over the water directly in the next skuller between London Bridge and Limehouse or London Bridge and Fox hall		2*d*

From London to Gravesend whole fare 4s 6d, with company 9d
From London to Graise or Greenhive whole fare 4s, with company 8d
From London to Purfleet or Eriff whole fare 3s, with company 4d
From London to Woolwich whole fare 2s 6d, with company 4d
From London to Blackwall whole fare 2s, with company 4d
From London to Greenwich whole fare 1s 6d, with company 3d
From London to Deptford whole fare 1s 6d, with company 3d
From London to Chelsey, Battersey, Wansworth whole fare 1s 6d, with company 3d
From London to Putney, Fulham, Barn Elms whole fare 2s 6d, with company 6d
From London to Hammersmith, Chiswick, Mortclack whole fare 2s 6d, with company 6d
From London to Brentford, Isleworth, Richmond whole fare 3s 6d, with company 6d
From London to Twickenham whole fare 4s, with company 6d
From London to Kingston whole fare 5s, with company 9d
From London to Hampton Court whole fare 6s, with company 1s
From London to Hampton Town, Sunbury, Walton whole fare 7s, with company 1s
From London to Walton, Weybridge, Chertsey whole fare 10s, with company 1s
From London to Stanes whole fare 12s, with company 1s
From London to Windsor whole fare 14s, with company 2s

Privilegia Londinensis (1702), 390–2

3

Government and politics

54. Purchase, patrimony, marriage and personal pledges gain freemen's privileges at Wells, 1456–58

1456

John Powle, junior. Fine paid the same day.
Willaim Lang, brasier. Mar. dau.
William Wodehele. Pl. John Godwyn, Henry Clerke.
John Chewe, junior. By patrimony.
John Sylcok, tailor. Pl. John Sadeler, John Chewe, senior.

1457

Maurice Goldsmyth. Pl. John Attewater, Thomas Horewode.
John Came, butcher. Mar. wid.

1458

John Stowell, freemason. Pl. John Sadeler, William Wodehele.
Thomas Hone. Pl. Thomas Horewode, John Sadeler.
John Hows, tailor. Pl. John Attewater, John Grype.

D. O. Chilton and R. Holworthy (eds.), *Wells City Charters*
(Somerset Record Society, XLVI, 1931), 149

55. Women admitted to the franchise at Queenborough, Kent, 1476, 1480–1

[16 April 1476] Mariorya, the widow of Edward Kyng came before us Alan Jacob, mayor of the town of Queneburgh and sought the privileges of our said town for the safety and welfare of her body and her goods and she was admitted and received by us on the 16th day of the month of April in the 16th year of the reign of King Edward IV.

[11 January 1480–1] Memorandum that on 11th day of the month of January in the 20th year of the reign of King Edward IV after the conquest,

Elizabeth Howell came and petitioned for frankpledge from Richard Rande then deputy mayor and from his brethren burgesses of the town of Queneburghe in the year and on the day aforesaid, to which she was admitted.

'Memoranda from the Queenborough Statute Book'
in F. Hull (ed.), *A Kentish Miscellany* (Kent Archaeological
Society, Kent Records, XXI, 1979), 93–4

56. Edward IV reassures the beleaguered town government at Lancaster, 1480

Edward, etc. To our trusty and well beloved John Curwen, our mayor of our town of Lancaster, Christopher Lemyng, and Robert White, bailiff there, and to all the burgesses of the same, greeting. For as much as we understand by credible report made unto us, how that upon Thursday next after the feast of Saint Luke last past, when you should have elected amongst yourselves another mayor and also bailiffs of the same our town according to your usage and custom there, you were so hindered and disturbed in that regard, through the assault and menace, as well of various strangers amongst you there as of others, being of the livery and retainers of certain gentlemen of your neighbouring countryside, that you did not dare at that time, for fear and jeopardy of your lives, to perform the intention of your said election, to the grievous trouble and annoyance of you all, so that the said mayor and bailiffs are not as yet from your said offices. We therefore will and charge you that you continue and exercise the same unto the end of this year in like manner as you have done the other year past and that you in the most effectual manner endeavour to see to the due conservation of our peace and other good and fitting rules to be kept within our said town. And whereas we are credibly informed that by means of the said gentlemen who have heretofore induced divers and many of our subjects inhabiting amongst you within our said town to be retained with them, you in time past have often been interrupted from correcting and reforming such offences, trespasses, and misbehavings, as within the same our town have been used or attempted, contrary to the liberties and franchises granted by us unto you, to your right great hurt and grief, the which, if it should be hereafter suffered, might cause our said town to fall into great ruin and decay, which we do not desire. We charge and command you that in our name you make open proclamation within our said town that no manner of person, stranger or other, inhabiting in the same, from henceforth be retained with any kind of gentleman or other by clothing, cognizance, oath, or otherwise, contrary to our laws and statutes ordained in that case, except only with us. And if any person or persons presume to attempt against the same, we will that you do certify us of his or their names to the extent that we may provide for their sharp punishment in that matter, commanding you strictly, on your fealty, that you see this our intent and pleasure in the foregoing to be duly observed and kept, as you and everyone of you will avoid our great displeasure and answer unto us at your perils. Given at London the 15th December, the 20th year of our reign.

By letter under the signet, signed with the sign manual of the king himself.

By the king.

P. R. O. Duchy of Lancaster Warrants, D. L. 42/19/ff.
85b, 16a. in A. R. Myers (ed.), *English Historical
Documents IV: 1327–1485* (1969), 1108

57. The capital witnesses, and accommodates, changes of political fortune, 1484–5

This yere, the ixth day of Novembre, the Mayr, and his brethern thaldermen, wt the citezeins in violet clothyng, fet in kyng Richard, metyng wt hym beyond Kenyngton, and so brought hym to the Warderobe at the blak ffreris, where he was loged. And this yere was takyn sir Roger Clifford, knyght, abowte Hampton, and so brought to London; and there drawne from Westminster taward Tower hill, and when he come at Seynt Marteyns gate by meane of a ffrere one of his confessours his cordes were there cut, and he likly to have tane seynt Martens; howe be it he was let, and newe boundyn, and drawen to the place of execucion, and there behedid. Also this yer died Richard Chester, Shiref, for whom was chosen Rauf Astry for the residew of the yere. Also this yer xxij day of August was the ffeeld of Bosworth, where kyng Richard was slayne, and the Duke of Northfolk upon his party, and therle of Surrey, son unto the said Duke, was taken upon the said ffeeld, and many other men slayn, as Brakynbury and other, by the power of kyng Henry the vijth. And after the ffeeld doon, the said kyng Richard was caried upon an hors behynd a man naked to Leyciter, fast by the ffeeld; and there buryed wt in the ffreres. And the xxvij day of August was the said kyng Henry brought in to the Cite, wt the Mayr, Aldermen and the ffelishippys clothed in violet; and so to the palays at powles, and there loged.

C. L. Kingsford (ed.), *Chronicles of London* (Oxford, 1905), 192–3

58. Bristol prepares to repel Cornish rebels, 1497

Johannes Drewes, Maior. This yere the Cornyshmen rebelled ageynst the King, and the lord Awdley arose with them. And the King met with them at Blak heth, and ther had victory of his enemyes rebelles, and the saide lorde Awdley was taken ther and behedded at [Tower Hill]. The same lord when he was at Wells with the blak smyth callid Mighell Josef, Capteyn of the Cornysh men, having with them [40,000] men, sent to the Maire of Bristowe to ordeign loddgyng and vitaill for [20,000]. But the Maire sent them worde that they shuld come no nere, and if they wold come ner, at their oune adventur. And then the Maire mustred and made redy to withstond the said rebelles, and garnished the town walles with men harnessid and with gonnes, and brought shippes and botes aboute the mersshe, garnisshed with men, artillery, and gonnes. And the said rebelles hereng of this chaunged theire purpose, and toke another wey.

L. T. Smith (ed.), *The Maire of Bristowe is Kalendar* (Camden Society, 2nd Series, V, 1872), 48–9

59. The bailiffs at High Wycombe made personally responsible for fee-farm payments, 1498

Memorandum: that on Wednesday the feast of Saint Antony in the thirteenth year of King Henry VII, in full gild and in the whole community of the borough of Wycombe, they agreed unanimously that if the bailiffs for the time being after the date of this present have not paid the fee farm of the bailiwick, it shall be lawful for the mayor for the time being to enter and distrain on all their lands, tenements, and goods to supply the default of the aforesaid unpaid farm, even to the sealing up of their doors until the sum of the aforesaid farm shall be fully paid up, and according to the custom of the town.

R. W. Greaves (editor and translator), *The First Ledger Book of High Wycombe* (Buckinghamshire Record Society, XI, for 1947, published 1956), 51

60. A successful defence of the common lands at Nottingham, 1500

1500, July 20. And they say that Robert Wyly, of Sneinton, in the County of Nottingham, husbandman, having gathered to himself divers other unknown men to the number of sixteen persons arrayed in warlike manner, on the twenty-fourth day of April, in the fifteenth year of the reign of King Henry, with force and arms, to wit, with clubs and knives, spades and shovels and other defensive arms, unjustly broke, dug up and turned up the common soil of the Mayor and Burgesses of the town of Nottingham in the holding of John Seliok at Nottingham, aforesaid, near Robynhode Well, to the grievous detriment of the said Mayor and Burgesses of the town aforesaid and of the said John Seliok, and against the peace of our said Lord the King, etc.

W. H. Stevenson (ed.), *Records of the Borough of Nottingham* (Nottingham, 1882–1914), III, 75

61. The Southampton elected 'cursus honorum', 1500–10

Year from Michaelmas	Mayor	Sheriff	Court Bailiff	Water Bailiff	Steward
1500–01	Robert Bishop	John Bawdwyn	Robert Young	Robert Wright	John Payne
1501–02	William Justice	Ralph Calton	James Nicholls	Nicholas Cowart	Peter Stoner
1502–03	Thomas Dymmok	Robert Young	Robert Wright	George Cokks	John Favor
1503–04	John Fleming	John Gough	Nicholas Cowart	Peter Stoner	Thomas Bethewey
1504–05	John Fleming	Robert Wright	Richard Hill	John Favor	John Harrison
1505–06	John Godfrey	Nicholas Cowart	Richard Wotton	Thomas Bethewey	John Owdale
			Peter Stoner		
1506–07	John Bawdwyn	Richard Hill	John Favor	John Grigge	Thomas Yevan
1507–08	Robert Bishop	Peter Stoner	John Grigge	Thomas Yevan	John Perchard
1508–09	Robert Bishop	John Favor	William Chalke	John Perchard	William Westmyll
1509–10	Nicholas Cowart	John Grigge	John Husee	William Westmyll	Thomas Lister
1510–11	Nicholas Cowart	William Chalke	John Perchard	John Owdale	Robert Mills

A. L. Merson (ed.), *The Third Book of Remembrance of Southampton 1514–1602* (Southampton Records Series, II, 1952), I, 64

62. The mayor, burgesses and inhabitants of Wilton try to settle their differences, 1526

M[emorandum] a comyncacion had by twene the maier and all the burges of Wilton the xxvjth day of July the xixth yere of the reign of kyng Harry the viijth that where there hathe ben of long tyme greate variaunce and trobill by twene the maiers, burges and other inhabitaunce withyn this borough at suche tyme & tymes as they hathe byn comaunded by the maier to assemble withyn ther councell house or yelde hall ffor the comen welthe and other necessary reformacion to be had amongeste the forseid inhabitauntes by rehersyng of dyvers sedicious wordes and unhoneste wordes oone to another for lighte causes by the meanes wherof the gode governaunce and quyete levyng hathe ben oftyn tymes subvertyd to the greate displeasure of god and to the greate hurte & inquyetnesse of the inhabitauntes of this towne. Wherfor nowe the premysses considered hit is fully agreid and determyned by the maier & all the burgesses of this borough and trewly by this presentes dothe bynd them & every one of them & ther successours ffrom hens forthe that what maior or burgess doo call any maier or burgess or reherse any sedious wordes whiche dothe sounde to the dishoneste of any brother at any tyme in courte, councell howse or any other place withyn this towne or borough or saith owte prevely or openly in the way of anger other wise than by ther righte namys so that hit may be dewly provyd by ij persons apon ther othes by ffore the maior or in his absens by fore his deputie that then the party for every tyme so offendinge shall fforfete to the comen box xs to be levyed of his godes and catels withyn this towne and that to be preised by the aldermen at the nexte courte ffolowyng provided alwey that the maior for his tyme beyng shall not fforfete no fine for the rebukyng or reformyng of any of his officers to hym chosen for that yere any thynge contayned in this acte to the contrary notwithstanding.

Also at the same day & yere above wreten hit is fully agreid by the maior & all the burges that from hens forth at all suche tymes & owres as the burges of the borough shall be ordered to be beffore the maior in ther councell howse or els in the churche of the trenyte for any mater concernyng this borough that the seriauntes for the tyme beyng or his deputie shall toll or cause to be tolled apon the grettest bell of the trynyte churche at the owre that the burges be comaunded for to apere xxx strokes and the seriaunt make defaute in tollyng of this xxti strokes at the owre assigned for the perfit warnyng of the maior or his deputie come not immediatly apon the laste stroke for the shorte spedyng of the burges towardes ther besynes he shall fforfete for every time making suche defaute to the comen box viij*d* and every burges for every tyme makyng such defaute iiij*d* to be levied of ther godes and catels and the same to be preised by the aldermen of the same borough etc.

Wiltshire Record Office, Wilton General Entry Book,
G26/1/25, fo. 116

63. The government of Great Yarmouth examines its documented liberties, 1542

A serche made for charters & recordes
Fyrst att this assemble arne ordeynyd and electid William Borow, Robert Alysaunder, Raffe Assheley & Robert Ladde of the xxiiijties John Hardyngham Thomas Hunt Nicholas Fen jun' & Thomas Kynge of the xlviijties to serche advyse and peruse all suche charters recordes & wrytynges as do remayne in the common hutche of the seid towne and diligently to take out & abstract suche matters and causes conteynyd in the seid charters recordes & wrytynges as shalbe most expedyent for the commodite and profight of this towne and that thei or vj of them shalbe alweis in redynes att the commaundment of the baylyffes after Tuysday next commyng as oft as thei shalbe requyred to do ther besy awys in the premysses.

P. Rutledge and D. L. Richwood (eds.), *Great Yarmouth
Assembly Minutes, 1538–45* (Norfolk Record Society,
XXXIX, 1970), 43

64. The government of Great Yarmouth enlists noble support, 1545

*Magna Jernemvtha. Communie consilium tentum in le communie aula
die martis proxima post festum decollacionis sancti Johannis anno regni
regis Henrici viijui xxxvijmo (1st Sept. 1545).*
[Great Yarmouth. Common council held in the common hall on Tuesday next after the feast of the beheading of St John the Baptist in the 37th year of the reign of King Henry VIII. (1st September 1545).]

The graunt to my lordes grace of Norfolk & the Erle of Surrey
At this present assemble yt ys fully & holly condyscendyd and a greed
that my lord the Duckes grace of Norfolk dewrying hys graces lyff shalbe
heigh steward of thys towne of Yermought and after hys deceas to my
lorde of Surrey dewryng hys lyf.

P. Rutledge and D. L. Richwood (eds.), *Great Yarmouth
Assembly Minutes, 1538–1545.* (Norfolk Record
Society, XXXIX, 1970), 65

65. The development of Cambridge's liberties rehearsed, *c.* 1550

... the town of Cambridge is an ancient borough, and existed from all time,
and was of late in the possession of the lord Henry the son of William the
Conqueror sometime King of England, the ancestor of the lord now King,
and that the said Henry sometime King had in the same borough his
bailiffs, which bailiffs at the time when that borough was in the hands of
the aforesaid King Henry had cognizance of pleas, as well touching lands
and tenements being in the same borough and the suburb of the same, as
also touching trespasses, covenants and other contracts whatsoever arising
in the same borough and suburb, and held pleas thereof before the said
bailiffs at Cambridge, and that the said Henry sometime King, by his
charter, which they produce in court, which is without date, delivered
and to farm let, to the then burgesses of Cambridge, his town of Cambridge, to hold of himself the then King and his heirs by the same farm
which the sheriff of Cambridge was wont to render to him; and that the
said Henry sometime King &c., by another charter of his which they
produce in court, which likewise is without date, granted that if any one
should forfeit there, he should there do right. And they say that by virtue
of the aforesaid grants the bailiffs of the aforesaid town, who then were,
held all pleas, as well touching lands and tenements being in the said
borough and suburb, as concerning trespasses, [covenants,] and other
contracts whatsoever arising in the said borough and suburb. And they
say that afterwards Henry son of the Empress, sometime King &c., by his
charter which they produce &c., ordered that his burgesses of Cambridge
should have and hold as well and peaceably and rightly all their liberties
and free customs in the river-banks and in all other things as the charter
of King Henry his grandfather witnessed to them. And they say that, as
well in the time of the aforesaid King Henry son of the Empress &c., as

of the aforesaid King Henry the grandfather &c., the bailiffs of the aforesaid borough, for the time being, likewise held before them all pleas arising within the said borough and suburb in form aforesaid; And they and all their successors likewise, afterwards have held before them all the aforesaid pleas in form aforesaid. And they say that the lord John sometime King &c. by his charter in the sixth year of his reign, granted to his burgesses of Cambridge a gild merchant, and that none of them should plead beyond the walls of the borough of Cambridge concerning any plea, save pleas of external tenures, except his moneyers and servants, and that they should have their lands and tenures and pledges and all debts, no matter who should owe the same, and that touching their lands and tenures which are within the borough, right should be holden to them according to the custom of the borough, and concerning all other their debts, which were lent at Cambridge, and concerning pledges there made, pleas should be holden at Cambridge. And further they say that the said John sometime King &c., by another charter of his, in the eighth year of his reign, granted and by his said charter confirmed to his burgesses of Cambridge the town of Cambridge with all its appurtenances, to have and to hold for ever, of him the then King and his heirs, to them and their heirs, rendering therefor yearly to his exchequer the ancient farm, namely forty pounds blanch and twenty pounds by tale by way of increase, for all service by their hands at the two exchequers of the year; and that they and their heirs should have and hold the aforesaid town with all its appurtenances, well and peaceably, freely and quietly, wholly and fully and honourably, in meadows and pastures, mills, water and pools, with all their liberties and free customs; and that they should make from among themselves a reeve whom they would and when they would. And they say that, after the aforesaid grant, the burgesses of the aforesaid town in every year chose their reeve and bailiffs of the aforesaid town on the morrow of the Nativity of the Blessed Mary; and the said reeve and bailiffs always held before them at Cambridge all the aforesaid pleas, to wit, concerning lands and tenements they held their courts and gave for this five days yearly, namely, on the Monday next after the feast of Saint Matthew [Sept. 21] the apostle and evangelist, and on the Monday next after the feast of Saint Lucy the Virgin [Dec. 13], and on the Monday next after the Sunday in Mid Lent, and on the Monday next after the feast of the Holy Trinity, and on the Monday next after the feast of Saint James the apostle [July 25]; and also they held pleas touching trespasses and other contracts and covenants made by those within the town on every Tuesday throughout the year; and concerning all manner of trespasses, contracts and covenants and other matters between strangers and those within the town, and between strangers and strangers [they held plea] from day to day; and likewise they held their court of the gild merchant, between merchants and merchants, concerning their merchandises, from day to day and from hour to hour, according to the exigence of the complaint; and likewise the aforesaid reeves and bailiffs held there in every year two leets, namely, one after the feast of Saint Michael and the other after the feast of Easter, and received presentments concerning all articles which pertain to the leet and the view of frank-pledge and took thence the penalties of delinquents; and likewise all their successors, bearing the aforesaid offices in the aforesaid borough, held all the aforesaid pleas before them in form aforesaid; and the aforesaid liberties and customs the lord Henry son of King John, sometime King of England, by his charters which they produce in court, afterwards granted and confirmed to his then burgesses of the aforesaid town; of which charters one is dated at Westminster on the twenty-first day of April in the eleventh year of his reign, and the other charter is dated at Westminster on the twelfth day of April in the fortieth year of his reign; and moreover the same Henry granted that henceforth they should be able to plead within the aforesaid town all pleas touching their liberty, as well concerning vee de nam [replevin], as concerning other pleas which they could plead without his Justices, so that no sheriff or other bailiff of the King himself should meddle with any matters relating to their liberties, except upon default of the aforesaid burgesses or of their bailiffs of the same town; and that the said burgesses might be able to choose from among themselves and create coroners in the aforesaid town, to make attachment of the pleas of his crown arising within the aforesaid town of Cambridge, until the coming of his Justices, as pertained to his coroners elsewhere; and the same King forbad under a penalty of ten pounds that any one should presume to vex, molest or disturb them against such liberties and grants. And they [the burgesses] produce here in court the aforesaid charter testifying the premises, and dated at Westminster on the eleventh day of April in the fortieth year of his reign. And [they say that] afterwards the lord Edward sometime King of England, the great-grandfather of the now lord King, inspecting the aforesaid charters and confirmations of his ancestors, and ratifying and according the said gifts, grants and confirmations, did for himself and his heirs, as far as in him lay, grant and confirm the same to the aforesaid burgesses, their heirs and successors, as the aforesaid charters reasonably testify; and moreover, the said King, wishing to confer an ampler favour on the said burgesses, granted to them aforesaid for himself and his heirs, that, although they theretofore had not fully used all or some of the liberties and quittances aforesaid, nevertheless they, their heirs and successors aforesaid might reasonably enjoy and use the liberties and quittances aforesaid and any of these henceforth, without let or hindrance by the King or his heirs or any his ministers, and that concerning trespasses or contracts made in the said borough and its suburbs, they should not plead nor be impleaded outside that borough unless the matter should concern the King or his heirs; and that concerning such trespasses and contracts or other internal affairs they should in no wise be convicted by foreigners, but only by their fellow-burgesses, unless the matter should concern the King or his heirs or the commonalty of the borough aforesaid. And [they say that] afterwards the lord now King, inspecting the said charters of his ancestors, and ratifying and according the gifts, grants, confirmations, liberties and quittances contained in the aforesaid charters, did for himself and his heirs, so far as in him lay, accept, approve and ratify the same, and by his charter did grant and confirm the same to the said burgesses, their heirs and successors, in such wise as the charter aforesaid of the aforesaid Edward his great-grandfather reasonably testifies, and in such wise as the said burgesses always, from the time of the granting and making of the aforesaid charter, have been wont reasonably to use and enjoy the liberties and quittances aforesaid. And they produce here in court the charter of the lord now King, testifying the premisses, of which the date is at Westminster on the eighth day of December in the first year of his reign.

F. W. Maitland (ed.), *The Charters of the Borough of
Cambridge* (Cambridge, 1901), 81–9

66. The penalty for slandering a town officer at Canongate, Scotland, 1567

Pennultimo Octobris Anno &c. lxvijo
Bessie Tailyefeir to be brankit [brought] and set upon the [market] Croce. The quhilk same day Bessie Tailzefeir being accusit be the bailleis [aldermen] and counsall of the sclandering of Thomas Huntar baillie sayand that he haid in his hous ane fals stoip [measure]. And thane eftir tryall tane thairof be James Selkrig officer fand the samyn nocht to be of veritie, And thairfoir the baillies and counsall ordanit the said Bessie to be brankit the morne and set upone the croce of this bruche [borough] thair to remane the space of ane houre.

Miscellany of the Maitland Club (Maitland Club, LI.2,
Edinburgh, 1840), 303

67. The Earl of Shrewsbury crushes Chesterfield's attempts at autonomy, 1568

1. Imprimus, where it is evident and without question that the said burgesses have not any authoritie or warrant from the prynce to have, electe, or chuse any aldermen or chamberlens within the said town of Chesterfield. It is therefore ordered that from henceforth they shall not take upon them to have, elect, or chuse any such officer or officers, and that the bailiff shall rule there as bailiff for the lorde.

2. Item touching the nomber of burgesses. It is ordered that there shall not be at any tyme within the said town above the nombre of twenty burgesses over and besides such burgesses as are and shall be presented, admitted, and sworne burgesses by reason of their burgage. And those twenty burgesses to be admitted from tyme to tyme by the said erle and his heirs. And further, that all manner of burgesses hereafter to be admitted shall, before his or their admittance, be sworn in the lord's court amongst other lawful things truly to maintain to their best powers all the lordes liberties, without deteigning or withdrawing from the said erle or his heirs any their lawful suyte, service, customs, dueties, or profetts within the liberties of the said town, and without procuring or consenting to any other person or persons to the same, and none to be made burgesses hereafter that shall be a retayner or shall weare any other liverie then the lord's.

3. Item, that from henceforth no manner of person or persons shall demande, levie, or exact of any the inhabitants of the said town, or of others coming or resorting to any faires or markets of the said erle within the said town any manner some or somes of money by the name of cutting money or by any other name whatsoever to the use of the said town, but that all manner of persons shall have free liberty according to the laws to occupy, bye and sell, at all times, there paying onelie unto the said erle his heirs and assigns their toll duties and rights of ancient tyme used and by the laws of this realme to them due and payable, and shall have places in the market at the appointment of the lord's officers.

P. Yeatman (ed.), *Records of the Borough of Chesterfield*
(Chesterfield, 1884), 114–15

68. The accounts of annual expenses at Bath, 1569

Charges of the holle yere. – The chargys of Mydsomernyght xl*s* iiij*d*, a loke and a kay for the chyste in the pantre ij*s* viij*d*, to Byrde for a loke and a kay for the palles viij*d*, a pottell of wyne to my Lorde Bysshopes chaplayne viij*d*, for clothe, pyche, rosson, tallowe and cordes xvij*d*, to the bellman for the same worke vj*d*, for rydinge to Brystowe, Mr Gybbes, Welshe and I, ij*s* ij*d*, for makinge the waulle at Goodwyffe Busshes iij*s* vj*d*, to Birde to mend the towne crokes and a loke to Bakars dore ij*s*, to Chaundler for viij krokes in the newe howsse iij*s* ij*d*, to a carpenter to worke the polles viij*d*, a quere of papre for the Yelde Haull iiij*d*, for the carege of bukettes to Stybbes ij*s*, to a pursavant fyrste for the lottere v*s*, payed for Mr Brytes horssemeatt for the yere before ij*s* vj*d*, a cotte clothe for the bagepype player viij*s* vj*d*, to the Erle of Worcyters playors iij*s*, to John Dallemie for waynskott xxxij*s*, for wyne and suger geven to Syre Raffe Hopton ij*s* j*d*, loste in the prysse of a oxe ix*s* viij*d*, for clothe, rosson, pyche and tallowe and cordes at Waukotes Lane ij*s* j*d*, for blewe slatt bowt for the bellhowsse xx*d*, ij carpenters for settinge up the same howsse iij*s* ij*d*, for bordes for the same howsse vj*s* viij*d*, for nayelles for the tymbre bordinge and for the slattes ij*s* vj*d*, the tylor for hys workemaneshype ij*s*, for mendinge Saynt Jeames pype xvj*d*, to the waytes of Brystowe agaynste my Lorde of Pembrokes comynge v*s*, to a pursyvant v*s*, for mendinge the pypes in Waulkotes Lane in the twelfe dayes for clothe, cordes, pyche, tallowe and rosson xvj*d*, to the belman for ij dayes worke there viij*d*, a tyler one day apone the Yelde Halle x*d*, to a pursyvant for stayinge of shypes iij*s* iiij*d*, to John Belman for v yeardes of frysse v*s* x*d*.

F. D. Wardle (ed.), *The Accounts of the Chamberlains*
of Bath 1568–1602 (Somerset Record Society,
XXXVIII, 1923), 4–5

69. Potential defenders and the town armour at Bridgwater, 1569

Borough of Brigwater, with Castell Diche

Ablemen

Robt. Mewe	... archer.		Jno. Paine	... archer.
Wm. Gyett	... "		Robt. Sprake	... "
Jno. Andersey	... archer.		Leonard Cone	... archer
Darbye Carren	... billman.		Wm. Hoskens	... billman.
Thos. Townesend	... archer.		William Collens	... "
Raphe Thack	... "		Tege Leyry	... "
Thos. Lappe	... "		Thos. Pope	... "
Henry Cornishe	... "		Jno. Chepman	... archer.
Richd. Wod	... billman.		Wm. Thomas	... "
Jno. Phelpes	... pekeman.		Hewe Culverwill	... "
Jno. Bowde	... "		Thos. Palmer	... billman.
Wm. Curry	... "		Richd. Wodd	... "
Wm. Forde	... "		Wm. Thomas	... "
Anty Love	... "		Wm. Bowk	... gonner.
Richd. Larke	... "		Jno. Chepman	... "
Alex. Protte	... billman.		Wm. Thomas	... billman.
Mathew Weste	... archer.		Thos. Weithers	... "
Walter Wyat	... gonner.		Wm. Stocke	... archer.
John Trebell	... billman.		Jno. Coppe	... billman.
Jno. Cornish	... "		Jno Thomas	... archer.
Wm. Thorne	... "		Wm. Heys	... "
Jno. Tyler	... "			

Armor

The Borough, ij corslets, ij harquebuts, ij jacks, ij bows, ij sheafs of arrows, ij swords, ij daggers, ij sculls, ij paire of almain rivets.

Castle Diche, one tithing corslet furnished.

Robert Mullens, gent., one corslet furnished.

James Boyes, gent., one corslet furnished.

Jno. Nethercott, one corslet furnished.

Nicholas Chewet, one paire of almain rivets.

John Hammon, one corslet furnished.

Philip Holworthe, with others } one paire of almain rivets.

Jeffery Shercon, with others } one paire of almain rivets.

Jno. Edwardes with others } one paire of almain rivets.

Jno. Sanders, a bow, a sheaf of arrows.

William Golde, Richard Castelman, with others } one paire of almain rivets.

Roger Goodyer with others } one paire of almain rivets.

Alex Jones, one paire of almain rivets, one harquebut.

William Waterman, one harquebut.

Jno Oder, one harquebut.

William Jones, one harquebut.

Jno. Dey, one Harquebut.

Richard Hyat, one harquebut.

There is containing in this tithing, xij bills, ij bows and ij sheaf of arrows.

Sum of the ablemen in the saide Hundred, xliij whereof

Gunners	... ...	v
Pikeman	... ...	vj
Archers	... ...	xvij
Billman	... ...	xv

Sum of the armour in the borough aforesaid.

Harquebuts, with Calivers	... ...	v
Corslets	... ...	vj
Almain rivets with jacks	... ...	ix

E. Green (ed.), *Certificates of Muster in the County of Somerset 1569* (Somerset Record Society, XX, 1904), 137–8

70. The constables at Lewes hand over to their successors, 1576–7

That wee Thomas Shearman & William Covearte have delyvered unto John Otteringame and Gorge Cockky constabuls sucksedinge, the toune boxe wyth locke & ij kayes wythe the toune seale and the seale ffor vacabons: one aunsyent one drum ij drumstickes one partisen and iiij stattute bockes: xij lethere bucketes ij great eyrne whockes wth chaines uppon

them & ij greate poles mad ffor the youse of ffyre if ned requyre wthin
the toune; one locke of the weste gate wyth ij kayes which gate & house
are ye prissons ffor the toune: and ij chestes ij lockes ij kayes in the
toune house: lackethe of ye gatheringe of the toune charges xiij*s* iiij*d*
and for that yt was not gathered before the said constabells made there
accounte: the costom of the toune is thate yt shouldebe loste: at the
charges of the said Thomas Shermann & William Coverte: etc' Quiete.

L. F. Salzman (ed.), *The Town Book of Lewes 1542–1701*
(Sussex Record Society, XLVIII, 1946) 24–5

**71. Town office, burgess status and privileges on the common lands
enshrined in 'The Orders and Constitutions' of Calne, 1589, 1597.**

Calne 1589. Here followeth the orders & constytutions of the Booroughe
and Towne of Calne aforesaide, made, ordeyned & constytuted by the
generall consent, and assente of the burgessez there as herafter ensueth,
wrytten and regestryed by Phyllip Rytche, clarcke, there.

IN PRYMIS it ys ordered and agreed, that when the Quenes lawe daye
shalbee assomoned tooe bee holden and kepte, that then ymmedyatlye the
burgessz shall coome together tooe the place accustomed, and then the
constables; with the consente of the Burgessez; shall choose twooe newe
constables and presente theire names unto the stewarde at the law daye
aforesayde.

Item it is agreed, that the Soondaye (before Saynte Mathias daye)
[24 February] in the afternoone of the same daye, the burgessz tooe
come toogeather: to the place accustomed and then the burges stewardes
with the consente of the burgessz shall choose twooe newe stewards, and
tooe have them nomynated yn the pulpytt at eveninge prayer, and they
beinge soe nomynated, than tooe enter tooe their charge: on Saynte
Mathewes [*sic*] daye. And the olde stewards tooe geve upp theire
accomptes the Sundaye followinge, on payne of forfeitinge of suche
soomes of mooney as they have, or shouldehave receyved yn theyr yeare.

Item it ys agreed that when they make anye newe burges thatt then the
burgessz dooe coom tooe geather tooe their accustomed place and there
choose hym, by the consent of the whole burgessz. And beeinge so elected
& chosen then tooe be sworne at the prynces cowrte: tooe be holden at
Oggborne nexte after suche choyse. Note that where the whole burgessz
are named, yt is mente, the moste parte of the burgessz.

Item it ys ordeyned and agreed, that everye chieffe, or head howse-
holder that dothe watch and warde, maye put yn three kyne or bullocks
yntooe the Porte Marshe and Alders at the stewards appoyntement, and to
paye at the puttinge yn of them fowre pence, a pece, and paye the hurde
his accustomed wagis. And the cattall tooe goe there from the thyrde daye
of Maye, untill Saynte Martyns daye [12 November], and no man tooe
have an oxe bullocke tooe feede there aboove the age of twooe yeres. ...

Item it [is] ordeyned and agreed: that yf anye inhabytante within the
booroughe, shall stubburnlye resyste the orders sett downe by the burgessz,
and wilfullye denye tooe paye and tooe dooe accordinge tooe the true
meaninge of the same orders, shall then ymmedyatlye hee shalbee dys-
fryanchised: and putt from all and all manner of commodyties, and
proffetts that he hath had of and in the Porte Marshe and Alders aforesaide. And soe tooe stand dysfranchysed, yett yf hee bee one of the
burgessz tooe bee also dysburgessed and dysplaced untill hee or they dooe
submitt them selves untoe the burgessz, tooe keepe theire orders and tooe
paye a newe fyne.

Item it ys ordeyned, concluded, and agreed that noe owte coomer or
stranger, coominge yntoe our boorroughe tooe dwell and ynhabytt there,
at anye tyme hereafter, hee shall not have, noe comodyte, yn nor uppon
oure commons, for the tyme & space of three yeres, after habytation
there, neyther then, but uppon his honest & good beehavyor, and that
with the consent and agreement of the burgessz there, or the greater parte
of them.

Item it ys ordeyned, concluded, and agreed the 28th daye of Decembre
An[n]o D[omi]ni 1597 (and yn the fortieth yere of the rayne of owre
soveraigne ladye Quene Elyzabeth etc.) by the burgessz of the booroughe
of Calne, that the burgessz stuards there, shall furthe of their common
purse paye tooe [the] undershryffe yerelye at Chrismass xx*s*, as a fee, tooe
dyschardge the burgessz there of & from all sutes and services of assyses,
seassyons, ynquestes and juryes, whatsoever, accordinge tooe the libertie
of their charter, for that yn tyme paste they have benne myghtelye
wronged & injured, by beeinge returned yn *venires* and other services at
the assizes and else where — By those burgessz whose names are here sub-
scrybed.

[Here follow the names of the burgesses who agree to these orders.]

Wiltshire Record Office, Calne General Entry Book, G18/1/1

72. A defence rate against Spanish invasion raised at Maldon, 1590

At this Court it was considered by the Bailiffs, Aldermen and head burgesses then and there present that for so much as they have lately received knowledge by letters from her Majesty's Deputy Lieutenant that there is great preparation and show of the foreign enemy, the Spaniards, to make some attempt shortly against this land; and thereupon have laid some further charge upon this town already and more very shortly is like to ensue; and for that there is not any money in the common chamber of this borough to defray the charge of this service when the same should be presently required but must be forced to tarry a general collection to be made through the town for the accomplishment of such urgent affairs and dutiful service to the danger of rebuke and displeasure of personages in high authority ... it is therefore ordered and constituted that every person within the borough now cessed to the subsidy shall pay for every pound cessed in lands 16*d* and for every pound in goods 10*d* which may appear to amount to the sum of £16 or thereabouts.

A. C. Edwards (ed.), *English History from Essex Sources,
1550–1750* (Essex Record Office Publications, No. 17,
Chelmsford, 1952), 21

73. The elected mayor excused from serving at Portsmouth, 1598

*Election of Mayor, 26th September 1598. Mr Thomas Bysson having been
elected.*

Whereuppon the said Mr. Thomas Bysson alleadged that he had once before served in that office and was nowe owlde and weake and wanted [lacked] a wyf, and was altogeather unfurnished and unable to execute and dyscharge the said offyce and therefore did earnestly desyre the maior and burgesses that he might be released and dyscharged from the said office and that they woulde accept this ffyne wch was vj*li* xiij*s* iiij*d* accordinge to an auntient constitution of the said towne and soe p'ced to a newe ellection. Whereunto the maior and burgesses then and there assembled did consent and agree havinge duly and advysedly considered thereof and p'sently p'ceeded to a new ellection and then Mr. Owin Totty was chosen to stande wth Mr. Richard Leonard for the office of maior of the said towne for this yeare followinge.

R. J. Murrell and J. R. East (eds.), *Records of the Borough
of Portsmouth* (Portsmouth, 1884), 213

74. The corporation of Leicester petitions the king for the extension of borough jurisdiction into the bishop's fee, 1605

Memorandum that we whose names are underwritten are parsuaded that yf it bee his Majesties pleasure to give authoritie, to the Maior and Burgesses of Leicester to apprehend evil doers and to punyshe misdemeanors in those howses and tenements called the Bysshopps fee adjoyninge and intermingled together with thee howses of the towne, itt will effecte a muche more quiete and orderlie government of the whole towne, and of the saide tenements called Bysshopps fee, and be noe waye prejuditiall, but rather an ease to the Justice of the Peace for the county.

Thus muche we are content to subscribe for our opinyons howe profitable it would be to have the towne and the said other howses unyted under one government, not intending thereby to prejudice the lawfull righte or libertie of anie man, of whiche, those whom his Majestie hathe sett in authoritie are to judge and not wee. And further it is not intended to keepe oute anie of the countrie artisants from trafique in the towne of Leicester, otherwise then of auncyent tyme (for three hundred yeeres past) hath been used, and by lawes and statute of this realme is provided.

H. Stocks and W. H. Stevenson (eds.), *Records of the Borough of Leicester.* (Cambridge, 1923), IV, 44—5

75. The mayor and corporation of Bedford make enquiries about town government to the city fathers of Oxford, 1608

1. Imprimis whether doe you chose the mayor and sheriffs of the cytie of Oxford by the freemen of your cytie or by all the inhabitants of the same?

For answeare to the first demaund, knowe yee for certentie that our mayor and bayliffs are chosen onely by freemen of the cytie, none other intermedling; every citizen with us being a freeman is a burgesse, and whosoever is not a freeman, wee call him a forriner and such have not to meddle with any affaires of the cytie.

2. Whether may the mayor, sheriffs or chamberlins of the cytie of Oxford being elected unto their places refuse to execute the same, and whether doe you punishe the contempt by fine, imprisonment or both?

The mayor, bayliffs or chamberlens being chosen may not refuse the place uppon payne of being fyned, the mayor x*li*; the bayliffs and chamberlens are offices that are desired and therefore never fyned.

3. Whether is not the steward and towneclark of the cytie of Oxon for the most parte always resident within your corporacion? or have you not a place or offyce wherein your records of your courts are continually kept? or doth not your steward or townclarck commonly keepe the same?

The towneclarcke alwaies is and ought to bee resident and dwelling within the cytie or suburbes, and he keepeth the office that the cytie hath by the yeldhall, where all records of later tyme doe remayne under his custodie, and those that are more ancyent are laid in a place by the yeldhall called the exchequer; and the townclarck or his sufficient deputie is daylie to be attendant at the same offyce for entring of plaints daylie, for examining of felons and other the cytie's businesses.

4. Whether may not the mayor and corporation of the cytie of Oxford remove the steward, townclarck or any other offycer that hath his offyce by patent for terme of his lyfe for abuses by him committed against the mayor, sheriefs or corporacion?

As the townclarck is chosen by the most part of the whole commons, becaus he is clericus communitatis, so by the greater part of them he may bee removed if he deserve it, as by non user, abuser or other misdemeanor. But wee doe not use to graunte the office by patent, but by act of common counsell, which is implyed to bee for his lyfe, if he bee not removed for lawful causes. If the towneclarck, nor his sufficient deputie, give attendaunce, the cytie and countrie would by their absence be much wronged and especially for want of entring of plaints, wee having courts kept twice a weeke.

5. Whether may any freeman arrest or impleade any freeman of the cytie of Oxford in any other court without your Jurisdiction, and may any freeman being impleaded within your courts bring any the King's Majesty's writts for removing of the cause depending in your courts?

It is the parte of every freeman's othe not to impleade another freeman out of the courts of the cytie, if that he may have right within the courts of the cytie. If any doe the contrarie, it is good to disfranchise him, but any freeman may remove any cause that is there brought against him by another freeman, either by habeas corpus, certiorari or priviledge in any the courts at Westminster.

6. Whether do you make lawes, constitutions or ordinaunces within the cytie of Oxford? and by what companie doe you make the same lawe and constitucions and by whom are they ratifyed, confirmed and allowed to bee good and justifiable by lawe?

Wee doe make lawes and ordinaunces by act of common counsell, that is by the mayor, aldermen, bayliffs, chamberlens and all that have beene bayliffs or chamberlens or have compounded for the place of bayliff or chamberlen in the said cytie, and by foure and twentie other citizens that are out of the commons chosen to bee of the Common Counsell which have never borne office, unless happilie [*sic*] thoffice of constableshippe, and they are to give their voices in graunting of leases and all other busy-nesses, except it bee at the eleccion of the mayor, aldermen, bayliffs, chamberlens or towneclarck; for at those eleccions the whole commons come togeather and the foure and twenty come not in the counsell howse, but give their voices in the hall with the residue of the commons ...

9. Whether may any freeman of the cytie of Oxford use any more trade than that he was made free unto? and whether will the other companie whose trade he doth use, sufferr the same? or what is your order for the suppressing of the same?

Wee doe not maynteyne that any freeman may use any other trade but such as he hath beene apprentice unto by the space of seaven yeares according to the statute, but yet sometymes our freemen doe sett uppe any other trade that they list to use, but shoe-makers, fullers, and weavers by ancyent charters, and taylors and glovers by graunts from the cytie under the common seale, and by acts confirmed by the justices of assise, so solelie hould their trades without any others intermedling with them, unlesse he bee a freeman of the cytie, and also free of that company ...

13. Are not the freemen of the cytie of Oxford free in any other place within the King's Majesty's domynions? And doe you make them patents and letters ad testificandum under the seale of your offices? and what is the fees due for the sealing of the said patents? and to what use is it paid?

The words of your charters and ours doe almost agree, that wee may buy and sell in all places as in London and other places without paying scott or lott, stallage, pontage or any such custome; and wee doe make our freemen patents and letters ad testificandum, that they are free of our cytie and therefore ought to bee acquited of all toll, custome, stallage, pontage and all such other things according to the words of our charters. For the seale of the mayor's office thereunto everie one at the sealing payeth vis viiid to the mayor for his fee ever accustomed; and for the drawing and ingrossing iiis iiiid to the townclarck ...

20. Is the charge of the renewing of the charter of the cytie of Oxford borne by the chamber and stock of the cytie, or by taxacion of the freemen of the cytie?

If there be a sufficient stock in the chamber of the cytie wee have not used to charge private mens purses for obteyning our charters. Otherwise wee thincke it lawfull and reasonable to use taxacion of the citizens for any such purpose, if need bee. And for relief of all such as are visitted with the plague, and for watching to keepe them in their howses or other places when they are removed, wee use taxacion of freemen and all inhabituants towards their relief and keeping.

H. E. Salter (ed.), *Oxford Council Acts, 1583–1626* (Oxford
Historical Society, LXXXVII, Oxford, 1928), 343–50

76. A would-be M.P. solicits support from the Aldeburgh electorate, 1639

Gentlemen,
His Majestie havinge published a parlement, I did thinke with my selfe that if I might be one of that body I might do some good to seamen. I bethought myselfe of some place upon the sea coast where men of my owne sort do inhabit (to request ther favor that they would chusse me if it might be no prejudice to them). I thought upon your towne of Aldbrough hopinge I might speed with you in regard I am known to most of you. And to that purpose I dessiered my Lord High Admiral's letter which you shall receave with this. My Lord had recomended another man whome you know not, one Mr Hugh Potter, yet I prevalled with him to recomend him to another place and to recomend me to you. Now I stand not upon recomendation only but upon your loves, and if it shall pleasse you to make choyce of me I hope you shall not have causse to repent. I promisse to deale faithfully in anythinge that shall conserne religion or the commonwealth accordinge to my understandinge and leave the further consideration to your owne ffree will and rest your lovinge frend.

In what I am able.

William Rainborow

London, this second of Dessember, 1639.[1]

[1] Rainborow was sucessful in his bid to become M.P. for Aldeburgh and was re-elected to the Long Parliament. He died in February 1642. Hugh Potter became M.P. for Plymouth, Devon (Mary F. Keeler, *The Long Parliament, 1640–41* (Philadelphia, Pa., 1954), 320,312

Suffolk Record Office. Aldeburgh records. EE 1/K4/1

77. The city and suburbs of London are put in a state of defence by the Corporation, 1643[1]

That a small fort conteyning one bulwark and halfe and a battery in the reare of the flanck be made at Gravell lane end. A horne worke wth two flanckers be placed at Whitechapell wind-mills. One redoubt wth two flanckers betwixt Whitechapell church and Shoreditch. Two redoubts with flanckers neere Shoreditch church wth a battery. At the windmill in Islington way, a battery and brestwork round about. A small redoubt neere Islington pound. A battery and brestwork on the hill neere Clarkenwell towards Hampstead way. Two batteries and a brestworke at Southampton house. One redoubt wth two flanckers by St Giles in the Feilds, another small work neere the turning. A quadrant forte wth fower halfe bulwarks crosse Tyborne high way at the second turning that goeth towards Westminster. At Hide parke corner a large forte wth flanckers on all sides. At the corner of the lord Goring's brick wall next the fields a redoubt and a battery where the court of Guard now is at the lower end of the lord Goring's wall, the brestwork to be made forwarder. In Tuttle feilds a battery brestworke, and the ditches to be scowred. That at the end of every street wch is left open to enter into the suburbs of this citty defenceable brestworkes be made or there already erected repayred wth turnepikes muskett proof, and that all the passages into the suburbs on the northside the river except five vizt The way from St. James towards Charing Crosse, the upper end of Saint Giles in Holborne, the further end of St. John Street towards Islington, Shoreditch church and Whitechappell to be stopped up. That the courtes of guard and the rayles or barrs at the utmost partes of the freedome be made defensible and turnepikes placed there in lieu of the chaynes all musket proof. And that all the shedds and buildings that joyne to the outside of the wall be taken downe. And that all the bulwarkes be fitted at the gates and walls soe that the flanckes of the wall and streets before the gates may be cleared and that the gates and bulwarks be furnished with ordnance.

[1] For the background to this document see B. Manning, *The English People and the English Revolution, 1640–49* (1976).

R. R. Sharpe, *London and the Kingdom* (1895), III, 431–2

The civil war politics of the Newcastle-upon-Tyne coal trade, 1644[1]

12 November, 1644: The Committee's Declaration dated at Newcastle
The Committee of Both Kingdomes, after many meetings and serious debates amongst themselves and the hearing of sundry persons well experyenced in the colleyries and the coleworkes about the towne of Newcastle, and haveing taken into there seryous considerations sundry propositions for the good of these workes, and the driving on that trade for the benefitt of the parliament and the pay of the army, have at length concluded and agreed amongst themselves that some of the most notoryous delinquents and malignants, late coleowners in the towne of Newcastle, shold be wholly excluded from intermeddlinge with any shares or parts of colleyries or intrest in any coles whatsoever, that former-ly they have laid claime unto. That the rest of the said delinquents deserve not to have any benefitt of the said coles and colleryes, but in regard the delinquents and malignants belonging to those coleryes were very many in number, they did not conceive it for the service of the parliament or the army to put them all out at once, and so to hazard the retarding of the present setting on of the workes and ruining of the same, in regaurd they were furnisht with matteryalls and utensells, and had things ready at hand, and did best know where to fynd workemen, which strangers wold have had difficulty to fynd, and cold not possibly on the sodden sufficiently provide themselves to set on the workes, and havinge made tryall to let some delinquents colleryes. And for this purpose haveing treated with some well affected persons what profitts might bee raysed, and how they might be let for the most beniffitt to the parliament, were constrayned for the present rather to make use of some of those delinquents in working theire owne colleries as tennants and servants to the parliament then to ingadge our freinds upon incertainties and hazard theire losse as our owne hindrance in setting forwards the workes for the use and benefit of the parliament, wherefore the Committee of Both Kingdomes, seing the necessity of dispatching away the shipps that every day call upon us for there layding and lye at charges in expectation of getting coles for there mony, have thought fitt to make this ffollowinge declaration to all but such as are excepted as before mentioned, and whose names are hereafter written.

That for the present tyme there be allowed on the behalfe of the rest of the late coleowners 10 shillings sterling upon every chalder of shipp coles for defraying the charges in the workes under ground, carriage therof to the staythes, and from thence in keeles to shipps, paying the townes dues as was formerly paid, viz: 13*d* for the towne and 3*d* for the garrison p chalder the the usuall and accustomed rents for the pitts, and as a competent consideration for the support of the said late owners themselves. And this allowance is made as well for the coles at the staythes and pitts ready wrought as those to be wrought. The said owners colleryes and workmen being alwayes obleiged to sett on fott with all diligence and mayntaine their cole workes, make ready their keeles and all other necessaryes fitt for the same, and the cole workers, who ar to receive the benefitt of payment as abovesaid for their worke out of the coles already above ground, ar obliged to continue in working the said coles att the ordinary rayt and condytions as was formerly accustomed. And whatsoever more price the said chalder of coles (being sould to merchants or mrs of shipps) shall yeild above the said 10s, and together with what custome and impost is or shalbe put upon the same and the ould custome of one shilling upon the chalder formerly paid by the owners to his Matie to be imployed for the pay and maintenance of the army upon accompt to the parliament of England or their Committees.

2. That the coales already wrought above ground ether at the pitts or staythes belonginge to freinds have like allowance of 10s upon the chalder, they paying the said townes dutyes (viz.) 13d to the Towne, and 3d to the garrison p chalder. And the supplus of the price which they shall yeild (being sould to merchants or shippmrs) to be imployed for the said publique use by way of lane, and that they have the publicke fayth for the same. The owners, taxemen, and workers being alwayes tyed to put on foot and mayntaine the said workes, remittinge to the determination of the parliament what other condytions they wilbe pleased to grant them for the coles henceforth to be wrought.

3. Itt is thought fitt that the price of coales bee fifteene shillings p chalder, which with the assesse of fower shillings upon the chalder, and the ancient 12d to the Kinge, is 20s for every chalder to the merchant or skipp for all coles vended in this port of Newcastle, and for those exported to pay the same rayte and such further custome as is ordeyned by the Booke of Raytes.

4. That certification bee made to the severall owners, of which we doubt not our freinds will take speciall notice and instantly apply themselves to set on their workes, that if presently they use not all possible dilligence in getting on foote their severall coleworkes and in mayntayning therof in that case to bee declared uncapeable of any future benefitt which they might expect out of their said colleyries, and that other persons shalbe imployed for workinge the same for the publique use and benifitt of the Parliament and Army.

The parties named excepted out of this declaration and agreement as before mentioned. Sir Jo: Marley Knt., Sir Tho. Riddell,Knt., Sir Thos. Liddell, Knt., Sir Alexa. Davison, Knt., Sir John Mennes, Knt., Sir ffrancis Anderson, Knt.

Will. Rowe, Secr. Comm[issione]rs

[1] R. Howell, *Newcastle-upon-Tyne and the Puritan Revolution* (Oxford, 1967) provides the context for this document.

Extracts from the Records of the Company of Hostmen of Newcastle-upon-Tyne (Surtees Society, CV, 1901), 81–3

79. Plans for the rebuilding of Liverpool with timber from Royalists' estates, 1645

Die Mercurii [*Wednesday*] *17 Septembris 1645*
Ordered that 500 tuns of tymber be allowed unto the towne of Liverpoole for rebuilding the said towne in a great part destroyed and burnt downe by the Enemie, and that the said 500 tuns be felled in the groundes and woodes of James, Earle of Derby, Richard, Lord Mollyneux, William Norris, Robert Blundell, Robert Mollyneux, Charles Gerrard, and Edward Scarisbricke Esquires. And that it be referred to the Comittee for Lancaster that are members of this Howse to take order for the due and orderly felling of the said tymber and for apporceninge the quanteties to be allowed to the persons that suffered by the burninge of the said towne for the rebuilding thereof.

G. Chandler (ed.), *Liverpool under Charles I* (Liverpool, 1965), 363

80. The Convention of the Royal Burghs of Scotland elect representatives to take part in discussions concerning union with England, 1652

The commissioners of the free burrowis of Scotland now convened by authoritie of the parliament of the commonwealth of England for electing sevin persones to represent all the saidis burrowis consenting to the unione of Scotland in an comounwealth with England, to attend the parliament of England or such as they sall appoint, as is directed by the declaratione bearing dait the 25 day of Merch 1652 yeiris and to have power for effecting the matteris expressed in said declaratione, considdering that the personis undirwrittin, viz., Mr Patrick Hay, Thomas Sydserff, William Dundas, and Mr Robert Gordoun ar elected comissioneris frome the burghis of Anstruther Eister, Bamff, Quenisferie and Dornoch, by vertew of the several comissionis granted to them, which comissioneris, althocht they be allowed by the honorabill English comissioneris appointed for reveising of the comissionis as agreeable to the forme of the comissione set doun in the declaratione emitted by the parliament of the comounwealth of England, yit considdering that the above-mentioned comissionis ar in materiall pointis concerning the qualificatione of the personis comissionated contrar to the liberties and practisses of the saidis free burrowis of this natione in all former tymes observed towardis the electione of comissioneris to publict meiting and conventionis, as namelie, that it hes ever bein thair especiall richt and custome to elect no comissioneris but such as ar memberis of the incorporatione of the burgh, actuall inhabitantis within the same, and who bearis burding therwith in the extent rollis, taxationis, and comoun burthingis, such as non of the above named persones comissionated ar, being strangeris and not actuall induellaris in the burghis from whome they have their respective comissionis, who never have borne anie comoun burding therwith, and although they be admitted burgessis of the burgh yit that being onlie ane honorarie favor frequentlie gevin to strangeris or done at this tyme for pryvat respectis not tending to the publict good to such as ar not thair actuall inhabitantis and who wndirgois no comoun burthingis with theme. And the saidis comissioneris of the free burrowis of this natione now conveined as said is, forbearing at this tyme to pres strictlie thair liberties and former practissis, and desyring in an unanimous way, with the least contradictione that may be, to advance the publict good and endis proposed in the declaratione of the parliament of the comounwealth of England, doe thairfoir protest that the admiting of the foirsaidis persones to be comissioneris with them in this present meiting is and salbe without prejudice to the burrowis of thair liberties in tyme cuming and that this thair giving way to the saidis comissionis at this tym salbe no preparative or prejudice to the burrowis in any other caice whatsoever in any other tyme cuming.

J. D. Marwick (ed.), *Extracts from the Records of the Convention of the Royal Burghs of Scotland, 1615–76* (Edinburgh, 1878), 361–2

81. An opponent of the restoration of the monarchy, Haverfordwest, 1660

Reasons why Sam[pson] Lort is a very unfit person to act for the town and county of Haverfordwest, certified by the mayor and common council.

1. During the late eleven years since the myrther of our gracious sovereign he was a potent and a most violent actor under the several changes and especially against this place. By his procurement a mulct was laid on the town having no such power by the then ordinance of parliament for so doing. Poor blind widows were mulct as well as those that were capable of hostile actions, and the moneys so raised never accounted for but converted to some of his relations' purses.

2. He was a most impetuous instrument for the ejecting of orthodox and godly ministers insomuch that he would not suffer an orthodox lecture to be set up in this place but procured his agents, being all of his kindred, to frame articles against them to the terror and deterring of those godly ministers from doing such soul saving offices. Instead he advanced cobblers, hatters, weavers, tailors and other orderless mechanics.

3. The aldermen were summoned by warrant from him to appear at the town of Pembr[oke] seven miles from this town, being a thing never offered to them. Instead of hearing their just grievances he sent [them] home with the denominations of barking dogs; on the least surmise would imprison such of the aldermen and others that he thought fit, for no other cause but that 'we' stood firm to 'our' oaths with God and man to defend the king's royal prerogative and privileges of parliament according to the laws of this kingdom, he having utterly cast it behind his back insomuch that he was made captain of the county troop. No motto could befit his disloyal colours but 'noe kinge, noe lorde wee are ingaged' which was taken out of the said colours within this month but it is much feared that it hath too deep an impression in his heart.

4. As for those he made of his party here, partly for fear and partly for reward, they are most of them troops and such as farmed the ejected ministers' livings upon slender accounts, informers, door keepers to the said commissioners for ejection, and such like instruments under him in the violent actings under the several changes, people encouraged always to be averse to government and governors by which encouragement every one of those thinks himself as fit to govern as those that are in authority over them being of the loose and 'phanaticall' principles of those of Munster.

5. Henry Jones, the present mayor, went to Lort to complain how hardly he was used, being charged with a horse and arms above his estate.

Instead of bearing of him [he] was bid begone like a malignant rascal, being a person of known integrity who was never in arms against king or parliament in his life.

6. Lort in [16]53 encouraged one John Sharpe, a pedlar, a fellow of desperate fortune, to question the then mayor, sheriff, bailiffs and some of the aldermen for bearing offices in the town which they could not avoid without incurring a fine, and caused them to expend much money besides their several journeys to London. Sharpe told Lort that he could not bring the defendants to a commission. Lort answered that he would force them to it, he [Sharpe] being a commissioner for him. This and much more they can prove by good testimony if they may procure a commission for the examining of witnesses, the town not being able to send up by reason of the violent dealing of these eleven years.

[*In another hand:*]

7. Charles Steward of Poole-chrohan, being brought into the court of Haverford in a caus that Sampson [Lort] did not well relish, was catechized who gave him that name, etc.: told him of a k[ing] by his name and that the name of C. Steward was odious.

B. G. Charles (ed.), *Calendar of the Records of the Borough of Haverfordwest, 1539–1660* (Cardiff, 1967), 169–70

82. Manchester celebrates the return of the monarchy, 1661

After sermon from the church marched in their order the burrough-reeve, constables, and the rest of the burgesses of this town not then in armes, accompanied with Sir Ralph Ashton Kt. and Bar. and divers neighbouring gentlemen of quality, together with the said Warden, Fellows of the said Colledg, and divers other ministers, with the town-musick playing before them upon loud instruments through the streets to the cross, and so forwards to the conduit, officers and souldiers in their orders. The gentlemen and officers drunck his Majesties health in claret running forth at three streames of the said conduit, which was answered from the souldiery by a great volley of shot, and many great shouts, saying, *God save the King*. This being ended, the gentry and ministers went to dinner, attended with the officers and musick of the town, the auxilliaries dineing at the same place. During the time of dinner, and until after sun-set, the said conduit did run with pure claret, which was freely drunke by all that could, for the croud come near the same. After an houre, or something more spent in dinner, the drums did beat, and the souldiers marched into the field again, giving three great vollies and shouts, makeing the country therewith to eccho. From thence through several streets, bringing the said Major Byrom to his own house, where making an halt, the Major began his Majesties health in sack to the officers, the souldiers standing in rankes and files likewise drank the same, and ecchoed it forth with several vollies and acclamations of joy. So from the Major's house marched round about Salford, fireing and shouting all along; and again at the door of the Major's ensign's house another halt was made, and the companies were drawne round in single file in the street, there freely entertained with sack and claret, returning of thanks with vollies of shot and great shouts – marched back into the town, and after some few vollies and shouts, were taken up with raine. Bonefires being in every street, and thereby preventing from marching. The bells continued ringing night and day; some fire-works runing upon cords the length of one hundred yards, and so backwards, with crackers in the ayre, which sport continued till almost midnight, but spectators much disappointed by the raine, all the day being very clear and glorious, bonefires burning above a week.

J. P. Earwaker (ed.), *Court Leet Records of the Manor of Manchester* (Manchester, 1887), IV, 283–4

83. The dismembered body of the Marquis of Montrose is taken down from the gates of Edinburgh, 1661

5th January 1661

Forsameikle as his Majesties Commissioner and Parliament of this kingdome by their act of Parliament of the fourt of this instant have resolved that the body of the lait Marquesse of Montrose, his head and uther divided members thereof, be raised and taken doun from the places wherupon they wer sett, be gathered together and honourablie interrd. And Moonday nixt appoynted to be done with all solemnitie the Counsell appoynts four companyes of the nighbours to be in armes that day to attend the Counsellis ordours and ordaines the thesaurer to cause erect a scaffold upon the top of the Tolbuith for the dountaking of the head and to be at such uther chairges and expensis requisite for that effect ...

M. Wood (ed.), *Extracts from the Records of the Borough of Edinburgh, 1655–65* (Edinburgh, 1940), 227

84. The faithful expect their due reward. Maldon, 1661

To the King's most excellent Majestie,
The humble petition of the aldermen and free burgesses of the borough
of Maldon in Essex

Humbly sheweth

That although we your Majestie's faythfull subjects doe now finde the reward of that loyalty for which many of us have deepely suffered, in that we have lived to see the happy restauration of your sacred Majestie. Yett we cannot hope to enjoy the full influence of your Majestie's gracious reigne so long as the government of this corporation is in the hands of such persons whose disloyalty to your Majestie (some of them having bin in actuall armes against your Majestie at Worcester and elsewhere), whose disaffections to the Church (being for the most part members of schismaticall congregations), whose irreverence in proclaiming your Majestie, and whose neglect in administring the Oath of Allegiance are so notoriously evident. They have also for many yeares last past impoverished the Corporation by exhausting our rents and revenues and still do continue the same designes by granting freedom to, and advancing to offices persons of the same principle with themselves.

May it therefore please your most sacred Majestie to take into your royall consideration the redresse of these enormities, that we your Majestie's faythfull subjects may be put into a capacity of testifying that loyalty and obedience that by the lawes of God and the land are due to your Majestie. And we shall alwayes pray etc.

Essex County Record Office. Maldon records. D/B 3/12/2

85. The convention of the Royal Burghs of Scotland instruct their London agent, 1671

13 October 1671

1. [As authorised by the 22nd and 28th acts of last general convention the commissioners appointed William Andersone, provost of Glasgow,] to be our agent, giving him heirby our full, free, plaine pouer, expres bidding, mandament, and charge, for us in our names and our behalf, to repaire to London to attend at court, and particularlie upon the Erle of Lauderdaill, and there to agent and negotiat in the forsaid affair of burrowes according to the instructions given by us to him or that shall be heiraftir direct from

us or any deligat from us to him ... Followes the instructions sett doun be the commissioners of burrowes.

(1.) That he shall forthwith repaire to London to the said Erle of Lauderdaill and there to interceid with his lordship anent the doun getting of the fyftie solze of impost, upon the tun laid on by the Frensh King upon ships and vessellis belonging to this kingdome in France, and to advance and make payment to his lordship, whensoevir the same impost is taken off, the soume of fyfteen hundred punds sterling, which the said William Anderson by his acceptation of the said imployment as agent for the burrowes is heirby oblidged till advance and make payment to the said noble earle accordingly.

(2.) Secundly. That he doe his uttmost endeavour at court by the mediation of the said noble erle, for the obteining of the burrows freedom from the restrent of importing of forraigne salt from France or elsewhere, and thatt forraign salt be imported by the burrows as formerlie, seeing the same is greatlie prejudiciall to their tread and ane heavie burdeen upon the kingdome, and to mynd this particular as the speciall concerne of the burrows and insinuat no les thatt if this be not granted the doun getting of the fyftie solze upon the tun will not be of great importance to thair estate.

(3.) Item, to represent the great invasion made upon the priviledge of royall burrows by regalities and barronies and uther unfree places, especiallie in that incommunicable priviledge only competent to royall burghis of exporting and importing comodities; and in regaird there are severall process depending befoir the lords of session at the instances of perticular royall burghs against unfree places, therefor he is to doe his uttmost for procureing ane letter from the King's Majestie to the lords of session in favors of the royall burrows and in that particular.

(4.) Item, to endeavour that the restrent of importing Irish commodities be also taken off and that there be free trade with that kingdome.

(5.) Item, that sieing by the constitution of royall burrows they have pouer of regulation of metts and measures within their respectiue jurisdictions, and yett that they are trubled by severall persons who impetrats gifts from his Majestie destructive to ther said priviledge, that therefor the said agent wold doe his endeavour to procuire a letter from his Majestie to the lords of secreit councill that no execution should pas upon any such gifts of that nature alredie granted or that heirefter sould be granted by his Majestie in prejudice of the burrows, or that no opposition be made against the burrows anent thair tryell of their weights and measures within thair severall jurisdictions.

J. D. Marwick (ed.), *Extracts from the Records of the Convention of the Royal Burghs of Scotland, 1615–76* (Edinburgh, 1878), 630–31

86. The 'Act for the well governing and regulating of corporations'. Leeds replies to official enquiries about its operation, 1680[1]

Leeds 26th May, 1680

May it please yr lordships

Wee, his Matys most humble subjects, the p'sent maier and aldermen for the corporac'on of Leeds in the county of York, haveing received an order from certaine of yr Lordpps beareing date the fifth day of May instant, reciteing some heads of the act of parliamt made in the thirteenth yeare of his most gracious Matys raigne, entituled an act for the well governing and regulating of corporac'ons; and enjoyneing and requireing us in his Matys name to give a speedy account to his Maty att his Matys Councell Board, whether or noe the said act hath bene from tyme to tyme duely putt in execuc'on wthin the said corporac'on; and whether memorandum or entryes have bene kept of the same according to the said act. In obedience thereunto we doe notifie that the said act from tyme to tyme hath bene duely putt in execuc'on wthin the said corporac'on, according to the true intent and meaning thereof; and that the maior, recorder, aldermen, com'on councell, towne clerke, and his deputy, and all and every the members of and belonging to the said corporac'on, bearinge, or who since the said act have borne any office of magistracy, or places of trust, or other imploymt relateing to or concerning the goverment thereof, have at the tyme of theire taking the oath of theire respective offices, in due forme of law likewise taken the oathes of allegiance and declarac'on therein menc'oned. And alsoe have taken the sacrament of the Lords Supper according to the rites of the Church of England, wthin one yeare next before the elec'on of every of them into theire seu'all offices and employmts aforesaid, and that memorandums and entryes have bene made duely of the oathes soe taken and subscripc'ons soe made, wch have bene entred into the Bookes or Registers of the said corporac'on according to the act aforesaid; and wee doe assure you Lordpps that we will at all tymes take effectuall care for the peace and obedience of this place; and that all the matters and things contayned in the said act be strictly putt in execuc'on sthin the said corporac'on; all wch wee beseech yor Lordpps to imparte to the Kings most excellent Maty, whome god long p'serve, to the end his Maty and Counceli may receive full satisfac'on herein.

Please yor Lordpps

Yor Lordpps most humble Servants,

Jo. Bawmer, Maior,

Two of the aldermen now att London,   Hen. Skelton,

and one beyond Sea, soe as they could
not subscribe this letter.

To the Lords and others of his Matys
most honoble Privye Councell, sitting
att Whitehall these

humbly p'sent

Daniel Foxcroft,
Marma. Hick,
Godfrey Lawson,
Thomas Dixon,
Wm. Hutchinson,
Samuel Sykes,
Anthony Waide,
John Killingbeck

[1] On this subject see J.H. Sacret, 'The Restoration government and municipal corporations', *EHR*, XLV (1930).

J. Wardell, *The Municipal History of the Borough of Leeds*
(1846), 45

87. The mayor of Nottingham writes to the corporation's lawyer about the new charter, 1688[1]

Nottingham, August ye 25th, 88

Sir,

I received yours of ye 23 Instant, upon which I immediately went to our good freind, whoe adviseth that itt is not safe for us to take a new charter before judgment be legally entered against the last, and therefore desiringe to stay in towne att present, and when you finde that ye judgment is soe entered, to take a charter for us, bearinge date within as few dayes as shall bee thought fitt with those you are consearned with, still, consideringe that the nearer itt comes to the time of ye judgment, the safer itt will bee for us, least any actions should be doone in ye meanetime betwixt ye judgment and ye charter. But, as yett wee stand informed, wee doubt wheather itt bee not best for us to lett itt alone till the first day of the next Michelmas tearme, because wee doe not yett understand wheather or noe the judgment was entered in ye master of the office his booke last tearme, but must leave you to advice upon that poynt, when you see wheather itt was soe entered, and wheather itt bee safe for us or noe, if itt bee nott soe entered, which wee are advised itt will not be . And therefore, I pray, send us word what the result of the councell's opinion is in this case; all the precedent lines are his owne words, therefore esteeme of them, and use them, to the best advantage; consider them well; wee would have you gett a very learned and honest councell to advise with. Wish hime secresie, and give hime what money you thinke fitt; a ginney att least, or two if you see cause; wee leave itt to you, the case is intricate and materiall, and must not bee slightily doone; wee have confidence in you that you will act cautiously and faithfully; hee saith you may tell them that you are consearned with that you are ordered by those that imployes you for theire sollicitor, to stay in towne att present, to see after ye judgment as above said; I have somthing more to write, but will send itt by another hand. I pray: mind our warrant of attorney. This is all att present; the post stayes. I rest   Your affectionate freind and servant,

Geo Langford, Mayor.

The things that are desired to bee altered:

1. That in all elections of mayor and other officers of ye corporation, ye mayor may not have a negative vote upon ye whole bodye, but ye greater number of votes to make ye election, altho' ye mayor dessent, and if ye electors bee equally divided, that side to prevail which ye mayor for ye time being shall vote for.

2. The mayor and aldermen are justices of peace, the mayor only is of ye quorum; so that, in case of sicknesse or absence of ye mayor, ye sessions of peace cannot be held. 'Tis desired that ye Duke of Newcastle, recorder, and ye recorder for ye time being may bee made justice of peace, and that hee, and ye eldest alderman, may bee of ye quorum, as well as ye mayor.

3. The elections of mayor, aldermen, sheriffs, coroners, and other officers of ye corporation are made by ye mayor, aldermen, council, and burgesses who have born ye office of sheriffs or chamberlains, and those that have been sheriffs or chamberlains doe claim ye libertye of voting in these elections, though they are displaced from ye corporation, who, being many in number, will carry all elections of officers at their will.

'Tis therefore prayed that none but ye mayor, aldermen, and council may vote in ye said elections, and that ye Council of Six may bee increased to a greater number, to bee chosen out of ye chamberlains and sheriffs, and to bee called ye [   ] Council of ye said Town.

4. The mistake in ye late charter concerning ye electing ye mayor to bee rectifyed.

5. The two fairs granted by ye late charter to bee left out, and ye old fairs to bee restored.

6. To leave out ye clauses concerning ye takeing ye Oaths of Allegiance and Supremacye and Tests, and the King's approveing ye recorder and town clerke.

The reason why I intend to increase ye number of the Council of Six, is to let in such of ye burgesses as have been sheriffs and chamberlains, and are deserving persons, to a share in ye government, ye better to exclude ye others.

¹ See R. H. George, 'The charters granted to English parliamentary corporations in 1688', *EHR*, LV (1940).

W. H. Stevenson (ed.), *Records of the Borough of Nottingham*
(Nottingham, 1882–1914),V,343–6

88. Disaffection in Nottingham after the 1688 Revolution

1690, Monday, June 30

Whereas the common counsell hath been this day credibly informed, that there is and hath been a very dangerous designe, contrived and carried on by a disaffected party of this towne, for the disarmeing of all or most part of their Majesties' best and most loyall subjects here, who, at the King's first comeing in, shewed themselves most forward with their hands and purses for the carrying on of that excellent revolution, and have ever since been most zealous and ready to serve their Majesties, and to preserve the Government with their lives and fortunes to the utmost of their power. And the counsell considering ye dangerous consequences of such an attempt, and how much it may prejudice their Majesties' interest, and advance the late King's, at this time especially, have this day ordered, that a speedy and diligent enquiry be made into this thing, and that if it appear to be soe that when notice be immediately given thereof to their Majesties, and their most honorable Privy Councell, that such order may be taken therein as they shall thinke fit. And it is also further ordered by this Councell, that application be further made to Master Hutchinson, one of our representatives in Parliament, to desire him to acquaint the Right Honorable, the Earl of Kingston, as soon as may be, with this order, and to let his Lordship know, that if he will please to give this corporation leave, they will informe his Lordship who in this towne they have reason to suspect are disaffected to the government, that care may be tooke of them; and, further, to signifie to his Lordship that this corporation is alltogether ignorant of anything they ever said or did to disoblige his Lordship. But, if they have, and they may but know it, they are ready to acknowledge it, and beg his Lordship['s] pardon for it, and also to let his Lordship know that the councell wonders to hear that Master Rippon should say that his Lordship would be revenged of some of us and ruine us, which they hope is utterly false. And, therefore, if his Lordship desire it, the Magistrates are ready to call Master Rippon to account for it. And it's further ordered by this councell, that a true coppy of this order be sent to the said Master Hutchinson, to be presented to and left with the said Earl, for his Lordship['s] sattisfaction, and their vindication.

1690, Tuesday, July 1

Whereas there came a warrant this day from the Earle of Kingston for the searching for armes in the houses of all disaffected persons, and particularly of Master Mayor and the aldermen and councell of this towne; and the militia officers, by vertue of the same, did take several armes from the mayor and others of their Majesties' loyall subjects, to the great discouragement of this government and their Majesties' subjects under the same; therefore, it is unanimously resolved, that the aldermen and councell request Master Major to do that service for their Majesties and this corporation, as to go forthwith to London, and deliver our addresse, under our common seale, to her Majestie, in the name of this corporation; and, further to solicete for this corporation as in his wisedome he shall thinke fit. And his charges to be borne by this corporation, and that one of his serjeant[s] waite on him thither.

W. H. Stevenson (ed.), *Records of the Borough of Nottingham* (Nottingham, 1882—1914), V, 365—6

4

Law and order, and public welfare

89. A benefactor to provide a women's prison at Norwich, 1454

Assembly on Friday after St Hillary [18 Jan. 1454]
It was announced by the mayor, that of the good will and attachment which Ralph Segrym bears to the community he proposes to construct a prison for detaining women therein and for separating them from the society of men, and for avoiding crimes which might arise. And this to be done of the goods and at the cost of John Wilbeye.

W. Hudson and J. C. Tingey (ed.), *Records of the City of Norwich* (Norwich, 1906), II, 91

90. A siege in Southampton, 1460

Thomas White violently naled up the saide dore upon herre [Christina Nymithalf] and kept herre in the saide chambre and ij yong chyldern with herre and wolde not suffre herre to goo furth nether to gete herre mete drynk ne fewell to succor herre ne herre chylder with but that oonly a sister of herres delyvered herre such mete and drynke as she hadde and put it in a bagge and tyed hit to a corde whereby she drew hit up in to the saide chaumbre and burned herre bedbordis and bed straw for lake of fewell to warme her childer by ... and he caused a gonner to shote gonnes oute of the saide tenement at the kynges liege peple so that noon of theym for fere of dethe durst com.

A. A. Ruddock, *Italian Merchants and Shipping in Southampton, 1270–1600* (Southampton Records Series I, 1951), 177–8

91. Orders for the watch at Norwich, 1471

Assembly on Tuesday after St Augustin 11 E. IV. [28 May, 1471]
It is agreed that watches shall be made by persons equipped for defence [defensibiles], every night in the form which appears at the assembly held here on the 23rd day of July in the ninth year of the present king [1469]. So that in every aldermanry one alderman and one constable and eight other equipped persons shall be present every night and to watch from the 9th hour to the second hour. And because it would be too burdensome for the constables to watch every second night, therefore, 24 other persons with the 24 constables are appointed. So that one of these 48 persons may always be present with the alderman in every aldermanry. And thereupon these 24 persons are elected having power equal to the said constables.

W. Hudson and J. C. Tingey (ed.), *Records of the City of Norwich* (Norwich, 1906), II, 100

92. The private charity of a widow at Bury St Edmunds, 1492

Margarete Odeham of Bury. 1492
In the name of God Amen. I Margarete Odeham, of Bury Seynt Edmund's, wedowe, with an hooll and clere mende [mind], beying at Bury aforseid the viij day of October the yere of our Lord God Mlcccclxxxxij, make my testament and last wyll in this wyse: Fyrst, I bequethe my soule to God Almyghty and my body to holy chirche to be buried in the chauncell of the chyrche of Seynt Jamys be myn husbond. Item I bequethe to the hygh aughter in the chyrche of Seynt Jamys vjs viijd. Item I bequethe to the convent to [*sic*] the monastery of the chyrche of Seynt Edmunde in Bury v marks for a dirige and a messe of *Requiem*. Item I bequethe to every hows of fryeres in Cambredge, Lynne, Norwiche, Thetford, Clare, Sudbury, to eche of thes howses vjs viijd. Item I bequethe to the convent of Babbe-welle by Bury iijli. Item I bequethe to every nunne in the howsys of the townys of Thetford, Shuldham, Wygnale, Blakbowr, Cambredge, Chaterys, Swaffham, Denny, Iklyngton, Crabows, Broseyerd, Campsey and Flixton xijd. Item I bequethe to the howsys of frerys in Colchester, Ipswyche and Walsyngham, to eche of them vjs viijd. Item I bequethe to the convent of Ixworthe xiijs iiijd this I wyll have do[ne] as hastely after my deth as it may convenyently be don or ellys before my deth. Item I wyll that every priest beyng at my diryge at my buryeng day and at my xxxti day have

xij*d* savyng I wole that the paryssh priestes and Seynt Mary priestes of both chyrches have eche of them xvi*d*. Item every paryssh clerke vj*s*. Item every other clerke at mannys age ij*d*. Item every chylde with a surplyce j*d* and every chylde withoute a surplice *ob* [halfpenny]. Item I wyll that myn executors vysite the pore men and others that be dysposed to take almes eche man and woman and chylde to have *ob* and every bedredman j*d* as hastely as it may be don after my deth. Item I wyll that myn executors do make a good dyner as hastely as thei may conveniently after my dethe to my neyghboures and other good lovers. Item I wole that the prisoners be refresshed with mete and drynke at the day of my dener, and I wole that every prisoner have j*d*. Item I wole that the torchys that shall [be] leve after my yeere day be departed iij to Seynt Jamys chirche, oon at the aughter of our Lady, oon at the aughter of Seynt John and on at the aughter of Seynt Lauerens; and iij to Seynt Mary chyrche, oon at the aughter of our Lady, oon at the aughter of Seynt Petyr, and oon at the aughter of Seynt Thomas. Item I wole that vj poore women have vj blak gownes lyned wyth blanket and vj blak dobyll hoodys, and the cloth that it be j*d ob* in wode. Item I bequethe to every servaunt that is dwellyng with me whanne I dey have a blak gowne and vj*s* viij*d*. Item I bequethe to the wyffe of John Banyard a blak gowne. Item I bequethe to John Malbourgh my sone my best silver salt with the curyeng, my beste standyng pece of gylte, and my best doseyn sylver sponys, upon this condicion, that he pay suche dettes as he oweth unto me, or elles the bequest to hym be voyde. Item I bequethe to John Ansty my sylver salt with the curyeng that I use dayly at my tabyll. Item I bequethe to a priest for to go to Rome x*li*, and I wyll tht the seid priest go to the stacyons and sey massys as is accordyng for a pylgryme, and in especiall I wole that the seyd priest abyde in Rome alle Lenton. Item I wole that Syr Edmund Castyr shall contynue in hys servyse alle the dayes of hys lyffe if he wyll. Item I bequethe to my systyr Isabell my best stondyng gowne furred with bever and my best kertyll [kirtle, outer petticoat]. Item I bequethe to my Lady Hogard my narowe gilte gerdyll and innamyld [enamelled, brightly coloured girdle]. Item I bequethe to the wyffe of Roger Drury of Haustede, for the love that I have unto her, my gerdell that ys velvett uppon saten. Item I bequethe unto Maister John Halowe my kynnysman a flatte piece of sylver, a blak gowne and an hood. Item I bequethe to Robert Halowe vj sylver sponys and a blak gowne. Item I bequethe to the wyff of Robert Halowe my best lyned gowne and my cloke. Item I bequethe to Maistress Tendale my flatte gylte cuppe with the curyeng. Item I bequethe unto the wyff of my sone Malbourgh my lytell gylte gyrdell. Item I bequethe to myn sone Ansty my grene worsted coverlyght.

Item I bequethe to Constans Aleyn a peyr of my best shetes. The resydue of all my goodes above not bequethed I geve and bequethe to my executoures, to dyspose for the sowle of me and myn husbond, and for the sowlys of them that I am bounde to prey fore, whom I make and ordeyn myn executours John Aleyn gentylman, Edmunde Castir clerk, and George Watton clerk; and I wole that eche of them shall have a blakke gowne, and ther rewarde for ther labour to be takyn as they thynk in ther conscyens and be the advice of the ordenary [local ecclesiastical official]. In wytnesse wherof I have putto my seall. Theese wytness, Jone Brett wedowe, Rychard Kyng mercer, John Brond, John Bamyard and Thomas Basse. Wretyn the day and yeer aboveseyd.

Proved 8 November 1492.

S. Tymms (ed.), *Bury Wills and Inventories* (Camden Society,
XLIX, 1850), 73—5

93. The Nottingham constables present an anti-social farrier and an eavesdropper, 1497

1497, October 9

And they say that the same Henry Gorall, of Nottingham, in the county of the town of Nottingham, horseleech, on the 26th day of September, in the 13th year of the reign of king Henry the seventh, with force and arms, to wit, with a club and knife, threw out a dead and putrid horse into the streets of our said lord the king at Nottingham aforesaid, to the grievous nuisance of the lieges of our said lord the king, and against his peace.

And they say that John Clitherow, of Nottingham, in the county of the town of Nottingham, weaver, on the twentieth day of September, in the thirteenth year of the reign of king Henry the seventh, and upon divers other days and nights, at Nottingham aforesaid, is a common listener at the windows and houses of his neighours to sow strife and discord amongst his neighbours, to the nuisance of his neighbours, and against the peace of our said lord the king.

W. H. Stevenson (ed.), *Records of the Borough of Nottingham*
(Nottingham, 1882—1914), III, 51

94. Royal authority for measures against famine at Bristol, 1522

Johannes Shipman, Major

This yere whete, corn, and other graynes rose at a dire price, by reason whereof the said Maire, of his gode disposition inclynyng his charitie towardes the comen wele and profite of this towne, authorized Mr. Ware and others, undre the comon seale of this said towne, to provide whete, corn, and other graynys necessary and beneficiall for the comons of this same towne, within the shire of Worcestre, or therabout, by vertue of the kynges moost gratious lettrez patentz to the said maire, at his meke supplication graunted; by reason wherof greate abundaunce of whete, corn, and other graynes was so provided, that the inhabitauntes of the said towne were greatly releved and comforted in mynysshing of the price of whete, corn, and other graynys, sold in the open markett of this said towne.

L. T. Smith (ed.), *The Maire of Bristowe is Kalendar* (Camden Society, 2nd Series, V, 1872), 49

95. Allegations of threatening behaviour with serious consequences for the town at Bath, 1534

The first interrogatory

Whether the said Crouche be a comen quareler and a mayntener of theves and vagaboundes and what be his yll demenors.

John Byrde, oon of the aldermen of the cittie of Bathe and oon of the kyng is justices of the pease there, of thage of liij yeres and more, saith that he hath knowen William Crouche sithens his furst comyng to Inglysshcombe within the countie of Somersett, which is vij yeres passed or there aboutes, as he remembreth, for he saith that vj years passed or there aboutes oon Robert Abyiare of the cittie of Bathe was then maire of Bathe, and used ther to make clothe, and dyd sett peapyll dayly in worke to the nombre of iijC persones or there aboutes, as he now remembreth. And the said Crouche then began to trouble and vex the said Robert Abyiare by the lawe for the havyng and usyng of the kyng is seale of the awnage within the said cittie of Bathe, which said Robert then hade a lease thereof; by reason wherof and of the lewde wordes that the said Crouche hade to the said Robert, as in my presence and heryng the said Crouche called the said Robert cankerd churl, knave, and other opprobrious wordes, the said Robert then beyng maire and the kyng is lieutenant there, for the greate mayntenaunce and beryng of the said Crouche dyrst nott abyde nether tarye within the said cittie, but departed and went from the said cittie of Bath untill the towne of Bristoll, wherby the said cittie is the wurse for his departyng and impoveryshing of the peaple within the said cittie Dc markes and more.

G. Bradford (ed.), *Proceedings in the Court of Star Chamber
in the Reigns of Henry VII and Henry VIII* (Somerset
Record Society, XXVII, 1911), 145–6

96. Problems with the relief of beggars and collection for the poor at Norwich, 1548

Convocation of Aldermen 1 June [1548]
Upon a compleynt made by ij men and ij women ayenst Purdy hurde and understond it is ordered by the corte that his staffe belonging to the master of beggers shalbe taken from hym, and he shalbe discharged of the office afforeseid and commytted to the stokkes.

Court on Wednesday, 4 July [1548]
Mr Davye, alderman, certifiyth to the courte that he herd saye that Thomas Cony and Richard Braye, gatherers ffor the releeff of the pore in the parisshe of saint Peter of Mancroft, on Sondaye the ffirst daye of Julye last past cam unto Andrew Quasshe in the seid chirche and axed hym money ffor the pore ffolkes. Wherupon the seid Quasshe axed them what it was and thei sied ij*d*. And therupon the seid Andrewe seid, I will geve you but j*d*, and therupon contemptuously threwe oute and shoke his hande, seying, So telle your alderman.

W. Hudson and J. C. Tingey (eds.), *Records of the City of
Norwich* (Norwich, 1906), II, 174

97. Part of the Norwich 'census' of the poor, 1570

North Consforth Ward: St Peter per Montergate
Robert Whitman, of 30 yeris, laborer, and Agnes, his wyf, of that age, that spyn white warpe, & hath 2 sons, the eldest 3 yeris. They dwel to gether & hav dwelt her ever, & ar now into Hetherset to hyr fathers for a tyme tyl they may have worke. hable [able].
In Heri Huntes house. No almes. Veri Pore.

Hery White of 30 yeris, laborer out of work, & Margaret, his wyf, that soyn white warpe, & dwell together; and 2 sons, the eldest 9 yers that spin white warpe, the other 3 yere; & hir mayde, Elizabeth Stori of 16 yeris that spyn also, & have dwelt 6 yere & cam from Below. hable.
Selecte. John Lynges house. Indeferent [moderately poor]. *No allmes.*

John Goslyng at South Conffor of 24 yere, carier that work at Dysse, & Margaret, his wyfe, of 24 yer that spyn mydle stuff; & a enfant of 3 yer, & have dwelt her ever. hable.
Veri pore. No almes.

Hugh Davi gone away of 18 yeris, gardener servant with the Deane, his wife dwell in Aylsham. hable.
Veri pore. No almes.

Thomas Paxe of 30 yeris, seafaringman out of work, & Elizabeth, his wyf, of 30 yer. She spyn white warpe & they kepe together; & 2 sons, the eldest 5 yere, & have dwelt here ever. hable.
Of the ospital house. Indeferent. No almes.

John Tomson of 36 yeris, a roge of no occupacon, & Tanyzen, his wyfe, of that age. She spyn white warpe & have dwelt here ever, but hir husbond non known from whence he cam. hable.
No almes. Veri pore.

Margaret Baxter, wedowe, of 70 yeres, that spyn hir owne work in woollen & Worketh not, & Agnes, hir daughter, the wyf of Richard Caly, Husbandman, who have bene from hyr this 8 yere, & she is 36 yere of age, & spyn white warpe, & have dwelt here ever. hable.
Mr. Haly house. 2d a weke. Indeferent.

J. F. Pound (ed.), *The Norwich Census of the Poor, 1570*
(Norfolk Record Society, XL, 1971), 28

98. The leet jury in action at Manchester, 1571

Ordinacoes. fact. per aucthoritat Curie. [Ordinances made through the
Court Leet's authority.]
The Jurie dothe order that Richarde Hollande esquier sonne and heare heir
to Edwarde Hollande shall come in and do his dewtie and fealtie unto the
lorde at the nexte courte heare holden. *Sub pena* xx*d* ... *misericordia*
[added later, as payment was not made].

It [e]m we order that whearas an order heretofore hathe bene made as
towchinge a dunge hill now or late in thoccupation of [*blank*] Bowker
widoe lyenge in the Fenell Strete we order that from hensfurthe the said
wiffe shall not at any tyme hereafterr sufferr the garbage or bloode of any
beaste to be layde upon the medinge [midden] or dunge hill there upon
payne for every tyme so doinge pen [alty] xij*d*.

It [e]m we order that wheare Richarde Marshall hathe made and sett
upp a pale and also a dunge hill upon the lordes waste at thende of a barne
by hym lately builded in the Mylne Gate, we order that the same shalbe
removed and taken away aswell the pale as the dunghill before the feast of
Saint Michael tharchangell [September 29] next comynge. *Sub pena* vs ...
factum est [it is done].

It [e]m we order that Thomas Romsdeyne do remove a pryvey in the
hedge betwixt Jamys Chourton and the said Thomas so that yt be not
noysom to the said James before the feast of Pentycost next. *Sub pena*
ijs ... *factum est.*

J. P. Earwaker (ed.), *Manchester Court Leet Records 1552–1846*
(Manchester 1884), I *(1552–1586)*, 138–9

99. The Glasgow town court settles some squabbles, 1574

7 April. The quhilk day, Margaret Hamilton is fund in the wrang, for
casting of stanes at Jonet Cowane, and chasyng and manassyng of hir on
the ferd of Ap'le instant, and als the said Margaret, and Robert Browne
and Jonet Broun hir barnys, in the wrang, in stryking and rugging of the
said Jonet Cowanes hair, and castyng hir to the erd: And siclike, the said
Margaret Hamylton in the wrang, for invadyng of Jonet Moresone, spous
to Johne Browne, and casting stanes at hir, and als for blaspheming be
injurious wordis and scalander, the saidis spouse and dwme gevin thereon.

John Smith (ed.), *Burgh Records of the City of Glasgow*
1573–1581 (Maitland Club, XVI, Edinburgh, 1882), 6

100. An attempt to exclude the migrant poor from Faversham, 1584

Yt ys agreayd and establyshed bye the foresayde mayor, juratts and
commynaltie at thys wardemoothe appearynge, that everye of the foresayde overseers of the poore people commynge and goinge in the foresayde three streetes, that shall not make everye monythe durynge the
tyeme of their foresayde offyce, presentemente to the mayor of the
foresayd towne, for the tyeme beeinge, of sooche poore people as shall
come into the same towne, there to inhabyte or remayne bye anye space
of tyeme, wherebye the same poore people maye bye order of lawe be
avoyded from the same towne and by pasporte sente to the places where
theye laste dwellyd bye the space of three yeres, or where theye were
borne, accordynge to the lawe, shall forfeyte for everye tyeme that theye
shall make sooche defalte of presentemente 3s 4d, to be levyed bye waye
of dystresse at the common lawe uppon their goodes and chattells in
sooche and lyke cases used.

Elizabeth Melling (ed.), *Kentish Sources IV: the Poor* (Maidstone,
1964), 43–4

101. Measures to feed the people of Bristol in a famine year, 1594

Michaell Pepwall, Maior
This yeere Thomas Aldworth, alderman, did buy to the use of the
commones of this cittie, from Christmas till Mychellmas followinge,
1,200*li* worth of wheate and rye, and did bringe and caused to be brought
into the markett every markett daie a quantitie, and thother daies did
serve the Commons of the cittie, to the greate good of the whole comun-
altie of the cittie, as by accompt maye be seene.

L. T. Smith (ed.), *The Maire of Bristowe is Kalendar* (Camden
Society, 2nd Series, V, 1872), 62

102. A felon's possessions returned to his destitute family at Southampton, 1597

xxii⁰ die Julii 1597 per maiorem et aldermanos & c.

This daye was taken out of the custodie of Richard Cushin serjaunt into the townes possession to the use of her Matie, for' as felons goods, one flocke bedd, one fether bolster, one coverlett and a paire of canvais sheets; wch were the goods of one William Dewringe late of this towne saylor, latelie executed at Winchester for a robbery by him comitted uppon the highe waye, and about xii moneth past were delivered as pledge into the hands of the said serjaunte by the said Wm. Dewringe uppon an action of the case against him comensed at the suite of John Sedgwicke, wch action was never prosecuted in courte by the said Sedgwicke to this daye, and therefore his said action by law discontinued & these goods of right appertayninge to her Matie as the proper goods of the said Dewringe. The wch said goods were also this daye delivered into the hands of Agnes Dewringe, widow, the wife of the said William Dewringe, towards the reliefe & comfort of her & her three children, beinge verie poore & needie.

T. B. James (ed.), *The Third Book of Remembrance of Southampton, 1514–1602* (Southampton Records Series, XXII, 1979), IV, 38–9

[*For No. 103 see overleaf*]

104. The Stirling kirk session keeps an eye on known moral offenders, 1600

Mar. 27. — Compeirit George Kinros, and denyes sclanderus behaveour with Hellein Crufurd, except onely that quhen he cumis furth of his chalmer in the morning, she takis up out of his bed the bairne quhilk was gotin betuix thame in fornicatione of befoir; quhilk doing he promesis sall nocht be in tymes cuming; and for removing of sclandir in all tymis cuming, he promesis to tak ane chalmer in ane uther plaice, and sall abstein fra all appeirance of hurdum with hir.

Miscellany of the Maitland Club (Maitland Club, XXV. 1, Edinburgh, 1833), 134

103. The poor of St Nicholas's parish, Ipswich, 1597

Names and Conditions	Ages	Woorkes	Wage	Children	Ages	Woorkes	Releife	Wantes
An Thaxter	54	Knitt hose		2	12 9	Knitt hose	8[d]	8d Clothing
Robart Edwards, ympotent of mind	40	A scherman						12d
His wife, able but presently sick	30			2			8[d]	
John Tassell, able	40	Poldaveis weaver		4	8 6 4 2			Worke 4d
His wife, able	50							
Robinson, able		A knacker		4				12d Clothing Firing
His wife, great with child								
Symon Blith, blind	65			2	8 8		10[d]	12d Firing
His wife	60						8[d]	
An Jacksonne, widdowe	60	Gather russhes					6[d]	6d
Widdow Goffe	40	A sewster		4	14 13 5 2	Seweth	4[d]	12d
John Wilson		Laborer	2s	3	7 5 2	Spinne		6d Wheles and cardes
His wife		Spin woll						
Reynald Cleark	65	Tayler		2	14 12		8[d]	8d Firing
His wife	40							
An Martin		Spin flax					8[d]	8d

J. Webb (ed.), *Poor Relief in Elizabethan Ipswich* (Suffolk Records Society, IX, 1966), 122–3

105. Negligent constables in Nottingham, 1601

April 2, 1601

Forasmuche as heretofore great negligence hath bene had and used amongst the constables of this towne in th'ex[e]cution of theyr offices, namely in theyr slight and superficiall seekinge and searchinge for suspected persons upon huy and crye, and also in theyr disordered receyvinge and deliveringe and settinge forwardes of such huye and cryes accordinge to the course of the lawe, whereby great losse and damage may befall to the state of this corporacion, yf any advantage should be prosecuted for such defalts. And for that also before this tyme and att this tyme there hath bene and yet ys held and observed a very unequall coorse amongst the sayd constables in theyr receavinge and conveyinge away of creples and impotent persons out of this towne forwardes, accordinge to theyr assigned travells, for that the troble and burden hereof hath allwayes bene imposed and layd upon the constables dwellinge next to the ends and out passages of the towne, and the others beinge many in nomber dwellinge in the middle partes of the towne have not once tasted the burthen of such trobles, but most unequally have posted the same and such lyke busynes to the townsend constables, as aforesayd.

For remedye whereof, and also for the reformacion of some other lyke abusive negligences had, held, and used in the offyces of the sayd constables, itt ys this present day ordered by Maister Maior now beinge, the aldermen his brethren, and the Common Councell of this towne:

That from hencefurthe all huy and cryes and the ex[e]cution thereof, and all conveyinge of crypples and impotent persons shall be undertaken and performed by monethly turnes and servyce, *videlicet*, the constables in every ward to serve severally a moneth; and so to go forwardes succeſsyvely according to the seniority of the aldermen.

For better explanacion whereof yt ys lykewyse ordered, that the constables in Maister Bonner's ward, now maior, shall begyn the observacion of this order this moneth of Aprill, and that what busynes or occacion soever shall come to this towne touchinge eyther huy and cryes or creples this moneth, the same shall be undertaken and performed by the same constables and none other: which moneth being ended, then the constables in Maister Clarke's ward to serve in lyk suit the moneth next followinge; and so the constables in everye ward successively, accordinge to the auntyenty of the aldermen. And this order to contynew for ever.

Also, it ys ordered, that every constable to whom or to whose howse any huy and crye or creple shall be fyrst brought within this towne, shall presently send the same, or notyce thereof, to some one of the

..stables whose moneth ys then in beinge, yf the same happen not to come to him in his owne proper moneth.

Item yt ys ordered, that the constables att the end of every moneth shall deliver up in wrytinge a noate to the alderman of theyr ward what huyes and cryes have comen unto them that moneth.

Item yt ys further ordered, that when any creples shall be brought hither, then the constables whose servyce ys in beinge for that tyme shall have the lyttle cart now standinge in the Draperie, and shall hyer a horse att the townes chardge to convey such creple away on the sayd cart.

Item yt ys ordered, that every constable att all tymes when he shall go about any servyce apperteyninge to his offyce shall have his constable staffe with him.

It ys lastly ordered, that yf any constable now beinge, or which here-after shall be, doo offend or shall be negligent in the observing of the orders aforeseyd or any of them then such constable shall forfeyt and pay to the use of the Chamber of this towne for everie such offence vjs viijd without any pardon or dimission.

W. H. Stevenson (ed.), *Records of the Borough of Nottingham* (Nottingham, 1882–1914), IV, 256–8

106. The regulation of poor relief at Ormskirk, 1624

28 April 1624

1. Imprimis it is ordered by the Justices that the needye and impodent poore of this parish of Ormskirke shalbe att libertie to aske and have reasonable relieffe within this parishe, not troubling any howse above once a weeke, and that they shall behave themselves orderly and shall not begge in any other parishe.

2. Item yt is ordered that in every towne there shall bee a bedle chossen and hyred by the constables and overseers of the poore by consent of foure of the sufficient inhabitants of the towne to expell strangers and wander-ers of other townes of the towne wheare hee shall be bedle and to bee aydinge and assistinge the constables of the same towne.

3. Item that noe person inhabitinge within this parishe shall relieve, harboure, receipt or keepe in his or her howse any wanderinge rougue or begger beeinge noe inhabitant of this parish, upon paine of law.

4. Item that the constables of every towne shall and may from tyme to tyme cawse reasonable taxacons of money to bee taxed, laide and

gatherede for paiement of such wages as shalbee allowed for such a bedle.

5.   Item yt is ordered that if any inhabitante of this parish which is able to relieve the poore shall refuse to relieve the poore of this parishe accordinge to theis orders, than then upon prooffe and notice thereof to the said Justices or any of them the said persons shall bee taxed to paie money weeckly or monethlie towards the relieffe of the poore of this parishe, as by the churchwardens and overseers of the poore of the same towne by the consente of two or more Justices of Peace shall bee sett downe.

6.   Item yt is ordered that noe person which is able to worke shalbee relieved by begginge, if the said person can have worke and if such person asks for relieffe to have none given unto him or her but in a very slender manner.

7.   Item it is ordered that noe person within this parishe shall take or receive into his, her or their keepinge any inmate or woman with child or any other person which by any likelyhoode may bee chargable to the parish by begginge.

8.   Item it is ordered that from henceforth noe taxacons bee made or relieffe of any poore of this parishe untill further order bee taken to the contrarie.

9.   Item whereas the constables and overseers of the poore of this parishe have delivered the particular names of all such poore of the said parish att this meetinge yt is ordered that the constable of Lathome shall deliver unto every constable of this parishe a perfect note of the names of every of the poore and of theis orders the better to enable the inhabitants of every towne to knowe whom to relieve and the constables and bedle to knowe whom to permitt to passe and begge and whom to restrayne and punishe and to have twelve pence of every constable for the same.

10.   Item it is ordered that if any further order bee needfull to be taken for relieffe of the poore of this parishe and the banishinge of strangeres and wanderers, that the churchwardens and overseers of everie towne of this parish shall take such further order for that purpose and they shall thinke meet and convenient with the consent of foure of the said sufficient persons of everie townshippe wheareunto wee the Justices whose names are hearunto subscribed doe nowe give our consents.

William Leigh
Gregory Turner
Hugh Hesketh

Lancashire County Record Office. Quarter Sessions. QSB 1/22/30

107. Ordinances concerning the children's hospital in Norwich, 1632

This day the worshipfull Thomas Shipdham, late maior of this city, Mr Thomas Cory, Mr Alexander Anguishe, & Mr John Toly, alderman, surveiors of the hospitall called the Childrens Hospitall in the city of Norwich of the foundacion of Kinge Charles did certify and make knowne to Mr Maior & the residue of the aldermen here assembled that they upon the seaventh day of October last did mete at the said hospitall & did there upon readinge of the charter & other things concerninge the said hospitall consider & thinke fitt that theise ordinances followinge should be in that said howse from henceforth duly observed and kept,

First that there shalbe allowed to the keeper of the said howse for the tyme beinge for every childe that already is or hereafter shalbe admitted into the said howse yearely fower pounds six shillings and eight pence. In which allowance there is included the dyett of the said childe in such sort as is hereafter mencioned, & recompence for fower combes of oatemeale yearely & a ferkyn of sope yearely. The said monyes accordinge to the number of the said children shalbe payd to the said keeper yearely by the treasuror of the said howse for the tyme beinge within twenty dayes next after every of the fower feasts of St Michaell the archangel, the birth of our Lord, the anunciacion of our Lady & St John Baptist, that is to say one quarter's allowance alwayes before hand.

See the order made 29⁰ Septembris 1632.

2. The keeper shall have his wheat & rye from out the granery of this city at twelve shillings the combe, that is to say so much rye as wheat and shall pay for every combe as aforesaid twelve shillings, and shall have at that rate yearely five bushells for every childe.

3. The keeper shall allowe to every of the said children every day at their dynner six ounces of bread & a pynte of beere & at their supper also six ounces of bread & a pynte of beere & at breakefast every morninge three ounces of bread & half a pynte of beere.

4. And shall upon Sondayes, Tusedayes & Thursdayes every weeke & upon Christmas Day in every yeare allowe to every of the said children at their dynner beeff & pottage, videlicet an ale pynte of pottage & to every one of them six ounces of beefe weighed before yt shalbe boiled.

5. And for their suppers every night one ounce of butter and two ounces of cheese.

6. And upon every Monday, Wednesday, Friday & Satterday to every of them at their dynner one ounce of butter & two ounces of cheese, & to every of them at their supper upon every of those dayes the like quantety of butter & cheese & to every the said children at their breakefast every day throughout the yeare halfe an ounce of butter.

7. And no childe above the age of tenne yeares shalbe taken or admitted into the said hospitall nor contynue there after the age of fourten or fiftene yeares at the most, but be sent againe to the parishe from whence they were received.

8. And that every childe that shalbe admitted into the said howse shall bringe a testimony of his age under the ministers hand of the parishe where he was borne before he be admitted into the said howse & shalbe sufficiently apparrelled with two sutes of apparrell at the charges of the parishe from whence they shalbe sent.

9. A schoolemaster to be provided and recompenced to teach the children of the said hospitall to read English & to write.

10. And that the said boyes shall every sabbath day come to the sermon in the cathedrall church in blew coates & in cappes conducted by an officer for that purpose which officer shall have twelve pence a quarter paid him by the treasuror of the said hospitall for the tyme beinge. And the said boyes shall in like habitt attend upon the sword when warninge shalbe gyven to their keeper or the said other officer conducted in decent manner by the officer aforesaid.

11. And that the said boyes shall goe in their blew coates & in their cappes to the buryall of every person that is or hath bene a benefactor buryed within the city and in decent manner attend the corpes singinge a psalme without any recompence save onely a penny loafe to every body & twelve pence to their conductor.

12. And yf the friends of any disceassed person that is not a benefactor shall desire the attendance of the said boyes or so many of them as they shall thinke fitt they shall performe the like service in attendinge & singinge for which service the person requiringe the same shall pay for every boy so attendinge into the hands of the treasuror of the howse six pence a peece & to every of the said boyes attendinge a penny loafe & twelve pence to the conductor.

13. The keeper of the said hospitall for the tyme beinge shall give & allowe to the said children dayly such allowances for dyett as is herein before mencioned or some other such dyett & victuall as shalbe equivalent thereunto.

14. The said keeper shall keepe a booke wherein he shall sett downe the name of every childe admitted & hereafter to be admitted into the said howse & the apparrell & beddinge that shalbe allowed to every such childe duringe the tyme that he shalbe there remayninge which booke shalbe alwayes remayninge at the said hospitall & shalbe shewed to the maior, surveiors & treasuror of the said howse when they or any of them shall require the same. At the death or removall of every keeper it shalbe

delivered to the treasuror of the said howse for the tyme beinge together with such apparrell beddinge & other goods of the maior, sheriffs, citizens & commonialtie as at any tyme heretofore have bene or hereafter shalbe delivered or comitted to his custody.

15. The keeper of the said howse shall not at any tyme accept or take into the said howse or give dyett or lodginge to any childe but such onely as shalbe admitted in the Court of Maioralty by the maior and greater number of aldermen nor without a warrant under the hand of the maior & two or more of the surveiors of the said howse testifyeinge such admittance.

16. The present keeper of the howse and every keeper of the said howse hereafter to be nominated & appointed shall enter bond of such a suerty as shalbe allowed by the maior & aldermen to performe the orders before mencioned and such other orders as shall at any tyme be made by the maior & aldermen of the said city for the tyme beinge or the greater number of them. And yt is also ordered that yf such keeper shall depart this life after he shall have received his quarter's pay before hand and before the end of the quarter for which such payment shalbe to him made that then his executors administrators or assignes shall keepe the said children in such sort as is aforesaid yf the maior and greater number of aldermen of the said city for the tyme beinge shall so thinke fitt untill the end of such quarter, or else pay to the treasurer of the said hospitall for the tyme beinge. A proporcionable sume of the mony so payd, and of the corne by such keeper received accordinge to the tyme that shall remayne of the said quarter at the election & choyce of the maior & aldermen of the said city for the tyme beinge or the greater number of them. And shall also leave such wood and coale or pay for the same after a proporcionable rate accordinge to the tyme that shall happen betwen the death or removall of every such keeper and the first of August next after such death or removall of such keeper and accordinge to such order as shalbe agreed upon by the maior & aldermen of the said city or the greater number of them, and entred in the booke of the Courts of Maioralty of the said city.

17. And that the keeper of the said howse shalbe yearely allowed for fyeringe seaven chalder of coale to be bought before the first of August in every yeare.

W. L. Sachse (ed.), *Minutes of the Norwich Court of Mayoralty, 1632–5* (Norfolk Record Society, XXXVI, 1967), 15–17

108. Keeping swine off the streets, Maidstone, 1645

Order touchinge hogges

Whereas the goeinge of hoggs in the open streetes of this towne is found by dayly experience to bee very noysome and inconvenient both to the inhabitantes of this towne as alsoe to others his Majestie's subjectes haveinge recourse thereunto, it is therefore enacted and ordered by this present courte that proclamacion bee made by the cryer of this towne in the most usuall places uppon the two next market dayes that noe person or persons whatsoever shall or doe from and after the first day of September next ensueinge permitt or suffer his or theire hogg or hoggs to goe in the Highstreete, in the meadow by the Waterside, in Bullock lane, in Puddinge lane, Mill lane, Week streete, East lane, Gabriell's Hill or Stonestreete as farr as the house commonly called the Dolphin, in the churchyard or Knightrider streete, uppon peyne of fower pence for every hogg that shalbee found in any the places or streets aforesaid, which is allowed to the cryer of this towne for the tyme beinge, to bee recovered by accion of debt to bee brought by the chamberleyn or chamberleins for the tyme beinge.

Records of Maidstone (Maidstone, 1926), 117

109. Shovelling paupers to Barbados from Liverpool, 1648

Beggars to be sent for the Barbados

Forasmuch as dyvers yong children and beggers which are much prejudiciall to the Towne are found wandering and begging contrarie to lawe it is therefore ordered by the Worshipfull Mr. Mayor, the aldermen and the major part of this assembly that Mr. Edward Chambers, Mr. Thomas Hodgson, Edward Formby, John Chantrell, Raph Massam, Edward Williamson, John Sandiford, Robert Lurting, and Robert Cornell shall goe all through and about the towne and take their names and examine them and cause such as are fitt and able to work in the plantacions to be shipt for the Barbados or otherwise to be put apprentices if they belong to this towne.

G. Chandler (ed.), *Liverpool under Charles I* (Liverpool, 1965), 411–12

110. Presentment of offenders at Harwich, 1652

Anthony Deane, Knight, mayor of the burrowe aforesaid, to Benjamin Marshall and William Cook, sergeants att mace of the said burrowe, greetings. In his Majesty's name I charge and comand you that you sumon the parties whose names are here under written that they be and appeare before me and the rest of his Majesty's Justices of the Peace for the said burrowe uppon Tuesday the eighteenth day of this instant Aprill uppon the town hall of the said burrowe then and there to answer their severall presentments and indictments uppon their heads severally appearing. And hereof faile not. And this shalbe your warrant given under my hand and seale the eleventh day of Aprill, anno domini, 1652.

Henry Rands, William Cook and Joseph Hastead for takeing away the clay from the hill att Mr James's and sand att high water marke without licence.

The owners of the lighthouse uppon the green of the burrowe for suffering the quay to be out of repaire which makes an incroachment uppon the towne ground.

Captain Ratford for not paveing against the field att the towne gates.

Mr Newton for not paveing against his storehouse in the Church street.

Captain Radford and Mr Luzancey for not paveing before their doores in the Church streete.

James Islesse for laying tymber in the highway att Dovercourt.

The surveyor of Dovercourt for suffering the footepath leading to Dovercourt church to be out of repaire.

Mr Robert Seaman for useing his drayes with shodd wheele to the prejudice of the streete of this burrowe.

Mr John Browne for the same.

William Cooke for the same.

Henry Rands for the same.

Joseph Hastead for the same.

Robert Whinet Jun. for not paveing before his doore.

Widowe Martill for the same att her fore doore.

Mr Townes for not mending the passage downe to Evan's Staires.

Edward Boyce for not paveing before his shopp.

Essex County Record Office. Harwich Records. D/B4/136/8

111. Vigilance in Marlborough during the Great Plague, 1665

Munday, July the 17th 1665
Burrough of Marlebrough. By the Mayor and Comon Counsell of the said
Burrough.
An order for the watch and ward during the sicknes
Ffor asmuch as the sickness dayly increaseing in the cittyes of London and Westmr and other parts of this kingdome this burrough is in great danger of being infected therewith by the too frequent passing of travellers, comon coachmen, carryers and others into and through this towne and especially by their being received and lodged aswell in the private houses as publique houses or comon innes there. Therefore for prevencon thereof, it is now ordered by the mayor of this burrough by and with the assent & consent of the comon counsell of the same burrough that the constables of this burrough cause dilligent watch & ward to be kept both night and day by every householder or other inhabitant there in his owne person or by his or her very substantiall deputie allowed by the mayor for the time being to watch and ward there in his or her turne att all and evry the streets and passages leading into this towne. Then and there with weapons to keepe out all suspected passengers or strangers whatsoever comeing to this towne during the continuance of the said sickness, soe that none be permitted either in coach, waggon, on horse back, or on ffoote or other wayes to come into this towne by day or night without lycense from the mayor of this burrough for the tyme being, or in his absence by one or more of the justices of the peace of the same burrough, uppon paine that evry such person soe refuseing to watch or ward in his or her turne (being thereunto duely somoned) and uppon paine that evry constable and other persons neglecting the due observacon of this order in such their watching and warding, shall forfeit the some of ten shillings a peece to the use of the chamber of the said burrough, and to be levyed by distress and sale of the offenders goods by warrant from the mayor or justices of the peace. And whereas informacon is given that sevrall inhabitants of this towne have lately received sevrall of their children and others that came from London or other places infected with the said sickness to the great endangering of the said towne, it is therefore further ordered that none of the said persons that have soe received children or others into their houses doe pmitt them to come or goe abroad into the streets or elsewhere amongst company nor they themselves without the order or leave of the said mayor or justices of the peace. And that noe inhabitant of this burrough whatsoever as well private housekeepers as others doe not nor shall not receave or take into his or their house or houses any child,

children, servants, strangers, travellers, hackney coach, waggon,wayne, or other carriage whatsoever without such leave as afore said uppon paine that evry one offending there in, his her or their respective houses be shutt upp and secured as houses suspected to be infected with the plague or sickness. The which is ordered shalbe done accordingly. And for the better putting this order in execucon yt is alsoe ordered that the respective petitt constables within their sevrall wards doe dayly warne soe many of the substantiall householders and other inhabitants of this burrough to ward by day and watch by night as aforesaid as they shall be required or appointed by the said mayor and justices of the peace from time to time. And that all and evry of the said constables of this burrough, as well chiefe as petitt constable, shall watch and ward in their turnes in their owne persons, one of them evry day and night to superintend the said watch and ward and give orders and take care for putting this order in execucon dureing such tyme as this sickness shall continue or other order to the contrary. And to the end all persons concerned may have due notice thereof it is ordered this precept to be forth with published in every ward or streete within this burrough.

B. H. Cunnington (ed.), *The Orders, Decrees and Ordinances of the Borough and Town of Marlborough, Wilts.* (Devizes, 1929),
32–3

112. The re-building of London after the Great Fire: the proclamation of King Charles II, 1666[1]

13 September, A D. 1666

In the first place, the woeful experience in this late heavy visitation hath sufficiently convinced all men of the pernicious consequences which have attended the building with timber, and even with stone itself, and the notable benefit of brick, which in so many places hath resisted and even extinguished the fire. We do therefore hereby declare our express will and pleasure, that no man whatsoever shall presume to erect any house or building, great or small, but of brick or stone; and if any man shall do the contrary, the next magistrate shall forthwith cause it to be pulled down, and such further course shall be taken for his punishment as he deserves. And we suppose that from the notable benefit many men have received from those cellars which have been well and strongly arched, will persuade most men, who build good houses, to practise that good husbandry, by arching all convenient places.

We do declare, that Fleet Street, Cheapside, Cornhill, and all other eminent and notorious streets, shall be of such breadth, as may, with God's blessing, prevent the mischief that one side may suffer if the other be on fire (which was the case lately in Cheapside). The precise breadth of which several streets shall be, upon advice with the lord mayor and aldermen, shortly published, with many other particular orders and rules, which cannot yet be adjusted. In the mean time we resolve, though all streets cannot be of equal breadth, yet none shall be so narrow as to make the passage uneasy or inconvenient, especially towards the water-side; nor will we suffer any lanes or alleys to be erected, but where, upon mature deliberation, the same shall be found absolutely necessary; except such places shall be set aside, which shall be designed only for buildings of that kind, and from whence no public mischief may probably arise.

The irreparable damage and loss by the late fire being, next to the hand of God in the terrible wind, to be imputed to the place in which it first broke out, amongst small timber houses standing so close together, that as no remedy could be applied from the river for the quenching thereof, to the contiguousness of the buildings hindering and keeping all possible relief from the land-side, we do resolve and declare, that there shall be a fair quay or wharf on all the river-side. No house shall be erected within so many feet of the river, as shall be within few days declared in the rules formerly mentioned; nor shall there be in those buildings which shall be erected next the river, which we desire may be fair structures, for the ornament of the city, any houses to be inhabited by brewers, or dyers, or sugar-bakers. which trades, by their continual smokes, contribute very much to the unhealthiness of the adjacent places. We require the lord mayor and aldermen of London, upon a full consideration, and weighing all conveniences and inconveniences that can be foreseen, to propose such a place as may be fit for all those trades which are carried on by smoke to inhabit together, or at least several places for the several quarters of the town for those occupations, and in which they shall find their account in convenience and profit, as well as other places shall receive the benefit in the distance of the neighbourhood, it being our purpose, that they who exercise those necessary professions, shall be in all respects as well provided for and encouraged as ever they have been, and undergo as little prejudice as may be by being less inconvenient to their neighbours.

These grounds and foundations being laid, from the substance whereof we shall not depart, and which, being published, are sufficient advertisements to prevent any man's running into, or bringing an inconvenience upon himself, by a precipitate engagement in any act which may cross these foundations: we have, in order to the reducing this great and glorious design into practice, directed, and we do hereby direct, that the lord mayor and court of aldermen do, with all possible expedition, cause an exact survey to be made and taken of the whole ruins occasioned by the late lamentable fire. To the end that it may appear to whom all the houses and ground did in truth belong, what term the several occupiers were possessed of, and at what rents, and to whom, either corporations, companies, or single persons, the reversion and inheritance appertained. So provision may be made, that though every man must not be suffered to erect what buildings and where he pleases, he shall not in any degree be debarred from receiving the reasonable benefit of what ought to accrue to him from such houses or lands; there being nothing less in our thoughts, than that any particular person's right and interest should be sacrificed to the public benefit or convenience, without such recompense as in justice he ought to receive for the same: and when all things of this kind shall be prepared and adjusted, by such commissioners, and otherwise, which shall be found expedient, we make no doubt but such an Act of Parliament will pass, as shall secure all men in what they shall and ought to possess.

[1]For the context of this document the reader is referred to T. F. Reddaway, *The Rebuilding of London after the Great Fire* (2nd ed., 1951).

W. de G. Birch (ed.), *The Historical Charters and Constitutional Documents of the City of London* (revised ed., 1887), 227–9

5
Religion and education

113. Prolonged harassment of a Rochester vicar revealed, 1450

They present that Henry Hikkes of Rochester, gent., on 1 July 1429 assaulted Thomas Chamburleyn, vicar of the church of St. Nicholas, Rochester, at Rochester, and then and for 20 years after made him so many threats of prosecution and imprisonment and so vexed him with false prosecution and legal actions, that the said Thomas was impeded in carrying out divine service and the other duties of his cure; and Henry did not desist from these actions until on 3 June 1447 the said Thomas granted to him an annual pension of 6s 8d for life and a robe worth 13s 4d.

F. E. H. du Boulay (ed.), *Kent Records: Documents Illustrative of Medieval Kentish Society* (Kent Archaeological Society, Kent Records, XVIII, 1964), 222–3

114. A Hull draper makes arrangements for church celebrations after his death, 1490

Nov. 3, 1490. Thomas Wod of Kyngeston upon Hull, draper and alderman. To be beried in the Trinite church, in the north ile, besides the grave of John Whitfeld, merchaunte, late mayre of this towne, undre a new marbill stone bought and lade there by the said Thomas Wood. To Sir Thomas Wod preste, my cousyn, vli, willing hym to syng where as I was borne, or at Caumbrege, if he continue ther, at his pleasor, for my soule. To Marion Mathew, my servant, two hundreth of Spanyssh iren. I will that myn executores shal sell a litle maser bounden with silver and gilte, which that I bought upon Palme-sondaie in the furst yere of the reign of king Edward the iiijth; and the money there of received to be given to poure people. To John Wodde, my cousyn, j pece of silver uncovered, j gowne of blewe furred with feches. To the Trinitie churche one of my best beddes of arreys werk, upon this condicion suying, that after my decesse I will that the same bedd shall yerely cover my grave at my *dirige* and *masse*, doone in the said Trinite churche with note for evermore; and also I will that the same bedd be honge yerely in the said churche at the feste of Seynt George Martir emong other worshipfull beddes; and, when the said beddes be taken downe and delyvered, then I woll that the same bedd be re-delyvered in to the revestre, and ther to remayne with my cope of golde. [Proved 15 Nov. 1491.]

Testamenta Eboracensia: a Selection of Wills from the Registry at York (Surtees Society, LIII, 1868), IV, 60

115. Action for rents in support of the free school at Nottingham, 1517

William English, merchant, and William Barwell, clerk of the mayor of Nottingham, guardians of the free school in Nottingham, complain of Robert Stables, gestronmaker, of a plea of debt of 22s 11d, which he owes them, etc. And whereupon the same guardians in their own proper persons say that whereas the aforesaid Robert, on the third day of April, in the sixth year of the reign of the present king, here at Nottingham, etc., received from divers tenants of property belonging to the Free School the aforesaid 22s 11d, which he ought to have paid to them, etc.; and, although often, etc., not yet, etc.: to the damage of 3s 4d; and therefore, etc.

W. H. Stevenson (ed.), *Records of the Borough of Nottingham* (Nottingham, 1882–1913), III, 141

116. The spoliation of Reading Abbey reported to Cromwell, 1538

Pleasyth youre lordshyp to be advertysed, that att my comymg to Readyng I dyd dyspatche Mr. Wrytheslys servaunt wyth every thyng accordyng to youre commaundment, wyche amountythe to the some of cxxxj*li* ixs viij*d*, as appeyrythe by the partyculers herein inclosyd, and parte of the stuffe reservyd for the kynges majestyes use, wyth the whole house and churche undefasyd. I and my fellowes have left hytt by indenture in the custody of Mr. Penyson, and as for the plate, vestementes, copys [long vestments], and hangynges, wyche we have reservyd also to the use of the kynges majestye, we have lefte hytt in the custody of Mr. Vachell by indenture, wych shalbe conveyd to London ageynste my comyng hyther; and, thangkes be to God! every thyng ys well fynysshyd there, and every man well contentyd and gyvythe humble thankes to the kynges grace. I wythe my fellowes intend on Tewesday next, God wyllyng, to take oure journey frome Readinge, as knowythe God, who ever preserve youre good lordshyp. Frome Readyng, the xv daye of Septembre.

Your owan assuryd to command,

Rychard Pollard

T. Wright (ed.), *Three Chapters of Letters Relating to the Suppression of the Monasteries* (Camden Society, Old Series, XXV, 1843), 220–1

117. Violent anti-clericalism at Perth, 1543

May 28, 1543. Mary, by the grace of God, queen of Scots, etc. Forsameikle as it is humbly meant and complained to us by our devout orators the prior and convent of the Friars Predicators of Perth, upon Alexander Chalmers of Potty, John Henry, George Crighton, Walter Pyper, John Davidson, James Rynd, John Mason, whilk with their complices and servants, of their causing, command and ratihabition, recently, upon the 14th day of May instant, betwixt eight and nine hours before noon, our said orators being actually occupied in divine service, came to their said place, and struck up their front gate, broke the locks and bands of the same, and siclike broke up two inner doors of the thoroughfare on the north side of the said cloister, and took away with them the locks of the said doors; and broke up the water door, and took away out of it chandeliers and glasses; and broke their kitchen door, and took off the fire their kettle with their meat, and carried it about the town, and yet withold the kettle and the pewter dishes, one or more, from them; and also broke their enclosure gate, which was new made with great violence and contemption, to their great damage and skaith, and against justice if so be.

T. H. Marshall, *The History of Perth* (Perth, 1849), 48–9

118. The Corpus Christi shrine at York, 1546

An inventory at the juells thereunto belongyng, surveyed and exeamyned by the right reverend father in God, Robert archebisshop of Yorke, and other the kynge's majestie's commissioners, the 12th of May, anno regni Henrici Octavi, Dei gratia Angliae, Franciae et Hiberniae, supremi capitis, 38° [1546]. That is to sey,

First the said shryne is all gilte, havyng 6 ymages gylded, with an ymage of the birthe of our Lord, of mother of perle, sylver and gylt, and 33 small ymages ennamyled stondyng about same, and a tablett of golde; 2 golde rynges, one with a safure, and the other with a perle, and 8 other litle ymages, and a great tablett of golde havyng in yt the ymage of our Lady, of mother of perle; which shryne conteyneth in lenght 3 quarters of a yerd and a nayle, and in brede a quarter di. and inch, and in height di. yerd, over and besides the steple stondyng upon the same; estemyng the same shryne, beside the saide steple to be worthe above £120 0s 0d.

The said steple havying a whether cokke thereuppon, all gylte and a ryall of golde, 4 olde nobles, 2 gylted grootes hangyng upon the said steple, and also beyng within the same steple a berall, wheryn the sacrament is borne, havyng in the berall 2 ymages or angells of sylver and gylt, beryng up the said sacrament, the foote and coveryng of whiche saide berall is sylver and gylte, weyng togeder, with the golde and berall besides the said shryne, 181 onzes, at 4s 6d the oz. − Summa £40 14s 6d.

R. H. Skaife (ed.), *The Register of the Guild of Corpus Christi in the City of York* (Surtees Society, LVII, 1871), 296−7

119. The state of Lewes grammar school after thirty-five years, 1547

The grammer scole in Southover nexte Lewes, of the foundacion of Agnes Morly.

There is a grammer schole founded there to have a prieste scholemaister to teache children and to say masse for the founder, and to have for his labour and for an usher, £3, and the rest for reparacions yelie, and for other charges, to be kepte in a chest in which there is now £72 or there aboutes remaynneng for the receptes, wherof it were convenient to have your letter, lest they do bestowe yt otherwayes, which is lyke they will doo, which scholemaster and usher shulde alwaies be named by the prior of Lewes and his successors.

There is nowe no scholemaster there, but only an usher, and for that it is a populous towne and moche youth. The inabitauntes do require to have some lerned man to be admitted to the same, bicause nowe the kyng, in the right of the late monastery of Lewes, intituled to be founder; and the proffittes of the said landes, besides the scholehous, clere towardes the reparacions and charges aforesaid, £19 6s 8d.

There is one Otley, parson of Rype, which is very well lerned, mete to be scolemaster there, if he will take it uppon hym.

Continuatur schola quousque.

'The Testament and Will of Agnes Morley, widow, founder of the
Free Grammar School at Lewes' in *Sussex Archaeological
Collections*, XLVI (1903), 135

120. Destruction of images and introduction of the new liturgy at London, 1547

Item the v. day after in September beganne the kynges vysytacion at Powlles, and alle imagys pullyd downe; and the ix. day of the same monyth the sayd visitacion was at sent Bryddes, and after that in dyvers other paryche churches; and so alle imagys pullyd downe thorrow alle Ynglonde att that tyme, and alle churches new whytte-lymed, with the command-menttes wryttyne on the walles.

Item the xvij. day of November at nyghte was pullyd downe the Rode in Powlles with Mary and John, with all the images in the churche, and too of the men that labord at yt was slayne and dyvers other sore hurtte. Item also at that same time was pullyd downe throrrow alle the kynges domyn-yon in every churche alle Roddes with alle images, and every precher preched in their sermons agayne alle images. Also the newyeresday after preched doctor Latemer that some tyme was byshop of Wysseter preched at Powlles crosse, and too sondayes followyn, &c. Also this same tyme was moche spekyng agayne the sacrament of the auter, and some callyd it Jacke of the boxe, with divers other shamfulle names; and then was made a proclamacyon agayne shoche sayers, and yet bothe the prechers and other spake agayne it, and so contynewyd; and at Ester followyng there began the commonion, and confession but of thoys that wolde, as the boke dothe specifythe. And at this tyme was moche prechyng agayne the masse. And the sacrament of the auter pullyd downe in dyvers placys thorrow the realme. Item after Ester beganne the servis in Ynglyche at Powles at the commandment of the dene at the tyme, William May, and also in dyvers other pariche churches. Item also at Wytsontyde beganne the sermons at sent Mary spyttylle.

J. G. Nichols (ed.), *Chronicle of the Greyfriars of London* (Camden Society, LIII, 1851), 54–5

121. Letters patent establish the grammar school at Birmingham, *c*. 1550

The Letters patents of King Edward 6 for the schoole in Birmingham translated into English

Edwarde the Sixte by the grace of God Kinge of England Fraunce and Ireland defendor of the faithe, and of the church of England and also Ireland in erthe the supreme head, To all to whom these presents shall come greetinge. Know ye that we at the humble peticion of the inhabitants of the towne parishe and lordshippe of Birmingham in the countie of Warwick as of verie many others our subjects of th'ole contrey neare there about for a grammer schoole in Birmingham in the seyd countie of Warwick to be erected and established for the institucion and instruction of children and younge men, of our especiall grace certeyne knowledge and mere mocion, we will graunte and ordeyne, that from henceforth there is and shalbe one grammer schoole in Birmingham aforeseyd whiche shalbe callid the free grammer schole of kinge Edwarde the Sixte for the educacion instruccion and institucion of children and younge men in grammer forever to endure, And that same schole of one schole master and one usher for ever to continewe we do erecte make ordeyne and establishe by these presents, and for that our seyd entente maye take the more effecte, and that the lands, tenements, rents, revenues and other thinges to be given assigned and appointed for the mayntenance of the seyd schole maye be the better governed for the continuaunce of the seyd schoole we will and ordeyne that from hencefourth there be and shalbe twentie honest and discrete men inhabitants of the towne and parishe of Birmingham or of the lordshippe of Birmingham to the seyd towne adioyninge in the seyd countie of Warwick for the tyme being, whiche be and shalbe callid governors of the possessions revenewes and goods of the seyd schoole comonly callid and to be callid the free grammer schoole of Kinge Edwarde the Sixte in Birmingham in the countie of Warwick.

W. F. Carter (ed.), *The Records of King Edward's School, Birmingham* (Publications of the Dugdale Society, IV, 1924), I, 55

122. Some Cambridge churchwardens sell off redundant church furnishings and restore the gaps in the fabric, 1550–1

Thes be parcelles of ye chyrche wyche be sold by ye assent of ye parysherners ye fyrst day of may m ccccc & fyfty

Item sold to doctor blyeth a pyllow covered with velvet & gold & xix[ti] flowers of gold	v*s*
Item sold ij pyllows to Mr smythe on of sattyne of bryges & on of tyssew	viij*s* viij*d*
Item sold to Mr smythe a cote of grene sattyne wyche was be fore ye Image off mary	iij*s* iiij*d*
Item sold ye Rede cote & qwood that seynt nycholas dyd wer ye coler Rede to Jeams Ratlyff	vj*s*
Item sold Rychard atkynson ye vestment & cape that Seynt nycholas dyd wer	xj*s*
Item sold ye care clothe & paynted clothe that was before Jhesus to crystoffer Rusell	iiij*s* iiij*d*
Item sold wylliam borwell ij deskt clothes of blew chamblet & j vallantes that was of ye sepulter	xj*s*

Item Received for ye allter stans in ye chyrche	ix*s*
Item for tabenacles that stod on ye allters	ij*s*
Somma iij score powndes ij*li* xij*s* vj*d*	

Exspences & paymentes layd out by ye seyd chyrche wardens wereoff yei desyre to be alowyd ...

Item to Roger young ye glassyer for mendyng the glase wyndows abowt the chyrch	xlvj*s* viij*d*
Item to Jeamis dwellyng in benet paryshe for payvynge ye chapelles were the allters stode & stopynge sertyne holles in ye walles	vij*s*
Item to Mr merys for x boshyl lyme for ye seyd chapell	ij*s* vj*d*
Item to crystoffer nychollsone for xvj boshyll lym for ye same	iiij*s*

Item to Mr merys for pavyng stone & tylles for ye same	xij*s* j*d*
Item to wylliam dawnser for pavyng tyll for ye same	vij*s* j*d*
Item for sound for ye same	iiij*d*
Item paid to John capper for caryinge away ye mener in the chapell when Jeams had done	viij*d*

J. E. Foster (ed.), *Churchwardens' Accounts of St. Mary the Great, Cambridge, 1504–1635* (Cambridge Antiquarian Society, XXXV, 1905), 118, 122–3

123. Ordinances for Sabbath day observance at Portsmouth, 1551

Ordynaunce for all peple to resort to the Church on the Sabot daye.
Item it is farder ordayned at the said court that no vitailor within the towne suffer any townes men to eate or drynk in ther howses on the Sabot day during the tyme of matyns procession and communion but to stay all suche doinges until the communion be ended and that all housolders cause their wifes and servauntes and childerne to be present in churche duryng that service tyme acordyng to the kynges commaunement and upon such paynes as the kynges majestie hath set forth for the same.

Ordinacion cum pena xij*d.*
Item that no bocher, tailor, shomaker, nether any other handy craft may kepe open hys shoppe wyndos on the Sabot daye upon that every man that shall do the contrary shall lose and forfet xij*d*.

R. J. Murrell and J. R. East (eds.), *Records of the Borough of Portsmouth* (Portsmouth, 1884), 189

124. The re-establishment of the old religion at Peterborough, 1554–7

Particulers laid forth

In primis to pay for the sepulture [burial]	vj*s*	
Item a lanthorne		ix*d*
Item wasshing the churchwall	ij*s*	viij*d*
Item to Gyll for a baldryckes	ij*s*	
Item the glazar	xiij*s*	x*d*
Item a rope to ye funt		vj*d*
Item a chrismatorie	ij*s*	viij*d*
Item to Mr. Chaplyn for one graleo ij antiphoners and a psalter	v*li*	
Item for a roode and setting upp	xx*s*	
Item George Yonge for yren worcke	vij*s*	viij*d*
Item to Hackeman for mending the great bell	iiij*s*	iiij*d*
Item to John Vickers for mending ye funt	ij*s*	vj*d*
Item fagottes and neales		ij*d*
Item making cleane the church		v*d*
Item for tenterhookes and poyntes		ij*d*
Item for the great bell clapper	xxvj*s*	viij*d*

Item ij bell ropes	iij*s*	
Item neales to the churchegat		v*d*
Item for clappes		xij*d*
Item for a whyttlether hyde		xx*d*
Item to the plaster	xx*s*	
Item a rope for the lytle bell		x*d*
Item another rope		x*d*
Item for mending ii spowtes	x*s*	
Item for mending bawderickes		viij*d*
Item a paire of sensures	v*s*	viij*d*
Item a belrope	ij*s*	
Item for my lordes dirige	ij*s*	viij*d*
Item to ringgers	x*s*	
Item for wax		xiiij*d*
Item for mending the crosse		iiij*d*
Item wax to the sepulture		xvj*d*
Laid out for setting up Mary and John	v*s*	

W. T. Mellows (ed.), *Peterborough Local Administration*
(Northants. Record Society, IX, 1939), 164–5

125. Renunciation of Rome in the St Andrews kirk session, 1559

Sounday the [   ] day of februar 1559 Recantit thir Priestes
underwritten.

We confess with our hart unfenyeatlie without ony respect to particular
profiet movet alanarlie be the feare of God and his word that we haif our
lang abstractit ourselfis and beyne sweir in adjwning ws to Christes Congregatioun setting furth his honour and glorie of the quhilkis we ask God
mercie and this congregatioun. Item we hartlie renunce the Pape quhai
is the verray Antichriste and suppressour of Godis glorie with all diabolic
inventioneis as be purgatorie, the mess, invocatioun of sanctis and prayaris
to them worschipping of images prayeris in strange language and multiply-
ing of them to certane nwmer and all ceremonies useit in papistrie as be
hallowing of candellis watter salt and bread with all ther conjurationes.
And finalie all authoritie as weill of the wicked Paip as utheris that sup-
presis Goddis law and stoppis his word and planelie maynteynes idolators
and idolatrie with all lawes and traditiones inventiones of men maid to
bind and thrall mennis consciences and promeseis in tyme cuming to assist

in word and wark with unfenyeit mynde this congregatioun efter our powar and never to contaminate outselfis with the forsaidis idolatrie and superstitiones nothir for profiet nor feer. And we haif contrare our consciences Goddis gloir and his word grevouslie offendit. In thir forsaidis we ask God and his holy congregation mercie.

Miscellany of the Maitland Club (Maitland Club, LVII.2, Edinburgh, 1843), 216–17

126. The Salisbury tailors hire a preacher at the ancient Midsummer Feast, 1570

June 10th, 1570: It is agreed that from henseforth anye honeste learned man preachinge at the ordinarie ffeaste at Mydsomer, shalbe allowed for his sermon and paynes, takinge it oute of the Common Cheste of the Companie.

C. Haskins, *The Ancient Trade Guilds and Companies of Salisbury* (Salisbury, 1912), 172

127. Some puritan regulations at Northampton, 1571

The orders and dealings in the churches of Northampton established and sett up, by the consent of the bysshop of Peterborough the maior and bretherne of the towne there and others the queens maties justices of peace within the saide countie and towne taken and founde the vth daie of June 1571, annoque xiij regine Elizabeth.

(1.) The singinge and playeing of organes before tyme accustomed in quier is putt downe and the comen prayer there accustomed to bee said is brought downe into the bodie of the churche amongst the people before whome the same ys used accordinge to the quene's booke with singinge psalms before and after the sermone.

(2.) There is in the chefe churche every Tewsdaye and Thursdaie from ix of the clock untill x in the morninge redd a lecture of the scriptures begynnynge with the confession in the book of comen prayer and ending with prayer, and confession of the faith etc.

(3.) There is in the same churche every Sondaie and holydaie after mornyng prayer a sermone the people singinge the psalmes before and after.

(4.) That service be ended in everie parishe churche by ix of the clock in the morninge every Sondaye and holy daye to thende the people maye resort to the sermon to the same church and that every mynister gyve warnynge to the parishioners in tyme of comen prayer to repaire to the sermon theare, excepte they have a sermon in their owne parishe churche.

(5.) That after praiers don, in the tyme of sermon or catechisme none sitt in the streetes or walke up and downe abroade or otherwye occupie themselves vaynely, uppon such penaltie as shalbe appointed.

(6.) That youth at thende of eveninge prayer every sondaie and holy-daye before all the elder people are examyned in a porcon of Calvyns cat-echisme which by the reader is expounded unto them and holdeth an hower.

(7.) There is a general comunyon every quarter in every parishe church with a sermone whiche is by the mynister at comen praier warned fower severall sondaies before every comunyon, with exhortacon to the people to prepare for that daie.

C. A. Markham and J. C. Cox (eds.), *Records of the Borough of Northampton* (Northampton, 1898), II, 386

128. Proclamation of a public fast at Edinburgh, 1574

Sept. 2 − Institutioun of the Publict Fast. − The said day, the ministeris, eldaris and deaconis, as thai war wachemen ovir the flok committit to thair chargeis, and foirseing the greit appeirand scurges and immanent plageis of God hinging aboufe the heidis of this meserable colmoune walth amangis the rest, thai have aspyit and foirseine the greit plage of fameng and hunger throw this unmeserable intemperance of the air and woddar, quhilk I say threittinnis the said plag of famyne that commounelie followis ryatus exceis of bankatting, quhilk na wayis can be forbyddin nor inhibitit, athir be prevat or publict admonitionis, with the greit con-tempt of the puir, quhairwith this haill realme is replenisit; (alace) for awoyding of the quhilk, the saidis ministeris, eldaris and deaconis hes thocht guid and necessar to institute any Publict Fast and Humiliation, with ane ernist prayar adjunit thairto, within this burgh for the space of aucht dayis nixt to cum.

Miscellany of the Maitland Club (Maitland Club, XXV.1, Edinburgh, 1833), 97

129. Rules for the schoolmaster and scholars at Maidstone, 1575

In the tyme of Mr. Thomas Beale, mayor

Certen constitucyons, orders and ordinances tochyng the scole-master and scolers ther and for the preferrement of the good and vertuus estate therof exibited by Rowland Stoberfelde then scolemaster agreed on and confirmed at a Borowmote Courte or Common Counsell holden in the Common Hall or Towne howse in Maideston aforsaid the xxvth day of Aprill, 1575.

Orders concerninge the grammer schoole

1. Fyrst acknowlegyng God to be the author of all good giftes. The master withe all his scollers or the moste parte of them shall every day at vij of the clock in the mornyng humbly kneling uppon theire knees, make theire prayers to Almyghtie God in manner and forme thought good by the master, so yt be not contrary to the lawes of this realme.

2. After prayers ended the master shall continue in the scole teachyng and apposing his scollers until xj of the clock before none, at whiche hower they shall goe to dynner. After dynner the scollers shall retorne eftesone to the scole, so that the master with his scollers may be all present in the scole by one of the clock in the afternone, and their to continue, the master teaching and apposing his scollers untill v or vj of the clock in the evening, and then, makyng their prayers, to depart for that night.

3. The master shall have his howse and his wages duryng his lyfe, not beyng convicted of some notable cryme, as to be a commune gamester, or haunter of tavernes or alehowses, not sounde in religion, prodigall in apparell or other extraordinary expences.

4. Yf the master happen to be infected with any cureable disease or yf after long tyme spent in the scole he waxe unable throughe age or any other infirmitie to indure the laboure of teachyng neadefull in the scole, he shalbe favorably borne withe and his wages fully alowed so that his office be satisfied by his sufficient deputie.

5. If their happen to be any contagius disease, as the plage or such lyke, so that the scole, touching teaching, cannot contynue, nevertheles the master shalbe allowed his wages, being ready to teache when yt shall please God to cease suche sicknes.

6. None shalbe taught in this scole but first the master be spoken withe by his or their frendes, and the master shall doe them to understand suche poyntes of these statutes as perteine to the scoller that is to be admitted.

7. None shalbe admitted into this scole whoe for his evell demeanor hathe byn expelled any other scole.

8. Every scoller whose frendes dwell owt of the libertie and parishe of Maideston at his admission shall paye to the common boxe of the scole xij*d*, and every towne childe of Maideston or of the same parishe, herafter admitted, iiij*d*, whiche shalbe employed to the mayntenance of common bookes neadefull in the scole, as a dictionary and other lyke.

9. Also consideringe the coldenesse of the scole it is thowght good that every scoller within the scole shall paye yerely at or before May day *alias* the first of May yerely towardes wood and mattes, iiij*d*, and to have no more of any person for wood and mattes but only iiij*d*, and to employed to that use and to none other uses.

10. Lastly the master shall ons in the weeke call his scollers to accompt howe they have frequentid divine service and for their behavioure in the churche or sermon tyme.

Records of Maidstone (Maidstone, 1926), 26–7

130. A puritan in Chelmsford, 1586

The jury do present that Glascocke of Chelmsford, shoemaker, did rend certain leaves out of the Book of Common Prayer, containing public baptism, and being demanded the cause did answer, 'Because it is naught: there is in it named the water of Jordan for the washing away of our mystical sins; if that water washeth away sins, then Christ died for us in vain'.

Quarter Session Roll (Q/SR 96A/4) in A. C. Edwards (ed.),
English History from Essex Sources 1550–1750 (Essex
Record Office Publications no. 17, Chelmsford, 1952), 9

131. Anti-puritanism at Maldon, 1592

Thomas Pearce, Thomas Purcas and John Holdinge say that one Sturgion coming into the church of All Saints asked Mr. Palmer, minister there, being there present whether he would preach that day. The said Mr. Palmer made answer that he would not make him account. Presently after there came into the church one Richard Williams and John Pratt, who rang the bell there to a sermon and the said Mr. Palmer did forbid them, charging them in God's name, the Queen's Majesty's and his own to leave ringing. Then the said Richard Williams said though be forbade them to ring yet they might toll and (the said Mr. Palmer holding the bell-rope in his hand) took the same and tolled certain times, and said' that Mr. Giffard had showed forth an order from the Lord Bishop of London that he might preach then. The said Mr. Palmer made answer that Mr. Giffard should not preach there, nor none such as he was, except he did wear the surplice, administer the sacraments, make the cross in baptism and subscribe as he had done. They say further that the said Mr. Palmer forbidding the said Richard Williams and John Pratt to ring, plucked the bellrope out of the said Richard Williams' hand and with that thrust him on the breast.

Maldon Borough Records (D/B 3/1/8) in A. C. Edwards (ed.),
English History from Essex Sources 1550–1750 (Essex Record
Office Publications no. 17, Chelmsford, 1952), 8

132. The corporation of Leicester rallies to the defence of puritan preachers in a letter to the bishop, 1611

[Sept. 8, 1611.] Right Reverend, whereas of late it hath seemed good to your Lordship to make staye of the monethlie meetinge of the preachers at Leicester. We the maior and his brethren and other the inhabitants there in regarde of the greate good that our whole towne (and manie also of the country) have receaved by their learned and godlie sermons for the space of fortie yeares and more, have thought it our parts to yeilde this our true testimonye unto soe manye as have preached amongst us upon that occasion. That as our whole countrie thinketh them to bee men well worthie of theire place, not onlie in all other respects, but also for theire right judgment and good affection to the government established, so wee in theire sermons here have never harde anie cause to suspecte the contrarie of anye of them: nor ever seene, or knowne anie hurte or matter worthie of blame to have happened in theire meetings, or by meanes thereof. In consideracion whereof we are the more bold to intreate your Lordship (as earnestlie as wee maie) that by your good leave and favour wee maie be still partakers of theire godlie labors to the good of manye soules, as heretofore we have beene. So shall wee more hartelie both praise God, and praie unto him for your Lordship beinge often provoked and stirred up unto those dueties by our enjoyinge the aforesaid benefite, for that by your meanes wee have it continued amongst us. And so recommending

you unto the Allmighties most gratious protection in humble manner wee take our leave.
Leicester, the viijth of September.

H. Stocks and W. H. Stevenson (eds.), *Records of the Borough of Leicester* (Cambridge, 1923), IV, 115

133. Sabbatarianism in Manchester, 1616

Orders to bee observed wthin the countye of Lancaster sett downe & agreed upon at Lancaster upon Thursday the eighte day of Auguste in the fourteenth yeare of the Kinges Maties reigne that now is by the Justices of the peace theare prsent & by the apoyntemt of the Judge of Assise.

1. Fyrste that theare bee no wares or victualls sould or shewed upon any Sunday, (necessar[y] victualls onely excepted), and that noe butcher sell any flesh upon any Sunday afte[r] the second peale ended to morninge prayer nor yet at any tyme in the afternoone upon the sabothe day and that every person so offendinge prsently bee broughte by the constables before some justice of peace to bee bound by him to the good behavior and to apeare at the next assise after hee is so bounde.

2. That noe howshoulder after the beginninge of the last peale to morninge prayer suffer any personne (not beeinge of the howshould) to eate drinke or remeyne in theyre howse in tyme of devyne service but shall shutte theyre doores upp to the end tht all persons wthin the sayd howse may goe to the church yf any bee found in any alehowse in tyme of devyne service the sayd alehowse to bee putte downe & thenceforth not to be lycensed agayne.

3. If any alehouskeeper will not suffer the constables or churchwardens to search theare howses to see whether good order bee kept thearein, then upon complaynte made & due proofe theareof that any one justice of peace or moe shall discharge the sayd alehowsekeeper so offendinge from brewinge & not to bee lycensed.

4. Every alehowse keeper wth his wife & familie shall come to the church every Sunday as well upon payne to loose & forfeite xij*d* as to bee discharged from brewinge except they have a lawfull & resonable excuse to the contrarie.

5. Such persons as shalbee found walkinge talkinge or ydely standinge either in the church yeard or markett place in tyme of devyne service shall

pay xij*d* a peece and are to bee bound to the good behavior & to apeare at the next Assises.

6. If the constables, churchwardens or other officers for the church bee negligent or refuse to doe theare duties in these articles then such to bee bound to apeare before the Justic of Assise as aforesayd.

7. That theare bee no pipinge, dancinge, (bowlinge beare or bull beating) or any other profanacion upon any Saboth day in any parte of the day: or upon any festivall day in tyme of devyne service that the persons so offendinge bee bound to the good behavior & to apeare as aforesayd.[1]

8. That the justices of peace themselves sometymes searche whether the churchwardens & constables have done theare duties and that the minister or incumbent do reade these orders publickly once every qrtr of the yeare that the[y] may the better bee remembred & observed by the parishoners.

[1] A marginal note in the text at this point reads:
'[p]ipinge, dancinge, [v]altinge, leapinge, [s]hootinge, &c. [l]awfull upon sondaies [b]y the King's Declaracion.'
The 'King's declaration' referred to here is James I's Book of Sports. Local and national policy were clearly at variance.

E. Axon (ed.), *Manchester Sessions, 1616–1623* (Record Society of Lancashire and Cheshire, XLII, 1901), 15–17

134. Amendments to the statutes of the free school and almshouse foundation, Worcester, 1647

Forasmuch as the orders of the Free Schoole and the twenty foure almeshouses in the Trinity are at present quite out of all good order whereby we are like to lose the guift for not being imployed according to the booke of orders by reason of the distracted time that hath beene of late, wee thought it fitt to reduce it into its former right course as it should be as nere as wee can. Therefore

It is ordered by Mr. Robert Stirrup, now maior, and wee that are the governers appoynted, according to our grant and trust in us reposed, vizt, Mr. Edw. Elvines, aldn, John Cowcher, aldn, Roger Gough, aldn, Rich. Heming, aldern, Hen. Foord, alderman, that if the parents of such children as do come to the free schoole will not admonish their children to subscribe to the orders and ordering of themselves, that they keepe their children away and not suffer them to have their owne wille to the great disturbance of the schoole and neighbourhood. And whereas in some schooles they have been used at feastifull times vizt, Christide, Easter and Whitsuntide, to leave of for some few dayes before any such times, wee the governors do order that there shalbe given no such liberty of breaking up schoole till five dayes before christide and a few dayes after as shall be thought meete, and no play dayes but on Thursdayes after two of the clocke, and no other day without the leave of one or more of the governors. Wee finde it doth a great deale of hurt to the schollers; they lose more in a playing weeke then they gett at schoole in a month, &c.

And we do further order that the poore in the Trinity shall put away all children, and no young people shall dwell there, but shall avoyd and gett them other places, and there shalbe hereafter but two in one house, an olde man and a woman or two olde men or two olde widdowes, and that hereafter none shall come in by any favour or affection, or leave of any of us above named after the Feast of St. Michael next ensueing the date hereof, upon payne of forfeiting fortie shillings apeece to the freeschoole and poore in the Trinity. And wee do likewise order that those inhabiting neere the Trinity that make use of the pump shalbe contributors to the repaire of it, so often as it shall want repaire. And for the poore, if any shalbe so willfull as not to put away their children, cozens or friends (as they terme them) they shalbe put forth themselves, and have no habitation there. Dated this 8th of December 1647.

A. F. Leach (ed.), *Documents illustrating early education in Worcester, 685–1700*, (Worcestershire Historical Society, 1913), 283–4

135. Schools and schoolmasters in Glasgow, 1654

25 March 1654

Forasmuche as be ane former ordour of the counsell the magistratis and sundrie members thairof did visit the haill Scottis scoolles, and they finding efter tryell that sundrie persounes had takine upe scoolles no wayes being authoreizit by the magistratis and counsell, ([which] is against all reasone or forme ever heirtofoir observit in the lyk), and the saidis Scottis scoole-masters haveing this day compeirit according to ane warning maid to them, and sundrie of them having givine in thair supplicatiounes most humble requeisting warrand to continow in the keiping of thair scooles and uthers to tak upe Scottis who never had [blank] of befoir. After consideratioune thairanent takin be the saids magistrats and counsell, they did as they doe heirby warrand thir persounes, viz., Mr. Thomas Smeittoune, Mr. Thomas Muir, Mr. William Forrest, John M'Clae, James Clerk, younger, William Bogle, Johne Patersoune, and Mr. Gilbert Wilsoune to continow in holding and keiping of thair scooles as formerlie; and grants warrand to thir persones wha never had warrand to keipe scooles of befoir, to wit, Robert Forrest and James Selkrig, to tak upe and hold scooles for instructioune of youthe. But the haill foirnamed persones ar admittit to the foirsaid charge upon thir speciall conditions fallowing, and no otherwayes, to wit, that they carie themselfis religiouslie and honestlie as becomethe, without any kynd of open scandell, and that they keipe morning and evening prayers in thair respective scooles and uther discipline thairin as becomethe, and that they tak no mor scolledge nor quarter payment fra towne bairnes bot ten schilling quarterlie and double fra straingers, except it be the will of the parentis and freinds to whom they belong to bestow the samyne upon them, and that they teache and instruct all poore children whomsomevir wha or thair parentis or freinds shall requyre the samyne of them frilie without any kynd of payment or scolledge whatsoever; and that they subscryve thir presentis for the better keiping ordour thairanent. And becaus James Porter hes formerlie usurpit the priviledge of holding and keiping of a scoole, for the [which] he could produce no warrand of the magistratis and counsell as aucht and sould be, and he being warnit to have givin in his petitioun in maner forsaid, according as the rest of the foirnamed persones wer, and seeing he hes slichted and neglectit the ingiveing thairof in the maner as the rest hes done, the forsaids magistratis and counsell hes discharget and does heirby discharge the said James Porter from keiping or holding of any scoole within this brugh until he first be warrantid and authoreizit be the magistratis and counsell thairof as he aucht to be.

The foirsaids magistratis and counsell, taking to thair consideratioune how the James Porter is ewir craveing some stipend alledgit promittit to him out of the rentis belonging to the Merchand Hospitall, [which] ar only destinat for sustentatioune of the poore, and that for keiping of a scoole within this brugh, [which] is contrair to all reasoune and equitie seeing all Scottis scoolemasters at thair first admissioune to that charge does undertak to teache all poore childrein frilie without any scolledge or quarter payment. Also that the granting of the lyk stipend as he craives is contrairie altogither to the fundatioun of the said hospitall, seing all moneys or rentis belonging thairto ar destinat and appoynted for supplie of the poore allanerlie as said is, and so that the said James Porter, nor no uther scoolemaster or persone [whatsoever] aucht for that cause have any kynd of stipend granted to them out thairof. The foirsaids magistratis and counsell, therfor, does heirby, for the reasones and grounds above wryttine and for the great and many respectis they have to the said hospitall and guid thairof and to the commoune good of the towne also, does heirby not only ratifie, allow and approve the act sett downe be the deine of gild and his counsell of the merchand rank, anent the reshinding, casting and annulling, of all actis, statutes and ordinances, contractis or what ellis of that kynd, whilks wer formerlie maid be the late deane of gild and his brethrein of the merchand rank in favours of the said James Porter anent the payment making to him of the sowme of twa hundrethe merkis money cleamet be him out of the rentis of the said hospitall for the keiping of ane scoole, and specially they approve the act sett downe thairanent upon the thrid day of November last bypast; as also the foirsaid magistratis and counsell, according to thair bund dewtie, for respect they have to the publict good of this citie, do heirby reshind, cast and annull, all actis of counsell or contractis anywayes past heirtofoir by the magistratis and counsell for the tyme in favour of the said James Porter, or any uther person or persones, for the stipend foirsaid cravit by the said James Porter, or any uther of that kynd, so that the samyne heirefter sall be null and of none availl as if they had nevir beine granted.

Extracts from the Records of the Borough of Glasgow,
1630–62 (Scottish Burgh Records Society, Glasgow, 1881),
284–6

136. An order against 'Intruders into the Church', Maidstone, 1656

Whereas it is found by dayly and frequent experience that divers heady and turbulent persons doe wander up and downe and sometimes intrude into pulpittes and publique meetinge places by law designed and appointed for the due orderly and peaceable publique preachinge of the Word and dispensinge of the ordinances of God by persons lawfully authorized and orderly approved and allowed thereunto. Sometimes also in a confused tumultuous manner gather togeather great assemblies and concourses of people in open streetes and markett places and other open places of concourse uppon pretence of preachinge and publique teachinge whereas they have noe lawfull authoritie, approbacion, or allowance to be publique preachers or teachers. And in trueth theire intent and ayme is to vent theire owne giddy fancies sometimes in raylings and revileings against ministers, ministry and ordinances of God publiquely owned and professed in this nation, and sometimes in horrid blasphemies to the greate greife and trouble of spirite of all that beare any love or zeale to the trueth, institucions and ordinances of Christ, owned and professed as aforesaid, and oftentimes to the occasioninge of open contradictings, contests, debates, wranglings and quarrelings which sometimes proceed even to fightings and affraies and tumultuous breaches of the peace, the proper and naturall fruites and effectes of such kind of irregularities and disorders. The maior, jurates and commonaltie now assembled consideringe the premises for preventinge the aforesaid mischiefes and the secureinge what in them lies the peace and quiet of this towne in that behaulfe doe hereby signifie and give notice unto all whoe may be concerned that in case any person or persons shall intrude into the publique meetinge place or parish church of this towne uppon any suche pretence of preachinge or publique teachinge not beinge lawfully authorized or approved thereunto or otherwise not haveinge the consent and allowance of the publique minister of this towne lawfully or by publique authority invested in the said publique place that they will take care that such person and persons soe intrudeinge shalbe proceeded against by accion or suite at the common law as intruders or trespassers by suche theire unlawful entry into and possessinge themselves of the said publique meetinge place or parish church. And the care of such accion and suite is hereby recommended to the maior of this towne for the time beinge to be prosecuted in the name of the maior, jurates and commonaltie of this towne (in whome the freehold and inheritance of the said publique meetinge place or parish church is by speciall charter and graunt thereof to them and to theire successors) or in the name of the chamberlyn or chamberlyns of the said towne for the time beinge or in the name of such other person or persons as to the said maior for the time beinge by counsell learned in the law shalbe advised. And it is further ordered that this order and constitucion shall from henceforth immediatly be of force and not expect any further meetinge of another Burghmote any former order or constitucion in suche behaulfe to the contrary notwithstandinge and further the said maior, jurates and commonaltie doe recommend it to the care and diligence of the justices of the peace of this towne and parish to use all lawfull meanes for the timely preventinge and redressinge of the aforesaid confusions and disorders in the aforesaid beginnings of them which have such a naturall and direct tendency to the aforesaid disturbances of the publique peace by a timely proceedinge and dealinge according to law with the aforesaid authors and ringleaders of them, whether in the said publique meetinge place or other publique open place in the streets or elsewhere within the said towne.

Records of Maidstone (Maidstone, 1926), 136–7

137. The corporation of Birmingham endows university scholarships, 1676

To Dr John Eachard, St Catherine's Hall, Cambridge,
Reverend and worthy,
   As it hath been in our endeavours to raise 70 *l.* per annum towards the maintenance of 7 poor scholars that shall yearly be sent from our school in Birmingham, one each year to either university: and is now in our desires to improve, and settle the same to the greatest advantage for the said scholars: so being credibly informed of your readinesse to assist, and promote such a work, we have sent to you the bearers hereof (one a member of our corporation, and the other our cheif school mr) on purpose not onely to signifie our readinesse to settle the whole upon your Hall: but to treat with you about the mode of such a settlement, and in case you shall please to grant us such terms as may advance as well as facilitate our designe, you shall find what is undertaken by them shall be ratyfyed, and confirmed by us, who give you the tender of all due observance, and assurance that we are gentlemen
   Yor reall friends and humble servants
subscribed in the name and on behalfe of
the whole corporation by our baleife
                                                            Tho: Rowney
Birmingham April 7, 1676.

W. F. Carter and E. A. B. Barnard (eds.), *Records of King
Edward's School Birmingham* (Dugdale Society, XII, 1933),
III, 8

138. The endowment of a school for the poor at Stratford-upon-Avon, 1676

To the Magistrates of Stratford upon Avon,

Gentlemen,

Having considered with myselfe that there are many free schools for the teaching of the Latin tongue and none I can heare of to teach poore men's children to read English. And that they must first reade English before they can learne Latin I have therefore according to my small tallent intended to have 20 children taught gratis in your towne and therefore desire you to gett some auncient woman of your towne to teach them. I shall allow her £4 per annum for her paines not tying her to teach noe more but that she may gett as many as she can and bee paid for them, only that she teach those 20 which you shall send to her, boys or girls of the poorest men as you shall appoint. And if any of those 20 dye or goe away that you supply the number and so 20 may still bee taught. I shall therefore send books for them to learne in, viz.

20 horne books	20 Bibles
20 primers	20 catechises
20 psalters	20 writing bookes.

I desire that they may not bee given them all at one time but as they shall be fitt for them for else they will spoile them before they come to learne them. I desire also that theis 20 children bee taught to write, that halfe an hour after tenn o'clock they goe to the wrighting schoole and continew there till 12. And hee to have for his paines 50s per annum, 12s 6d the quarter ...

Thus I present theis things to your consideration and if you thinke fitt to take so much paines as to see them done I hope God will reward you for it. And I shalbe very thankfull for your paines and pray God to give his blessing to it. I desire that the children may be taught their catechises, twice a weeke, Tuesdays and Thursdays, when they are fitt to learne them. Also when they can read in the Bibles that they may have them to church with them and that they read them at home before their parents at least 3 tymes in the weeke (for parents are oftymes taken more with their children's reading than with that they heare at church).

And because I live out of London and know not where to send to the carriers that you would appoint some body in London to call for the books and mony at my sonn's shop at the Black Boy in Lombard Street at St Clement's Lane end, a wollen draper his name Mr Joseph Smart, and that they give an acquitance that they received so many bookes and so much money for your towne. And when you have received it that you send a writing under your town's seale that you wilbe carefull to see it disposed of and to what I have writ. The books are as before and the money you shall receave £4 for the schoolmaster and £4 6s for to buy corne for the poore for bread, viz. 20d a Sunday comes to £4 6s a yeare at 20d a weeke for 52 weekes. I have not sent mony for the writing maister because hee cannot begin till they can read and then if you will write to me I will send it by whome you shall appoint to receave it. And thus I doe every yeare as long as God shall continew my life. Doubt not but my sonn, if you bee carefull to see it don well, will continew. And thus gentlemen, I leave all to God's blessing and your care and say as David in the first of the Chronicles 29 chap., 14 verse "Of thine own have I given thee".

[Endorsed] The gift of Mr John Smarte of Rumford, Essex.

Stratford upon Avon Record Office. Borough Archives,
BRU 15/17/25

139. Suppression of unlicensed schools in Inverness, 1677

Hew Robertsone, Andro Shawe and Willeam Patersone being requyred to giwe in ther diligence anent ther wisiting of the unfrie shools conforme to a former act of counsell of date the 16 Apryle last did in anser therto declair that they did sie sewerall children learning the Prowerbs and sewerall other books in Rorie Sincler's hous & Issobell Fraser hir chalmer, & diwerse and sundrie children learneing to read & wrytt in George Anderson his hous; which report was made, and the Magistrats & counsell being therwith maturelie adwysed, and considdering the great prejudice that may aryse to Johne Innes, present precentor, and to this place also by reasone of keiping and upholding sewerall shooles without warrand had from tham; they therfor all in one voice have discharged, and be ther presents discharges the forsaids thrie shooles, with certificatione to the upholders of tham that iff they or aither of tham presume under whatsoever cullor or pretext to teach a shoole heirefter they salbe lyable in the peyment of 40 lbs. Scots *toties quoties*, & that by & attour the dischargeing of the shoole.

W. Mackay and G. S. Laing (eds.), *Records of Inverness*
(New Spalding Club, 1924), 273

140. The petition of a nonconformist distiller, Leicester, 1691

The Humble peticion of Thomas Pendford of the same burrough, distiller, sheweth,
That after your peticioner had served his terme of seaven yeares in that imployment by the divine hand of providence, came to this burrough (there being none then of that imployment that followed that way) did sett up the art & calling of a stiller, but some time after your peticioner was informed that it was irreguler and could not follow that imployment without first obteyneing the freedome of this auncient corporacion, after which your peticioner did address himselfe to some friends to mediate for him to become a freeman thereof, but could not be admitted upon his fine for the same unless hee would take the accustomed oath of a freeman. But your peticioner being then, & now is, of the persuasion it is not lawfull to sweare at all, and now their majesties by their late gratious Act of Parliament, has been pleased to indulge all discenters that scruple to take oathes, shall onely subscribe a declaracion & subscribe a profession of their christian faith which your peticioner is ready to doe.

Therefore he humbly desires, as their majesties have been pleas'd to graunt their indulgence to tender conscience christians and subjects soe your worshipps according to your canded respects will favourably graunt to your peticioner the freedome of this burrough, paying such reasonable fine as in your wisdomes shall be thought meete for such an inoffensive peticioner to any of that calling to which your peticioner shall readily submit.

Peticioner granted his freedome paying £20.

G. A. Chinnery (ed.), *Records of the Borough of Leicester.*
V: *Hall Books and Papers, 1689–1835*, (Leicester, 1965), 11

141. The churches of London at the turn of the eighteenth century

Considering how much it may tend to the glory of God, and the comfort and satisfaction of all well-dispos'd christians, to see the church prosper in spight of its enemies, I have endeavoured to give an impartial account of the good order, manner of divine service, and success of the churches within and about London, especially at present and since the late devouring fire which turned many of them into ashes and the most part of the city to which they belonged. And to encourage to the more punctual and due observation of that good and settled order I have annexed a short perswasive thereto.

In that unparallel'd and most dreadful conflagration on September 2, A.D. 1666 out of 97 parish churches then within the walls of this city 87 besides the great cathedral of St Paul and 6 consecrated chapels were burnt down or much demolished, some whereof suffer to this day. Yet by the blessing of God to the great confusion of Roman cruelty and grandeur of this nation, that vast loss was effectually repaired in a far shorter time than could reasonably be expected, by rebuilding 52 of them in a more splendid and magnificent condition than they had formerly been in and annexing 35 to those which remain yet unbuilt and are only set apart for burial places or other uses. And further that mournful day was by Act of Parliament render'd memorable to all posterity by solemn fasting and humiliation.[1]

And thus this royal city has risen, like the phoenix out of its own ashes, and so mightily increases (and long may it flourish and be enlarged) that now there are 64 stately parish churches and one cathedral beside the 35 parishes of the demolished churches and diverse chapels within its walls, in the suburbs 16, in Westminster 7 besides the Abby, in the out-parishes of Middlesex and Surry 15. And in my whole compass I have given an historico theological account of 200 places which have been set apart for the service of God, whereof there are 63 chapels but 35 of them are not. But as if all these had been too few the last session of parliament out of their godly respect to religion thought it necessary to order fifty new churches to be erected about it, which is twice as many as are in any city of Europe, and is not parallel'd in any city of the world beside itself, yea, little inferior to a whole kingdom.

I have given a short description of them in general as they lie in alphabetical order so far as is possible to be found or needful to be known. For which I have consulted the best authors on that subject, neither can things of that nature be otherwise known at such a distance of time. And if the curious antiquarian Mr Stow had not obliged the world with such observations, many of them had lain in perpetual darkness. And moreover, to inform the truly devout and religious who had rather frequent the house of God than loyter in the tents of wickedness I have particularly set down the special times or seasons of prayers, sacraments, and sermons with an account of the donors, occasions and present preachers thereof, which may stand for a common rule to incite, direct, and prepare them to attendance upon these parts of divine worship.

Herein may be seen the good order and conformity of our church to the right primitive constitution, and one may have a glance of its victory over both Roman cruelty and particular innovations, for many of them were profanely converted into stables, barracks etc in the time of the Civil War, and others some few years ago have been meeting houses. But most part of them were laid in ruinous heaps by the former though now they be stately temples.

¹ On the re-building of London generally see extract 112 above.

J. Paterson, *Pietas Londinensis, or the present Ecclesiastical State of London* (London, 1714), introduction

6

Social structure, social life and amenities

142. The Trinity Gild of Coventry celebrates a patron saint's day, 1458

Expenses incurred on the day of Saint John the Baptist. [1458 Jun. 24.]
First to the priests and clerks of Babbelack 6s 8d. Also for an oblation 12d.
Also to the master and other officers of the guild for a reward of ancient
time accustomed 3s. To the city minstrells 5s. Also for 'cirpis' and
'Berchyng-bowys'[1] 3d. Also for one gallon of tyre 12d. Also for one
potell of malmsey 8d.
      Sum 17s 11d. [*sic*, actually 17s 7d].

[1] Rushes and brooms.

> G. Templeman (ed.), *The Records of the Guild of the Holy
> Trinity, St. Mary, St. John the Baptist and St. Katherine of
> Coventry* (Publications of the Dugdale Society, XIX, 1944),
> II, 182—3

143. Improvements to the water supply at High Wycombe, c. 1497

Humfrye Welsborne, mayor. An Order for the course of water
Md that hit is greed bytwene Thomas Pymme John Peytevere and John
Upton by fore Humfride Wellysborne esquyre and mayre of Wycombe
that there shalbe a comen corse of water from the howse of Thomas
Pymme John Peytevere as ferre as his grounde goeth ynto the howse
and grownde of John Upton and he to Thomas Pymme and Thomas
Pymme to conveye the water thorowe his grownde as ferre as his grownde
goyth to the comyn streme and Thomas Pymme to make the pale bytwene
hym and John Upton and evry of them to geve a fote and di [half].

> R. W. Greaves (ed.), *The First Ledger Book of High Wycombe*
> (Buckinghamshire Record Society, XI, for 1947, published
> 1956), 49

144. The taxpayers of Great Marlowe, 1524

The towne of Marlowe Magna cum Membris

1524

Tuchard Bold, gent.	£40.	Henry Conrade "ducheman"	£2.
John Saunder.	£20.	Edmund Duffe.	£2.
John Draper.	£40.	John George.	£2.
Peter Gaffeney.	£20.	Richard Torner.	£2.
William Pryst.	£13.6.8.	William Shaftysbury.	£2.
Thomas Oderyngton.	£10.	Robert Robynson.	£2.
Thomas Goodfray.	£9.	Richard Kene.	£2.
Thomas Colard.	£15.	John Cary.	£2.
Edward Wolley.	£16.	John Gardyner.	W £1[1]
Richard West.	£12.	William Smythe.	W £1.
Davy Sherwode.	£8.	William Elys.	W £1.
John Gray.	£10.	Richard Hollmes.	W £1.
Nicholas Webe.	£6.13.4.	Thomas Robynson.	W £1.
John Burge.	£7.	John Peynter.	W £1.
Richard Ravenyng.	£7.	Thomas Flege.	W £1.
Ralph Dygnam.	£5.	John Barnes.	W £1.
Robert Pekeford.	£5.	John a Deane.	W £1.
William Hynkeley.	£5.	Thomas Hattyllyngton.	W £1.
Robert Laurens.	£6.	Thomas Welles.	W £1.
John Ravenyng.	£20.	John Drewe.	W £1.
William Tryll.	£4.	John Abowse.	W £1.
John Hawkewell.	£5.	Richard Gaffenaye.	W £1.
Robert Beamond.	£4.	Richard Deken.	W £1.
John Rowland.	£4.	George Gray.	W £1.
Thomas Asheburne.	£4.	Richard Butteler.	W £1.
John Barnard.	£5.	John Nayshe.	W £1.
William Webe.	£3.	John Taylour.	W £1.
Thomas Clerke.	£3.	William Luddenden.	W £1.
Richard Webe.	£4.	John a Dale.	W £1.
William Watur.	£3.	Nicholas Butterfyld.	W £1.
Thomas Fetyng.	£3.	Henry Carter.	W £1.
Thomas Broke.	£3.	William Frankelen.	W £1.
Robert Gray.	£3.	John Fysher.	W £1.
Nicholas Warden.	£3.	William Goodfray.	£1.
John West.	£3.	John Gray.	£1.
John Londrye.	£2.	John Carter.	W £1.
Richard Spence.	£2.	Robert Rowland.	£1.

Robert Draper.	£2.	Richard Tylar.	£1.
John Broker.	£2.	John Plumryge.	W £1.
John Porter.	£2.	Bennet Fysher.	W £1.
William Tytyng.	£2.	John Johnson.	W £1.
Thomas Crafforde.	£2.	John Langeley.	W £1.
William Carye.	£2.	Jasper Barnard.	W £1.
John Rowland the elder.	£2.	Richard Brwes.	W £1.
Raynold Shyrewode.	£2.	Nicholas servant with	
John Fernes	£2.	Bodes gent.	W £1.
William Brogson.	£2.	Richard Cowper.	W £1.
		Sum £13.8.2.	

¹ W = Wages.

A. C. Chibnall and A. V. Woodman (eds.), *Subsidy Roll for the County of Buckingham Anno 1524* (Buckinghamshire Record Society, VIII, 1944), 23

145. The first recorded horse-race at York, 1529–30

Whereas the running day of horses between William Malory esquire and Oswald Willesthorp, esquire, was the Tuesday after Saint George day, the 22 year of the reign of King Henry the VIII. at the city of York; thereupon it was concluded and agreed by both the said gentlemen, after that the aforesaid Oswald had won the silver bell before the right worshipful Robert Whitfield, alderman and lieutenant of the said city, at which day and place the said Oswald, having the said bell delivered by the said lieutenant to his custody, promised the same lieutenant to bring in the said bell that day 12 months, and to deliver it to the Mayor for the time being, and also to bring with him that said day a horse to run with any man both for the aforesaid bell and also a wager of 6s 8d or more money as they can agree.

A. Raine (ed.), *York Civic Records* (York Archaeological Society, Record Series, CVI, 1942), III, 131

146. The performers of the Norwich Pageants in the sixteenth century

Pageantes – i Mercers, Drapers, Haburdaisshers. – *Creation of the World.* iii Grocers, Raffeman. – *Paradyse.* ii Glasiers, Steyners, Screveners, Parchemyners, Carpenterz, Gravours, Caryers, Colermakers, Whelewrites, –*Helle Carte.* iiii Shermen, Fullers, Thikwollenwevers, Coverlightmakers, Masons, Lymebrennerz. – *Abell and Cayne.* v Bakers, Bruers, Inkepers, Cokes, Millers, Vynteners, Coupers. – *Noyse Shipp.* vi Taillours, Broderers, Reders and Tylers. – *Abraham and Isaak.* vii Tanners, Coryours, Cordwaners. – *Moises and Aron wt the children off Israel and Pharo wt his knyghtes.* viii Smythes. – *Conflicte off David and Golias.* ix Dyers, Calaundrers, Goldsmythes, Goldbeters, and Sadelers, Pewtrers, Brasiers. – *The birth of Crist w^t sheperdes and iij Kynges off Colen.* x Barbours, Wexchaundelers, Surgeons, Fisicians, Hardewaremen, Hatters, Cappers, Skynners, Glovers, Pynners, Poyntemakers, Girdelers, Pursers, Bagmakers, Sceppers, Wyerdrawers, Cardmakers. – *The Baptysme of Criste.* xi Bochers, Fisshemongers, Watermen. – *The Resurreccion.* xii Worstedwevers. – *The Holy Gost.*

W. Hudson and J. C. Tingey (eds.), *Records of the City of Norwich* (Norwich, 1906), II, 230

147. A royal proclamation attempts to stem the tide of poor entering London, 1531

The king our sovereign lord straightly chargeth and commandeth that all beggars and vagabonds being within the city of London and the suburbs of the same, or within any liberties, franchises, or places privileged of the same city of London, that they and every of them, this side the Feast of St. John Baptist next coming, do depart from the same city into their countries where they were born, or else where they last dwelled by the space of three years upon pain of such imprisonment as is contained in an act made in this present parliament the 31st day of March last past, prorogued unto the 14th day of October next coming.

P. L. Hughes and J. F. Larkin (eds.), *Tudor Royal Proclamations* (1964), I, 198

148. Some Lichfield families including dead spouses and children, 1532—3

Bird Street (Burge Strete)

William Bardysley, Ann, Constance, † Alice,[1] uxores eius, Agnes, Edmund, Katherine, Richard.

Thomas Wytmore, Cicely, uxor eius, † Henry, Richard.

Thomas Blest, Joan, uxor eius, Nicholas, † John, † Joan, Frances, Ralph, Joan.

Richard Terfford, Joan, uxor eius, Edward, Katherine, Agnes, John, Alice, Thomas.

John Snape, Ann, uxor eius, Joan, Ann, Henry, John, Michael, Henry.

Robert Sandbage, Elizabeth, uxor eius, Joan, Elizabeth, Margery, Agnes, Thomas, John, Maud, Joan, Edward, Isabel.

Henry Byrde, Joan, uxor eius, Isabel, Nicholas, Henry, Agnes, William, Hugh, John, Thomas.

Robert Swan, sengulman.

Ralph Herdyn, syngulman, John, Alice, parentes.

John Burgys, Margery, uxor eius, Margaret Ensdall, mater eius.

Richard Gardener, Margery, uxor eius, Alice, Margery, John, Elizabeth, Edward.

Hugh Clarke, Elizabeth, uxor eius, John, Margery, parentes, † Hugh, † Elizabeth, John.

Thomas Leyh, Margery, uxor eius, John, Katherine, † Alice, † Margery, Alice, Henry, Michael, Joan, Elizabeth.

Richard Balerd, Ann, uxor eius, Frances, John, Gregory, Isobel.

John Huntt vel Strynge, † Margaret, † Isabel, Alice, uxores eius, John, Elizabeth, John, Agnes, Edward, William Dayne, sp'us.

Robert Morley, Margaret, uxor eius, Robert, Katherine.

John Cradocke, † Elizabeth, Alice, uxores eius, † Richard, Nicholas, Chad, Richard, John, Joan, Edmund, Emmot, Ann, † Ralph, Alice, Martha, Richard.

William Hyll, Margery, uxor eius, Margaret, † Joan, Joan.

William Goslyng, Joan, uxor eius.

Thomas Browne, Joan, uxor eius, cum pueris, Ralph, Thomas, Joan, Elizabeth, Agnes.

John More, syngulman, † Thomas, pater, † Margery, mater.

Sandford Street (Sanford Strett)

Alexander Grene, Alice, uxor eius, John, Nicholas, Thomas, Alexander, Philip, Ralph, Elizabeth.

Richard Balderston, Margaret, uxor eius, Richard, Alice.

William Mason, Joan, uxor eius, Agnes, † John, † Thomas, † Richard, † Michael, † John, Alice.

William Hyncley, Joan, uxor eius, Ann, Ellen, Katherine, Edith, Margery, Elizabeth.

Thomas Godfrey, Elizabeth, Alice, uxores eius, Jeffrey, Thomas, Elizabeth, † Joan, † Margery, Ellen, † Agnes, † Thomas, † Elizabeth, Isabel, † William Everett, sp'us, Prudence, Agnes, Joyce, Joan.

John Janens, Elizabeth, uxor eius, John, Richard, Alice, Eleanor, † John, † Alice, † Margery, Thomas, † Richard, Simon.

Robert Garett, Agnes, uxor eius, † Robert, † John, John, † William, John, Alice, Joan.

John Brynton, Joan, uxor eius, Henry.

Thomas Penchall, Alice, Agnes, uxores eius, John, Margery, Elizabeth, Joan, Alice.

Thomas Bromsgrove, † Agnes, Agnes, uxores eius, John, Robert, William, Hugh, Richard Joan Wright.

Morgan Pulson, Joan, uxor eius, Margery, Agnes, Hugh, Thomas, John.

Thomas Smyth, syngulman.

William Bronrege, Joan, uxor eius, William, † Elizabeth, † John, Alice, Elizabeth, Eleanor, Richard, Joan, Margery.

William Evys, Margery, uxor eius, † John, † Thomas, † Ralph, Elizabeth, Alice, Roland.

William Reyde, Joan, uxor eius, † John, Agnes, John.

Thomas Ferrer, Cicely, Isabel, uxores eius, Dorothy, Joan.

Nicholas Hyde, † Elizabeth, † Alice, Ellen, uxores eius, William, † John, † Elizabeth, Richard Adleintes, Joan, parentes.

John Olfeld, Agnes, uxor eius, John, † Margery, Alexander.

James Morley, Margaret, uxor eius, Thomas, Margaret, Robert, Maud, Alexander.

John Rys, Elizabeth, uxor eius, † Elizabeth, Robert.

Thomas Renold, Agnes, uxor eius.

Nicholas Bronerege, Alice, uxor eius.

Thomas Byle, Katherine, uxor eius, Alexander, Thomas, John, Isabel Glover.

[1] The crosses indicate that an individual had died.

A. J. Kettle (ed.), *A List of Families in the Archdeaconry of Stafford, 1532–3* (Staffordshire Record Society, Fourth Series, VIII, 1976), 178–9

149. A Coventry Gild celebrates the memory of a long-dead burgess, 1533

Sent John Portlaten [May 6, 1533].
Expences ffor the obett of Rychard Spicarre[1] the vj day of May.

Payd ffor j dossen of cakes	xij*d*.
Payd ffor iiij galons ale	xij*d*.
Payd ffor j galon of gascoyn wyn	viij*d*.
Payd ffor j galon of sack	xij*d*.
Payd to the prestes and clarckes of Bablake	iij*s* vj*d*.
Payd in almes to pore pepull	vj*s* viij*d*.
Payd to the master to offre	viij*d*.
Payd to master meyre	xx*d*.
Payd ffor rusches and swepinge	ij*d*.
Payd to the bellman	iiij*d*.
Payd ffor hyre of pottes	ij*d* (*ob*.) [half penny].

Summa xvj*s* x*d*.

[1] Died in 1415.

G. Templeman (ed.), *The Records of the Guild of the Holy Trinity, St. Mary, St. John the Baptist and St. Katherine of Coventry* (Publications of the Dugdale Society, XIX, 1944), II, 155

150. An attempt to regulate the feasts of the wealthy at Norwich, 1543

Assembly on Friday, 11 May 35 H. VIII. [1543].

It is enacted that the mayer of this citie and his successours nor any of them shall not excede the nounber of six disshes at dyner nor at ony other oone mele. And that the aldermen and sheriffes and eny other inhabitaunt w^{t}in the said citie under the degree of a knyght, ther successours nor any of them shall not excede the noumber of v disshes at eny one meale. Except the mayer of the seid citie ffor the tyme beyng be present and then nat above vj disshes under the peyn of the mayer c*s* and every alderman and sheriff offendyng this acte shall fforfet xl*s* and every comoner xx*s*; the seid fforfettes to be devyded in thre partes wheroff the one parte shalbe to the mayer, the ijde parte to the commonaltie and the iijde parte to the presenter theroff. And every of the seid fforfettes to be levyed by distresse by the officers therto to be assigned by the mayer.

And the seid dyet and noumber of disshez to be had at gildes within the seid citie. And this acte to begyn ffrom and after Trynytie Sondaye next ensuyng [20 May].

W. Hudson and J. C. Tingey (eds.), *Records of the City of Norwich* (Norwich, 1906), II, 124

151. Paving at Winchester, 1550

For pavinge before the doers

Item that everi owner of landes or tenementes within the bowndes of the Highe stret and frome Newbridge to Estgate shall pave or cause to be pavyd the stret before there landes and tenementes at all tymes when thei shalbe therunto required by the mayor for the tyme beinge, and if anye refuse so to do, beinge so as aforesayd required, it shalbe lawfull to distrayne uppon the same landes and tenementes for the pavinge therof.

W. H. B. Bird (ed.), *The Black Book of Winchester* (Winchester, 1925), 182

152. The influenza epidemic spreads in Lancashire, 1557–8

And this yeare and the yeare before was great sickenesse in Liverpole, as was all the countrie of thiese parties in Lancashyre, and speciallye a great plage in Mamchester, by reason wheareof this towne was in great dreade and feare. And as Saynt Laurence daye was buried mayster Walker, that is Roger Walker, and alsoe a chyld of Nicholas Brayes at the Pole howsse, the newe howsse that Robert Corbet made. At the death of which sayd Brayes chylde was great murmur and noyce that the plage shuld be brought in to that howsse by an Irysshe man, oone John Hughes, comyng syckely from Mamchester, and brought his lynen clothes theder to be wasshed, which after cold not be found trewe by noe probacion before mayster mayre then beyng, nor mayster mayre then next after, which was mayster Corbet. But for all that ever after that daye the holle towne suspectyd it for the verry plage and pestilence of God, bycause ther was owte of the same howsse buried wyth in v or vi dayes late before [blank] persons. And soe after that, it encresyd daylye and daylye to a gret numbre that died betwix the sayd Sayncte Laurence daye and Martylmas then nexte after, the holle numbre of 240 and odd persons, under xiiitene score. And that yere was noe fayre kepte at Saynt Martyns daye, nor marcket tyll after the Christmas nexte.

J. A. Twemlow (ed.), *Liverpool Town Books, 1550–1862*
(Liverpool, 1918), I, 104–5

153. The giant, the devil and the three black boys for the Salisbury Tailors, 1570

May 24th, 1570: At thys assemblie, Gregory Clark dyd promisse, covenant and graunte to and with the wardens, chamberlaynes, stewards, and the rest of the bodie of the companie, for and duringe the hole tyme of fyve yeares from the feast of Saynte John the Baptyst next folloinge the day of this assemblie fully to be complete and endyd, to fynde and sett goinge for the accustomed pageant of Mydsomer feaste, the gyant, the thre black boyes, the bearer of the gyant, and one person to playe the divells part, at the proper costes and charges of the sayed Gregorye, as well in victualles of the parties aforesayed, as the repayringe of the gyant, and the wagis of all and singular the parties aforesayed. And the sayed wardens, chamberlaines, stewards, and the rest of the bodye of the companie for the part dothe promisse, covenant, and graunte to and with the sayed Gregorie Clark, that he the sayd Gregorie, in consideracion of the aforesayed chargis, and travell [work] of the sayd Gregorie, shall have the hole cost of the howse and garden, whereas now the sayed gyant standyth to his proper gayne and comoditie, with licence to lett and sett the same durying all the terme aforesayed, and besides shall receyve yerelie duringe the terms aforesayed of the sayd wardens, chamberlaynes, and the rest of the companye x*s* of good and lawfull money of England, to be payed at Mydsomer feaste yearlie. And it is agreed that for the repayreinge and new sowinge of the gyants coat, provision shalbe made that the sayed companie, or some of them, shall bestowe ther labor and payne without anye chargis to the sayd Gregorie, and he the sayed Gregorie promussetthed covenanthed and grauntheth, to render the sayed gyant hole and perfeyct in all his proporcions, with all and singular his implements and appurtenances, at the ende of his sayed terme, to the sayed wardens, chamberlaines, stewerds, an the reste of the companie, and yelde uppe under the

name of appurtenances, all as contayned in the divells apparell, and thre
payer of slops for the three blacke boyes.

C. Haskins, *The Ancient Trade Guilds and Companies of
of Salisbury* (Salisbury, 1912), 172

154. A survey of immigrants at Norwich, 1571.

Under the Court on Wednesday, 20 Oct. [1571]
A viewe of the straungers taken the xxiiijth of October 1571 viz. Men M^l
lvj [1056]. Women M^l iiij^{xx}xv [1095]. Childerne M^l viij^c xlviij [1848].
[Total] iijM^l ix^c xviij [3998, but should be 3999].

W. Hudson and J. C. Tingey (eds.), *Records of the City of
Norwich* (Norwich, 1906), II, 154

155. Unlawful games and their penalties at Kendal, 1577

Item it is ordeynyd and constitutyd by the alderman and burgesses and
xxiiijt assistannts off this borough that no maner off pson or psons either
inkepers alehowsekepers or other inhabytannts whatsoever at any tyme or
tymes hearafter have kepe or suffer any playe at cardes dyce tables bowells
or any other unlawfull games ffor moneye aile or beare or any other unlawfull things at or in any his hers or ther howse or howses gardyns or
yeards or any other place wthin the librtys hearoff eyther in tyme off
devyne svyce or any Sondaye or holy day or in any nyghte after tenn off
the clock upon payn to lose to the chamber off this boroughe ffor the
ffurste offence vj$s$ viij$d$ and for the second offence xiij$s$ iiij$d$ And every
player ffor the ffurste offence iij$s$ iiij$d$ and ffor the seconnd offence vj$s$ viij$d$.

R. S. Ferguson (ed.), *The Boke off Recorde or Register of
Kirkbie Kendall* (Cumberland and Westmorland Antiquarian
and Archaeological Society, Extra Series, VII, 1892), 102–3

156. Fire precautions at Northampton, 1586

Whereas there are dyverse inhabitings and dwellings within the precincts of the Checker, the Gutter and the Draperie that yearly do have in their dwellinge howses, strawe, brakes [bracken] pease straw, and turves, and have not conveniente howses and backsydes to laye the same in, whereby often times great casualties of fyer hath heretofore happened and herafter ys lyke to chaunce and happen yf reformation be not spedelye had and taken therein, and therefore it is enacted and by this present assembly established and agreede uppon that no person or persons dwelling and inhabitinge within the precincts of the Checker, Gutter nor Draperie havinge noe backsyde or out howses to laye in any strawe, brakes, pease strawe or turves shall laye any of the same in any parte of their dwellinge howses, but in barnes and other places fitt to laye such kind of fewell inne, whereby noe daunger may therebye ensewe either to themselves or their neighboures.

C. A. Markham and J. C. Cox (eds.), *Records of the Borough of Northampton* (Northampton, 1898), II, 243

157. Betterment by apprenticeship at Kingston-upon-Thames, 1587–8

Henrye Wescott sonne of John Wescott of Fetcham in the Countye of Surrey husbandman apprentyce with Thomas Paltocke of Kingston grocer for viii yeres from the feast of the Byrthe of Our Lord God last before the date of the indenture to be taughte the trade of a grocer and tallow chandler to do as an apprentyce and in thende to have duble apparell here of meete and sufficient for him for his wages and during his terme meate drinke apparell and lodginge etc. In wytnes [*In margin*:] Henr Westcott apprentyce with Thomas Paltock per Indenture dat' octavo Jannuarii xxx⁰ Regine Elizabeth irrotulatur primo Februari anno predicto.

Anne Daly (ed.), *Kingston-upon-Thames Register of Apprentices, 1563–1713* (Surrey Record Society, XXVIII, 1974), xv–xvi

158. Negro servants at Southampton, 1591

xxix^o die Julii anno predicto.

M[emorandum] that the daie and yere above written in the presence of those subscribed came Deonis Edwards and, beinge demaunded whether he would laye anie felonie or other charge unto or against two negroes, thone named Michaell late Mr. Holmes blackmore, and thother named [   ] Mr. Heatons blackmore, they beinge bothe before that comitted to prisson at his suite uppon suspicion of cuttinge & stealinge a cable from his barcke, aunswered that he would not laye anie thinge to there charge; Wheruppon (they denyenge the fact) weare punished in the stocks and so freed. [signed:] John Jackson maior, Richarde Goddarde, John Bollackar.

T. B. James (ed.), *The Third Book of Remembrance of Southampton, 1514–1602* (Southampton Records Series, XXII, 1979), IV, 6

159. The house of an Exeter apothecary, 1596

In the Hall. It. 2 chaiers, 8 stooles, a litell bord, 3 foot stooles & a pece of seling £1 3s 4d. It. a paier of copper andyrons a paier yron doggs, ffierpan and tongs all £2 10s 0d. Sum £3 13s 4d.

In the Parlour. It. a bedstead and truclebeed £2 0s 0d. It. a coverlett, curtains and valence to the same £1 15s 0d. It. a paier of blancketts 5s 0d. It. 3 ffether beeds and 2 bolsters £5 10s 0d. It. one great cypress chest and tow smale £1 6s 8d. It. one old wenskot chest 4s 0d. It. a low chaier and two stols covered with leather and a sid table bourd 8s 0d. It. a skryen and close stoole 8s 0d. It. a peece of leather 2s 0d. It. 2 paier of dogs and a paier of belloes 4s 0d. It. 2 window curtains and curtayne rodds and a litell painted cloth 5s 0d. It. 2 old window cushens 8s 0d. It. a basen and yeower 5s 0d. It. a lowking glasse and 2 brushes 3s 4d. It. a payre of vallance 3s 4d. Sum £13 7s 4d.

In the Chamber over the Hall. It. 2 flockbeeds with bolsters 10s 0d. It. a paier of blanketts and 3 coverings all old stuffe 6s 0d. It. a truckle beed and ticke 4s 0d. It. 2 teasters and stayned cloths 2s 6d. It. a cheast, an old bourd, a racke, a paier of hampers and a barrill 8s 0d. It. 2 paier of bouts and spurrs, a hanging table and a budgett 5s 0d. Sum £1 15s 6d.

In the Chamber over the Parlour. It. a lowe beedstead and canapie

13s 4d. It. a fether beed, flockbeed and bolster £2 0s 0d. It. a paier of blanckets and coverlet 6s 8d. It. a presse with a cuppbourd 13s 4d. It. a cupbourd and a box for bands 8s 0d. It. 2 chests 13s 4d. It. 2 litell coffers and a truncke 4s 0d. It. the stayned cloths and a wicker chaier 5s 0d. It. 3 old boxes 8d. Sum £5 4s 4d.

In the Chamber next to the street over the Parlour. It. 2 truckell beeds, a flock beed and coverings and bolsters 17s 6d. It. 1 old cupbord, 2 boxes, a old willy [willow basket] and wicker chaier 6s 0d. It. a hamper and 3 boxes 1s 0d. It. a teaster and stained cloth 2s 0d. It. 8 fether pilloes and 2 others 18s 0d. Sum £2 4s 6d.

In the Lowe Parlour. It. a table bourd and six stools £1 4s 0d. It. a yland chest £1 6s 8d. It. a chaier, 2 stooles, a coffer & glase cupbord 8s 0d. It. a window cushen, a carpett, 6 cushions, curtayne and curtayne rods 12s. It. 3 tabletts and a small mappe 5s. It. a paier of tables and a lowe stoole 2s 6d. It. a paier of yron Doggs 8d. It. a wrought border, 6 litell crowks and glasses 3s 0d. It. a greene carpett 6s 0d. It. a coloured carpett 8s 0d. It. a green cupbord cloth frenged 6s 0d. It. a litell greene carpet 5s 0d. It. 3 prenitados 4s 0d. It. an Arras coverlett £3 10s 0d. It. half a dozen cushens 15s 0d. It. half a dozen other cushions 10s 0d. It. a window cushion 5s 0d. It. a paier of cotton blanckets 8s 0d. Sum £10 18s 10d.

In the Kytchen. It. a table bourd, a settell, a cupbord and a pewter cupbourd 12s 0d. It. a casse of comfitt boxes with turned pillars 10s 0d. It. shelfs, a sugar barrill and asbole 2s 0d. It. 5 spitts 5s 0d. It. a paier of Andyrons & doggs with tongs, ffier pane and yron barr 8s 0d. It. 5 poterouks and 3 hangings 3s 0d. It. 3 potts and 2 possnetts £1 0s 0d. It. 4 gredyrons and 3 chaffen dishes 10s 0d. It. 4 chaffen dishes 2s 0d. It. a kettell of yron and yron pott 5s 0d. It. 3 pannes 10s 0d. It. 4 calderons 8s 0d. It. 10 skillets 12s 0d. It. 2 plate covers 1s 0d. It. 2 skomers, 2 labels and fleshouke 1s 8d. It. copper candelsticks 7s 0d. It. one Armor and 2 headpeces £1 0s 0d. It. a musket a calyver with furnytur £1 10s 0d. It a fowling peece, a rapier 6s 8d. It. a bowe and quyver of arrowes 4s 0d. It. a dagge 4s 6d. It. an earthen dish, 2 erthen chaffen dishes 6d. Sum £9 2s 4d.

In the Seller. It. tubbes, barrils, a old cupbourd & a coupe 6s 8d. It. 2 frying panns, 3 goosepanns 2s 0d. It. a copper panne 3s 4d. It. a beame and skales 3s 4d. It. coasts and powdering tubbs 12s 0d. It. 2 cuppboards 5s 0d. It. a lanterne, wood 2 bags and other stuffe 5s 0d. It. 2 stonne jugs, 6 carracke dishes [? foreign crockery] & one doz. of chease trenchers 5s 0d. Sum £2 2s 4d.

In the Upper Laught. It. 10 doz. of urynals and 6 bottells 11s 0d. It. 20 lb. of salzaperilia £1 10s 0d. It. half hundred of red lead 6s 8d. It. 20 lb. of Ratsbanne 6s 0d. It. old barrils, potts and hampers £1 0s 0d. It. a candle mould and a great chest 3s 4d. It. 7 tynn potts, a coate of meale 5s 0d. It. 7 tynning stills £1 0s 0d. It. 5 C of small boxes 5s 0d. It. 12 lb. of lynnseed 2s 0d. It. 20 lb. of gombe arabeck 6s 8d. It. 20 lb. of otroum and 20 lb. of rasons 3s 0d. It. one doz. of cupping glasses 3s 0d. It. a frame and cradle 2s 0d. £6 3s 8d.

M. Rowe and G. E. Trease, 'Thomas Baskerville, Elizabethan Apothecary of Exeter', *Transactions of the British Society for the History of Pharmacy*, I, 1970, 12–15

160. The freemen of York in 1604

2 Jac 1, Will. Greneburie, Majore. Arth. Brooke, Joh. Banester, Matth.
Topham, Tho. Key, Mercatoribus, Joh. Dicconson, Drap., Joh. Stable,
Dyer, Pet. Willmson, Sadler, Joh. Brownles, Bak., Camerariis

Xpoferus Dawson, taillour.	Henricus Wilson, carpenter.
Georgius Spence, bocher.	Marcus Allanson, carpenter.
Georgius Ellison.	Johannes Johnson, marcator.
Georgius Chapman.	Henricus Barnard, carpenter.
Robertus Baynes, cooke.	Marmadacus Potter, panyerman.
Nicholaus Emerson, haberdasher.	Robertus Mawmond, tallour.
Richardus Jackson, taillour.	Ricardus Addison, bocher.
Edwardus Rutleedge, talour.	Jacobus Allan, milner.
Johannes Stokedale, cordyner.	Petrus Jerrome, bower.
Michaelus Mosey, baker.	Radulphus Spencley, tallour.
Willehnus Wynter, imbroderer.	Georgius Lister, taillour.
Johannes Sleightholme, inholder.	Edwardus Rossendale, marryner.
Thomas Walker, dyer.	Thomas Mitley, glover.
Rogerus Dent, sadler.	Johannes Rigile, panyerman.
Franciscus Atkinson, tallour.	Georgius Atkynson, mussission.
Xpoferus Aplebie, inholder.	Robertus Ellis, grocer.
Launcelot Whitloke, locksmyth.	Nicholaus Dicconson, baker.
Reginaldus Todd, sadler.	Johannes Dodsworth, milloner.
Xpoferus Thompson, mussission.	Simon Loftous, tallour.
Thomas Holtbie, inholder.	Christoferus Joye, cordyner.
Johannes Shaw, brekelayer.	Franciscus Ledale, glover.
Petrus Clerke, cook.	Robertus Hemseworth, draper.
Johannes Barton, mussission.	Johannes Dent, tanner.
Johannes Peacke, porter.	Thomas Letbie, taillour.

Willelmus Palleser, milner.
Ricardus Atchison, taillour.
Johannes Ewerdyne baker.
Georgius Jackson, tapitour.
Michaelus Tyerman, inholder.
Johannes Browen, tiler.
Georgius Fynley, feltmaker.
Georgius Smyth, bower.
Willelmus Tennaund, inholder.
Robert Jackson, bocher
Johannes Ryveley, baker.
Thomas Ketland, baker.
Xpof. Wray, parchmentmaker.
Thomas Lawne, ropmaker.
Ricardus Wilson, marcator.
Arthurus Hustler, inholder.
Xpoferus Swaile, inholder.
Willelmus Stockedale, tallour.

Ricardus Smyth, taillour.
Josephus Booth, milner.
Henricus Hayburne, cordyner.
Xpoferus Croft, marcer.
Jacobus Byrkhead, barbour.
Willelmus Wharton, feltmaker.
Thomas Harrison, baker.
Nicholaus Ball, appothicarie.
Rogerus Reaveley, bocher.
Davidus Bewley, marryner.
Xpoferus Courte, glover.
Christoferus Thomlynson,
    mussission
Franciscus Hall, taillour.
Jacobus Blackburne, tanner.
Johannes Richardson, draper.
Johannes Killingeworth, taillour.

Per Patres

Robertus Womersley, milner, fil. Ricardi Womersley, latryver.
Robertus Sawer, smyth, fil. Roberti Sawer, smyth.
Johannes Wilson, cordyner, fil. Stephani Wilson, tanner.
Will. Hutchenson, goldsmyth, fil. Willelmi Hutchenson, goldsmyth.
Georgius Fawcett, inholder, fil. Edwardi Fawcett, aldermani.
Willelmus Wood, marcer, fil. Ricardi Wood, marcer.
Willelmus Brownles, baker, fil. Georgii Brownles, tallour.
Georgius Jakson, cordyner, fil. Georgii Jakson, tanner.
Arthurus Branton, blaksmyth, fil. Willelmi Branton, blaksmyth.
Radulphus Harper, grocer, fil. Roberti Harper, marcer.
Georgius Waite, haberdasher, fil. Willelmi Wate, baker.
Ricardus Sympson, glover, fil. Walteri Sympson, glover.
Georgius Wilson, haberdasher, fil. Thomæ Wilson, parchmentmaker.
Xpoferus Harbert, marcator, fil. Johannis Harbert, marcatoris.
Robertus Geldert, bocher, fil. Ricardi Geldert, bocher.
Thomas Tyrrie, blacksmyth, fil. Oliveri Tyrrie, blaksmyth.
Georgius Todd, blacksmyth, fil. Willelmi Todd, blaksmyth.
Samuel Wilkinson, cordyner, fil. Roberti Wilkinson, haberdasher.
Vincentius Sympson, taillour, fil. Petri Symson, cordyner.
Franciscus Cottame, sadler fil. Briae Cotam, inholder.
Willelmus Preston, feltmaker, fil. Abrami Preston, laborer.

Willelmus Bynkes, haberdasher, fil. Willelmi Bynkes, baker.
Laurencius Allanson, cordyner, fil. Johannis Allanson, cordyner.
Johannes Weddell, bocher, fil. Roberti Weddell, bocher.
Willelmus Roger, pewtherer, fil. Thomæ Roger, baker.
Johannes Morton, cordyner, fil. Roberti Morton, pynner.
Thomas Cowpland, taillour, fil. Lanceloti Cowpland, baker.
Petrus Richardson, ropmaker, fil. Johannis Richardson, ropmaker.
Radulphus Marston, inholder, fil. Willelmi Marston, sadler.
Ricardus Brear, armorer, fil. Ricardi Breer, baker.
Georgius Lenge, sadler, fil. Johannis Lenge, cutler.
Andreus [sic] Smyth, taillour, fil. Georgii Smyth, tallour.
Johannes Willmson, sadler, fil. Petri Willmson, sadler.
Johannes Cundale, marryner, fil. Johannis Cundale, marryner.
Georgius Midleton, milner, fil. Willelmi Midleton, porter.
Edwardus Mayneman, taillour, fil. Thomæ Mayneman, baker.
Willelmus Key, tallour, fil. Henrici Key, tallour.
Samuellus Persyvall, marcator, fil. Sampsoni Persyvall, marcatoris.
Willelmus Clerke, mussission, fil. Johannis Clerke, mussission.
Robertus Whitfeld, porter, fil. Johannis Whitfeild, cobler.
Petrus Batherstone, tyler, fil. Johannis Bawtherston, mussission.
Edwardus Wanopp, laborer, fil. Roberti Wanop, baker.
Jacobus Mynn, tanner, fil. Johannis Mynn, bottelmaker.
Robertus Peareson, inholder, fil. Willelmi Peareson, tallour.
Robertus Wilson, mylner, fil. Thomæ Wilson, mussission.
Georgius Stele, cobler, fil. Georgii Stele, cobler.
Ricardus Tebb, lokesmyth, fil. Ricardi Tebb, lokesmyth.
Thomas Nicholson, laborer, fil. Roberti Nicholson, pewtherer.
Adamus [sic] Smyth, girdler, fil. Johannis Smyth. girdler.
Georgius Dent, tallour, fil. Ricardi Dent, vittualler.
Henricus Nelson, joyner, fil. Petri Nelson, joyner.
Willelmus Mason, tallour, fil. Xpoferi Mason, lynwever.
Johannes Wrighte, cocus, fil. Johannis Wright, taillour.
Robertus Vause, baker, fil. Roberti Vause, coci.
Edmondus Fell, milner, fil. Milonis Fell, milner.
Franciscus Ketland, tanner, fil. Roberti Ketland, tanner.
Ricardus Smyth, haberdasher, fil. Henrici Smyth, caryer.
Henricus Lee, milner, fil. Percivalli Lee, milner.
Jacobus Hewit, haberdasher, fil. Willelmi Hewit, taillour.
Johannes Richardson, cordyner, fil. Henrici Richardson, tapitour.
Robertus Criplinge, imbroderer, fil. Johannis Criplinge, tallour.
Johannes Brice, inholder, fil. Laurencii Brice, spuryer.

Willelmus Hewthwate, glover, fil. Willelmi Hewthwate, glover.
Thomas Robinson, marcator, fil. Laurencii Robinson, aldermani.
Xpoferus Balland, cordyner, fil. Johannis Balland, cordyner.
Thomas Thomlynson, porter, fil. Milonis Thomlynson, walker.
Willelmus Hemesley, haberdasher, fil. Milonis Hemsley, baker.
Arthurus Doninge, grocer, fil. Georgii Donnynge, grocer.
Simon Pockley, silkewever, fil. Petri Pockley, cowper.
Robertus Weare, carpenter, fil. Thomæ Weare, carpenter.
Robertus Hoggell, laborer, fil. Thomæ Hoggell, marryner.
Thomas Fell, baker, fil. Willelmi Fell, baker.
Edwardus Kidson, upholdster, fil. Edwardi Kidson, tapitour.
Arthur Paige, sadler, fil. Gilberti Page, sadler.
Thomas Marr, letherdresser, fil. Nicholai Marr, letherdresser.
Phillippus Askwith, marcer, fil. Roberti Askwith, aldermani def.
Xpoferus Hudles, taillour, fil. Johannis Hudles, tallour.
Robertus Busfeild, pewtherer, fil. Jacobi Busfeld, pewtherer.
Thomas Sawer, pewtherer, fil. Roberti Sawer, blaksmyth.
Henricus Ledale, barbor, fil. Roberti Ledale, milloner.
Robertus Wilkinson, taillour, fil. Edwardi Wilkinson, tallour.
Jacobus Hutton, tapitour, fil. Thomæ Hutton, tapitour.
Brianus Nicholson, taillour, fil. Michaellis Nicholson, cordyner.
Johannes Nicholson, cordyner, fil. Michaellis Nicholson, cordyner.
Thomas Iley, tallour, fil. Johannis Iley, plomer.
Thomas Iley, plomer, fil. Joh. Iley, plomer fil. prædict. Joh. Iley.
Johannes Smyth, tanner, fil. Roberti Smyth, tanner.
Johannes Child, joyner, fil. Thomæ Child, skynner.
Jacobus Wilson, draper, fil. Thomæ Wilson, generosi.
Edwardus Lund, marryner, fil. Johannis Lund, marryner.

Register of the Freemen of the City of York. II: 1559–1759
(Surtees Society, CII, 1900), 49–52

161. Aldeburgh regulates the flow of immigrants, 1606

An order against lettinge howses to outdwellers
Wheras this towne beinge a maratime towne and verie populous and
much surcharged with poore people having noe towne lands or meanes
to meynteyne the same but by rates and ympositions out of men's
trades and adventures. And wher many owners of howses within the same

hath much ympoverished the said towne by lettinge ther howses to out townesmen haveing many children and being of verie poore estate not able to meynteyn themselves wherby the towne is many tymes charded with keeping of them to the great ympoverishinge hereof. For the avoyding whereof it is this day ordered by the bailiffe and chefe burgesses aforesaid being of the Common Councell of this towne that if any owner or owners of any howses, lands or rents within this towne shall lett to farme any howse or howses within this said towne to any person or persons whatsoever dwelling out of towne without the consent of the bayliffe of the same towne for the tyme being ffirst had and obteyned in wrighting under one of ther hands, or if any person or persons whatsoever dwelling out shall hire any howse or howses within this towne and come unto this towne to dwell or inhabitt without the consent of the said bailiffe or one of them for the tyme being first hold in writing under ther or one of ther hands that then each and every of such persons for everie tyme soe doing shall forfeit and lose to the use of the said towne the some of three pounds of lawfull English money to be paid into the hands of the chamberlyns of the said towne for the tyme being or one of them presently uppon the demand therof. And for default of payment therof or of any part therof it shall and may be lawfull for the said chamberlyns and each of them for the tyme being to levy the same by distres or distresses and to deteyne the same distres or distresses. And if that the said fforfeiture shall not be paid as aforesaid within fouer dayes next after such distresses taken that then it shalbe lawfull for the said chamberlyns and three of the cappitall burgesses to apprize and sell the said distresses to any person or persons and the overplus (the fforfaitures being payd) to paie the residue therof into the partie or parties offending or els action or actions for debte against such persons so offending in the Court of Record within this towne [shall be started].

Suffolk Record Office. Aldeburgh records. EE 1/E1/1/15

162. The brief existence of a playhouse in York, 1609

And nowe upon a peticion preferred by Richard Middleton and others wherin they requested that they might be permitted to erect a theater or playhowse within this citty wherin such as have bene borne and brought upp therin should imploye ther laborious expenses for the maintenance therof which might be a meanes to restrayne the frequent comminge therunto of other stage plaiers, and they would yeild x li per annum unto this corporacion. It is therfore thought good and agreed by this court that ther said requestes shalbe graunted unto them upon suche condicions as shalbe agreed upon hereafter by this court … And wheras Richard Middleton and others did heretofore of late make suite unto this court that they might be permitted to erect a theater or playhowse within this cittie, and this court then takeinge consideracion upon ther requestes did thinke good that before they should begyn to erect the same playehowse ther should be some condicions considered upon by this court which they should on ther parte performe. And forasmuch as this court doth understand that they have erected a theater or playhowse in this cittie, and have not attended this court to have receyved dyreccions upon what condicions they might have bene permitted, and have drawne unto ther companyes straingers that did inhabitt in the countrie, and likewise some of manuell occupacions in this cittie who do intend to give over ther occupacions and fall to [and] an idle course of life, it is nowe thought good and agreed by this court for that they have proceded in suche sorte as aforesaide that they shalbe discharged for kepeinge of anie playehowse in this cittie, as they will answere at their owne perell.

A. F. Johnston and M. Rogerson (eds.), *Records of Early
English Drama: York* (Manchester, 1979), I, 530–1

163. Innholders *versus* alehousekeepers in Maldon, 1630

To the right worshipful his Majesty's bayliffs and justices of his borrowe towne of Maldon,
    The humble petition of the said inhowlders of the ancient inns within the said borrough,
    humbly shewinge to your good worships that our said inns have time out of mind bene the receipt of all sutch passengers and travelers as have passed through or uppon theire occasions staid within the said towne by reason wherof the inhoulders have by theire reasonable gaines bene able to defraye their houshold chardges and from time to time to contribute to sutch comon chardges as we have nessessarilie bene called unto in the said towne. But soe it is, maye it please your good worships, that of latter times many perverse and ill disposed people to government and the good estate of the said towne have of theire owne authoritie undertaken and do continue to kepe comon alehouses and others by sinister respects and meanes

abusing by bad pretences the magistrates for the time beinge havinge obtained licenses to kepe sutch houses whoe beinge of smale credit doe drawe unto them all sorts of people wherby not onlie the benefit is taken from the older inns but alsoe by reason of the multitude therof and the abuses therin comitted the peace and quiet government of the said towne is mutch disturbed and the inns impoverished and the religion therin professed mutch more defamed and evell spoken of.

For thes reasons abovesaid and for many others which we are redie to tender to your grave considerations and ernestlie intreat to be admitted therunto, we humblie desire your worships would be pleased not only to suppress many alredye contrarie to the holsume statuts of this realme and civill constitutions of this corporation enacted, set up and in being, but alsoe without waighti considerations more that you would be pleased to forbeare to licence any other. And we shalbe bound not onlye to praye for your good worships but also willing and the better able to doe all sutch services as for the good and benefitt of the corporation we shalbe nesseralie called unto.

Essex County Record Office. Maldon records. D/B 3/3/199

164. Postal services in Maidstone, 1641

For as much as wee are very sencible of many inconvenientcies and greate disadvantage not only arriseinge to particuler persons within this corporacion but alsoe to the corporacion itselfe by reason of the unlimited nomber of postmen and incerteinty of the daies of those postmen which are or shalbee in goeinge to the citty of London whereby wee can neither send to London nor have retornes from thence as the weekely occasions of this towne and parish doe or shall require. And those postmen that would bee carefull are not able to subsist comfortablie in their said imployment by reason that many others take uppon them to bee posts. For the prevencion of all which inconvenientcies, disadvantages, and abuses aforesaid it is now inacted by the mutuall and unanimous consent of the maior, jurates, and commonaltie within this towne and parish that for the tyme to come there shall only bee three posts within this towne and parish and noe more, namely John Saywell, the elder, Samuel Skilton and Richard Baldwyn. And the posts aforesaid shall keepe theire sett daies to London in manner and forme followinge: that is to say, namely, Richard Baldwyn on every Munday weekely, John Saywell on every Wednesday weekely and

Samuel Skilton on every Fryday weekely. And that if any of theise posts after notice given hereof shall presume to goe to London as a post in any other day then the day before prefixed to them or faile to goe upon that day prefixed (except hee or they bee lett by extremitie of weather or sicknes) then the said post or postes soe presumeinge to goe or faylinge to goe as aforesaid shall forfeict to this towne for every such his or theire presumpcion or faylure as aforesaid (except before excepted) the some of five shillings. And if any other person or persons whatsoever within this towne and parish haveinge notice of this act (except the posts before mencioned or any other designed or appointed in theire place or places) shall presume to goe from this towne to London either directlye or indirectly as a post uppon any day or daies whatsoever then the said person or persons soe offendinge as aforesaid contrary to the true intent and meaneinge of this act shall forfeict to this towne the somme of tenn shillinges for every offence. All which said some or sommes of money are to be recovered by distresse or accion of debt or any other such way as is appointed for the recovery of debtes, yssues, fynes and amerciamentes due unto this towne. And it is inacted by the consent aforesaid that in the vacantcy of any of the three posts aforesaid by death or otherwise the maior for the tyme beinge, two of the jurates and three of the common counsell or the major parte of them whereof the maior to bee one shall have power to elect and nominate another person to supply his or theire place beinge soe vacant untill the next ensueinge burghmote. Provided allwaies neverthelesse and bee it enacted by the consent aforesaid that none of the posts aforesaid after the feast of Sainct Michael next shall take upon him to keepe a shopp whereby to trade in any retaylinge way for any mercery, grocery or chandlery wares upon peyne of forfeicture of his or theire place of beinge post for this towne and parish anythinge herein before mencioned to the contrary thereof in any wise notwithstandinge.

Records of Maidstone (Maidstone, 1926), 109–10

165. Regulation of football, Kendal, 1641

Item, it is ordered that whosoever do play at the football in the street and break any windows shall forfeit upon view therof by the mayor or one of the aldermen in the ward where the fault is committed the sum of 12*d* for every time every party, and 3*s* 4*d* for every window by the same broken and to be committed till it be paid. The constable is to look to it to present it presently at every court day.

R. S. Ferguson (ed.), *The Boke off Recorde of Kirkbie Kendall* (Cumberland & Westmorland Antiquarian and Archaeological Society, extra series, VII, 1892), 170–1

166. The rebuilding of Glasgow, 1652

25 June 1652

The saidis magistratis and counsell being conveinet, and finding it expedient for the better trying of the townis losses that the names of the heretouris of the haill burnt lands, with the tennents and occupyers thairof, be inventarit and takin upe. They have thairfor nominat and appoynted the persounes fallowing to goe about the samyne with all diligence, viz., James Bornis, John Walkinschaw, Edward Robiesoun, James Govane, James Kinkaid, Johne Andersoune, Dowhill, with Androw Conynghame, and James Bradwood, to survey to the effect foirsaid the haill landis burnt on the west syde of the Saltmercat and north syd of the Briggait. Item, Adame Wilsoune, Johne Buchanan, Thomas and Robert Scottis, Johne Glen, Johne Miller, maltman, John Cuik, to tak survey of the haill houssis as is aforesaid on the eist syd of the Saltmercat and southsyd of the Gallowgat. Item, Johne Herbertsoun, Johne Hall and William Stewart to tak a survey of the haill burnt lands above the cros as is above wrytin. Item, Patrick Park, Robert Merschell, John Wilson and John Kilpatrick ar to visie the haill houssis in Trongait on both sydis that ar burnt. And all of thame ar to tak upe the names of the heretouris and occupyers of these burnt landis, and to report thair dilligence this day betwixt and twa houris efternoon.

The foirsaidis magistratis and counsall, takeing to thair consideratioune the present hard conditioune of the towne, and for the better encouradgement to everie man to helpe to repaire his awne, seeing the work is lyklie to be great anent the building up and repaireing againe of the decayit pairts of the towne, and that the work is of suche a necessitie that it must be presentlie gone about, the necessitie of many poore people requyreing the samyne. They have thairfor statute and ordanit that the hail wreichtis and maissounes of the towne shall serve and work according to the pryces fallowing, viz., the maisterman his waidges to be threttein schilling four

four penneis ilk day, and the servand being fund ane sufficient qualefeit craftisman for ten schilling a day, and uther prenteisses according to thair worth. And seeing that the wreichtis and maissouns of this citie, for the better preservatioune of thair liberteis, ar first to be imployit in the said work, the samyne is granted to them wpon thair observatiounes of the cautiouns fallowing and no otherwayes, viz., gif so be they cannot get that work they sall be imployit in be the townes people tymeouslie wroght, according as they wha imployes them may get it done by others not exceiding the pryces foirsaid, it sall be lisome to the townes people to imploy any countreymen or others for working of thair said work. Item, that everie craftisman of the qualitie foirsaid sall work out and compleit the haill work they ar imployed to work within the towne and shall not leive the samyne, whither it be task wark or dayes wark, or seick any augmentatioune of thair pryce and workmanschipe, aither for task or daylie waidges, whill first the samyne be fullie compleit according to thair agreement with the pairtie. Item, that none of the saidis craftismen, naither maissounes or wreights, tak any mair work in hand nor that which they ar able to performe within the dayes aggreit upone betwixt them and the pairteis. Which cautiones if any of the said craftismen does transgresse it sall be lisome to any of the townes people to imploy any others for working of thair wark. And as for the exorbitancie of all task wark or insufficiencie of any work whatsomever to be wroght be any of the saidis persounes, upon a complaint maid by any pairtie whatsoever, the present magistratis ar to decyde thairupone and the samyn to be done according as they sall modifie. And this present act to stand and indure till the first day of October nixttocome.

Extracts from the Records of the Burgh of Glasgow, 1630–62
(Scottish Burgh Records Society, Glasgow, 1881), 230–2

167. Apothecaries and surgeons in Edinburgh, 1657

After consideration of a petition from the apothecaries and surgeon-apothecaries ... the council being sensible of the great concernement of that airt to the cittie and inhabitantis theirof and what prejudice may aryse to them if any burges at their awen hand sould profes and practise that airt without first giveing proofe of their qualificatioun in a decent and ordourlie way. And finding that no persones of whatsoever qualitie or degree ar so fitt and able for tryell and examinatioun of such who desyre to be admitted to the said airt as the petitioners themselffis and their successoris in the said professioun. And lykwayis that it is most necessar that tryell be made of all sort of drogs and siklyk that what other good overtures sall be made by the petitioners and their foirsaids to the counsell for the good of the people and weill of the said airt that the samen may be taken to consideratioun thairfoir the counsell have thoght fitt to statute and ordaine ... that from hencefurth no persone be admitted to the professioun and practise of the said airt of apothecarie within this brugh or liberties theirof but such as haveing obteind the friedome of being burges and gildbrethren ... sall make their addres by petitioun to the counsell for their recommendatioun to the apothecaries and chirurgian apothecaries and their successors for their tryell and examinatioun. And that report be made be the apothecaries and chirurgian apothecaries and their foirsaids to the counsell of their abilities and qualificatiouns in the said airt in which caice the counsell ar to admitt them to the said professioun. And the saids intrants [are] to be frie of anie exactioun or payment of any dewis whatsoever ather to the saids apothecaries and chirurgian apothecaries or to the counsell. And for that effect the counsell gives power warrand and commissioun to the saids apothecaries and chirurgian apothecaries and their foirsaids in all tyme comeing to try and examen the abilities and qualificatiouns of all such persones who intend to profes and practise the said airt within this brugh being recommended as said is and statutes and ordaines that na maner of persone or persones whatsoever within this brugh or liberties theirof in any tyme heireftir preysume nor take upon hand to profes and practise the said airts of apothecarie ... who sall not be fund qualified and admitted in maner abovewritten under the paine and punishment of the contraveneris in their persones and estaites. And siklyk statutes ... that the bailies ane or mae for the tyme with the dean of gild and twa or mae of the apothecaries and chirurgian apothecaries and their foirsaids to be nominat be the counsell being persones of most approven integritie and skill sall from tyme to tyme visite the sufficiencie of all sort of drogs within this brugh ... and seize upon such drogs as they sall find unsufficient and report the same to the counsell wherby the havers and users theirof may be condignlie punished in their persones and estaites according to the qualitie of their fault and their fynes and penalties applyed to the use of the good toun. And the counsell heirby desyres the petitioners and their foirsaids for their encouragement in the said airt to present to them from tyme to tyme sutch other good and reasonable overtures as may tend to the bettir improvement of the said airt and good of the people which they will take to consideratioun and doe theirin as they sall sie caus. The counsell doe heirby declair that this present act in favoris of the chirurgian apothecaries and apothecaries foirsaids is no way of intentioun to erect them in a corporatioun bot meirlie for the improvement of the said airt and good of the people and this without prejudice alwayis of the premissis in all poynts and ordaines the extract heirof ane or moe to be given out under the seall of office and subscriptioun of their clerk.

M. Wood (ed.), *Extracts from the Records of the Borough of Edinburgh, 1655–65* (Edinburgh, 1940), 51–2

168. Hearth tax assessments, Oxford, 1665

University of Oxon	
In Hart Hall	xxiii
John Galloway	v
Henry French	iii
	xxxi
In Edmunds Hall	xxiij
John Sampson	iij
Christopher Ayre	ix
	xxxv
Magdalene Hall	lj
New Inn Hall	xx
St. Mary Hall	xxvj
Gloucester Hall	xxxix
Alban Hall	xxvij
Queene Colledge	liiij
Corpus Christi Colledge	liij
University Colledge	lj
All Soules Colledge	lx
Penbrooke Coledge	liij
Exon Colledge	lxviij
Wadham Colledge	lxiij
Jesus College	lxv
Trinity Colledge	xxxix

Oriell Colledge	liiij
Lincolne Colledge	lij
Brazennose Colledge	lxv
Balliall Colledge	xl
Merton Colledge	lxxxij
St. John's Colledge	lxiiij
In New Colledge	liij
Christ Church	cxxvj
In the Great Quadrangle	xliij
In Peckwater Inn	xlvj
In Canterbury Quadrangle	xxviij
St. Mary Magdalene Colledge	cxij
	[1354]

Citty of Oxon. Southwest Ward
St. Martin's Parish

Thomas Box	iiij
Thomas Williams	iiij
Daniell Prince	iiij
Richard Houghton	iij
John Hancks	i
John Wildgoose	v
Francis Alder	i
Michaell Carter	v
Robert Sadler	ij
Richard Horne	iij
William Tustein	iij
Widdow Baker	iij
Widdow Ireland	iiij
Anthony Hall	viij
Richard Goodson	x
William Ward	iij
William Mitchell	vj
Nathaniell Slimaker	iij
	lxxij
William Tennge	ij
Robert Stapler	ij
—— Taylor widdow	i
Richard Wheelett	i
Edward Swift	i
	vij

discharged by poverty

St. Peters

Robert Pawlinge	iiij
William Shenton	iiij
John Kinge	v
John Boate	viij
Edward Adams	iij
Robert Rudley	iij
Thomas George	ij
George Lee	iiij
William Rancklin	iij
Richard Paine	ij
John Spencer	ij
Isaac Ovens	ij
Margarett Ovens	ij
John Smyth	ij
Robert Tippinge	iij
Thomas Meeres	v
William Greene	iij
Robert Prince	viij
Thomas Evatts	i
John Weavor	ij
Margery Coxeter widdow	vj
Robert Minn	ij
John Wildgoose	i
	lxxvij
Andrew Robinson	ij
William Sorrell	ij
John Showell	ij
John Shren	ij
James Dudley	ij
Richard Bunce	ij
Jerome Clarke	ij
John Wells	ij
Richard Alder	i
	xvij

discharged by poverty

M. B. Weinstock (ed.), *Hearth Tax Returns, 1665*
Oxfordshire Record Society, XXI, 1940), 78–80

169. The river polluted at Inverness, 1669

26 May

That day the magistrats and counsell, considering the great abuse and prejudice the inhabitants of this burghe have susteaned and ar daylie susteaneing by the washers of cloath at the riwer of Nes on both syds therof, and sicklyk by those that steipes thr hyds and skinnes in the said river, have, for preweinting therof in the futur, statute and ordayned that none presume to wasche any kynd of cloathes on this syd of the riwer abow the way that leads to the water wnder the kirk and kirkyeard, and that none presume to wasche on the wther syd of the water abow David Fouller his land, and that wnder the payne of tuentie punds Scots *toties quoties* and that by and attor punisching of the contraweiners persone. Sicklyk the magistrats and counsell have ordayned that none persun to weit or steip any kynd of leather in the said riwer in tyme comeing abow the said way wnder the kirk wnder the payne of fywe punds Scots *toties quoties*, and punisching the transgressors persone at the magistrats' discretione. And such as have any lether steiped abow the said place that they carie the samen away within tuenty four hours next efter publication therof, wnder the forsaid payne.

W. Mackay and G. S. Laing (eds.), *Records of Inverness*
(New Spalding Club, 1924), II, 234—5

170. Prostitutes in Glasgow, 1670

12 February 1670

The said magistratis and counsell taking to their consideratioune the great outcry made by many of the inhabitentis of this burgh, for that many of their weomen servandis therin hes theis divers yeares bygaine desertit their service, out of honest mens houssis, and hes tak wp houssis of their awine, wher som twa some thrie of them dwellis togither, wherby idle houssis ar keepit and many male [evil] reportis ar rysen by their bordle houssis so keepit and therby thei doe what thei can to bring the plague of God on this citie. Therfor the said magistratis and counsell being most willing to goe about all meanes to withhold Godis judgment from ws, and to benish away againe that ill practis that is risen among us, have concluded that twa of their number sall goe throw with the minister of ilk quarter, and some of the sessioune with them, as the minister sall appoynt, the haill quarter and

ilk particular hous therof, and to tak notice of ilk idle and orray woman
that hes takin wp houssis, and to mak them ether presently to returne to
service or then to act and obleis themselfes to remove aff the toune without delay, and to tak notice of theis persones who setis them the houssis
that thei may be punished conforme to the proclamatioune made in the
contrair; and for this effect the counsell appoyntit Johne Bell and James
Colhoune to goe throw with the parson his quarter. Dowhill, elder, and
Archibald Sheillis with maister Johne Bell throw his quarter, and the
deane of gild and deacon conveiner to goe throw with maister Williame
Stirling in his quarter, and Frederik Hammiltoune and Johne Barnes
elder to goe throw with maister Alexander Mylne his quarter: and to mak
report with the best conveniency.

Extracts from the Records of the Burgh of Glasgow:
1663–90 (Scottish Burgh Records Society, Glasgow,
1905), 126–7

171. Water supplies in Nottingham and Leeds, 1684, 1694

1684, Monday, September 1

Water Carts. — It is this day ordered by this Councell, yat those persons
yat shall continue the new use of carryinge of water from the River Leene,
or other places, for brewinge, washinge or other necessary uses, in carts,
or other carriages on wheeles, shall for the tyme to come use noe wheeles,
but such as shalbe clogg wheeles, and not bound with ironn or nayles;
upon payne to forfeite twoo shillings and sixe pence, to be leveyed by
distresse.

W. H. Stevenson (ed.), *Records of the Borough of*
Nottingham (Nottingham 1882–1914), V, 326

Whereas att a meeting of the maior, aldermen, and com'on councell,
Henry Gillert of Nether Soale in the County of Leicester, Esqr and George
Sorocold of the towne of Darby, gent., have proposed and doe designe to
lay an engine to convey water from the river of Aire, through the streetes,
to the ev'all houses within the towne of Leeds aforesaid, or to soe many
of them as shall purchase the same of them. This corte therefore takeing
the same into considerac'on, doe judge that it wilbe a worke of publique
benefitt, and deserves great encouragement. For the encouragement,

therefore, of the said undertaking and in considerac'on of the sume of forty pounds to be paid by the said Mr. Sorocold to the treasurer of this corporac'on, for the use and benefitt thereof, doe order and it is hereby ordered that the said Mr. Sorocold, his heires, executors, admistrators and assignes shall for ever hereafter be exempted, by reason of the profitts and rents which he or they shall make of the said water workes, of and from all and all manner of taxes, layes, and assessements, to and for the poore, constable, and highwayes, the mill by which the said Mr. Sorocold conveyes the water, and workes his engine, onely excepted. And that to be taxed and assessed att the onely usuall rate that it has been taxed and assessed att for seaven yeares last past.

J. Wardell, *The Municipal History of the Borough of Leeds*
(1846), 63

172. The inventory of a King's Lynn innkeeper, 1690

A true and perfect inventory of the goods and chattles, rights and creditts of Thomas Hardy late of King's Lynn in the county of Norfolk, innholder, deceased, taken and apprized this nineteenth day of May Anno Domini 1690 by us whose names are hereunder written.

	£	s	d
Imprimis his apparrell and things in his pockitt	4	0	0
In the kitching:			
Five iron horses, one hanging iron, a fore iron, a paire of cobb irons and other fire irons with fire spitts	2	10	0
A jack pully and weights		8	0
Six rush bottome chaires, one stoole, two white tables, a rack, a pewter case, a trencher case, a nest of spice boxes	1	10	0
Six and twenty pewter dishes	5	0	0
Three dozen and a halfe pewter plates	1	10	0
Seavteene pewter chamber potts and other small peeces of pewter	1	5	0
Eight pewter porringers, two pewter basons, two salts and a tanker		15	0
A warming pan and eighteen fine candlesticks		5	0
In the back kitching:			
One copper and fire irons	1	0	0

	£	s	d
Two brass potts, one brass kettle, a frying pann, two iron dripping panns, and one iron kettle	1	5	0
In the Great Parlour:			
One fire grate and fire irons, a brass candlestick	1	5	0
Nine rush chaires, a forme and a stoole		8	0
In the Hall:			
One cole grate and fire irons	1	10	0
Two tables, one dresser, one forme, fourteene rush chaires, one small table, two boxes, a stoole	1	10	0
Four lanthornes, a candlestick, a smoothing box and heates		6	8
Flagons and gillpotts	1	10	0
In the Pantry:			
Two sawcepanns, a chaseing dish, a powdering tubb, and severall other wood and earthenware with weights	1	10	0
In the Star:			
One fire grate with brasses, a purr, a firepan, a candlestick		10	0
Two tables and twelve chaires	1	0	0
In the Hall next the Star:			
One fire cradle and two oate tubbs		10	0
In the Billiard Roome:			
One billiard table, king, port, balls and stick	3	0	0
[Sub-total]	32	7	8
In the Dineing roome:			
One fire cradle with brasses, one table and forme		15	0
Tenn leather chaires	1	0	0
In the Dineing roome Chamber:			
Two bedsteads and furniture, two chaires and a forme	5	0	0
In the Crowne Chamber:			
One fire grate, a paire of tongs, a firepan and horse	1	0	0
Six Rushia leather chaires	1	10	0
Foure green chaires, one redd arme chaire and six cushions		15	0
Two tables, a nest of drawers, a stand and a looking glass	2	5	0

One bedstead, a suite of blew curtaine and vallence, a rugg and other furniture	6	0	0
Two bedsteads with two suites of greene curtaines and vallens and other furniture	11	0	0
One bed tyke and a paire of blanketts	1	10	0
Four silver cups, 3 tasters and 4 spoones	6	10	0
One side saddle, a pillion and cloath	2	0	0
In the Maid'shead Chamber:			
A fire grate and a fore iron		6	0
Tenn chaires and one table	1	5	0
Foure bedsteads and furniture to them	16	0	0
One chest, one box, and one trunck		10	0
Five and twenty paire of sheets	12	10	0
Sixteene paire of pillowbeeres	1	12	0
Seaven dozen napkins	2	2	0
Eight board cloaths	1	4	0
In the Gatehouse Chamber:			
One bedstead and furniture	2	0	0
One bedstead and furniture	1	0	0
One close stoole, three chaires and a table		10	0
In the Bell Chamber:			
Two bedsteads, matts, curtaines and vallens, two bedsteads with featherbeds and other furniture	8	0	0
Eleaven stooles and one table	1	0	0
In the Kitching Chamber:			
Two bedsteads with furniture and one bedstead	3	0	0
In the King's Head Chamber:			
One bedstead, curtaines and vallens, featherbed, blanketts and rugg, one other bedstead, curtaines and vallens	3	0	0
One table, one cubboard, a skreene, eight chaires and a glass case		15	0
In the Stable:			
One horse bridle and saddle	6	0	0
Lumber and goods forgott	2	0	0
	101	19	0
Brought over	32	7	8
[Grand total]	134	6	8

Norfolk Record Office. Inv. 65B/15

173. A newspaper in Edinburgh, 1699

The convention haveing considered the 35 article of the misive anent the proposall given in by Mr Donaldson for publishing of ane Edinburgh Gazet and what encouragement they think fitt to bestow upon him for containowing his newes, doe therfor appoint the agent to pay him the sowme of threty pound sterline for his encouragemnt to continow in publishing the Edinburgh Gazet to the nixt generall conventione, and recomends to all the royall borrowes as they think fitt to concert and aggree with the said Mr Donaldson for furnishing any of them the newes and gazets by everie post.

J. D. Marwick (ed.), *Extracts from the Records of the Convention of the Royal Burghs of Scotland, 1677–1711*
(Edinburgh, 1880), 286–7

INDEX
Numbers refer to pages